NATURALISM
IN AMERICAN EDUCATION

Naturalism in American Education

BY

GEOFFREY O'CONNELL, Ph.D.

PREFACE BY

Louis J. A. Mercier, A.M., Litt.D., K.L.H.

ASSOCIATE PROFESSOR OF FRENCH AND EDUCATION, HARVARD UNIVERSITY
LAUREATE OF THE FRENCH ACADEMY

New York, Cincinnati, Chicago, San Francisco

BENZIGER BROTHERS

1938

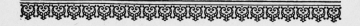

Nihil Obstat:
EDWARD B. JORDAN, D.D
Censor Deputatus

WASHINGTON, D. C., May 29, 1936

Imprimatur
✠ MICHAEL J. CURLEY, D.D.
Archbishop of Baltimore

BALTIMORE, Md., May 29, 1936

REPUBLISHED BY THE COURTESY OF
THE CATHOLIC UNIVERSITY OF AMERICA,
WASHINGTON, D. C.

To
MY FATHER AND MOTHER

PREFACE

"Naturalism in American Education" offers in its field what the French call *le bilan d'une génération,* the balance-sheet of a closing epoch. To all engaged in education, Dr. Geoffrey O'Connell's inexorable analysis must produce the same effect as would the sudden sight of the general staff's map of a large military offensive to one too long at and close to the front to have had a bird's-eye view of the operations.

Dr. O'Connell has done his plotting well, cautiously leaning throughout on original texts and on numerous standard reports from the various sectors, allowing them to speak for themselves except for the objective summing-up of their implications.

It is interesting to note that he brought to a task which he carried out so well as to be a model for such surveys, the fresh vision of a newcomer, representative moreover of the youth of one of the countries emancipated since the war. It is natural that there should be in such men a deep concern for the currents of thought in a world in which their own nation is facing a new future. Born of a distinguished family close to the influential circles of the new Ireland, just in time to see it left free to solve its own problems, he came to this country to widen his horizon. Accepted by the diocese of Natchez, Mississippi, where he became Director of the Society for the Propagation of the Faith, giving at the same time missions and retreats in nearly a third of the parishes of the diocese, he found his way finally to the Catholic

University of America and at once plunged into the study of educational problems. His Master's thesis, "The Educational Significance of the Irish Language Revival," was a real contribution to the solution of those of his native land. But, under the able direction of his professors, quickly sensing the breathtaking range of the American scene, he was soon caught by the challenge of our own cultural situation. The result was his doctoral dissertation which, going to its very heart, at once attracted so much attention that it was soon out of print, and that a call came even from non-Catholic educators that it be made available in permanent form.

This general interest should not be surprising, for what Dr. O'Connell forces us to realize, no matter how loath we may be to do so, is that what our most prominent American educational leaders have been doing in the last thirty-five years is to formulate and propagate such doctrines as must inevitably undermine American institutions and prepare the advent in the United States of atheistic totalitarianism.

The why is not far to seek. Alternative ideas are implacable in their consequences. American democracy is essentially based on the idea of inalienable personal rights stemming from God, the Creator; while the fact of God's existence, and of a consequent antecedent and transcendent righteousness as the source of natural law which individuals and social groups should try to discover and respect, is precisely what our more prominent American educators have labored to deny for the last thirty-five years, as Dr. O'Connell luminously establishes through his painstaking analysis of their writings.

The reason is that, under the influence of idealistic

and materialistic monism, they passed to such a conception of reality that they denied the possibility of any abiding element above or in the universe and man.

With Dewey, personal culture and social efficiency become synonymous but "there is nothing to which growth is relative save more growth," and that growth can only be attained by an education which develops "the flexible attitude which seeks to outgrow existing social conditions." There should remain no traditional ought or ought not. "Not even the aim of democracy in education and in society is permitted to lay an obligation or claim on human life." Kilpatrick, as the popularizer of the doctrines of Dewey, would also set the student against every established moral code and bid him be ready to make his own in the light of presumably unprecedented experience. Did not Dewey even say that "the institution of marriage and family that developed in medieval Europe, considered as the last and unchanging word," is but an example "of the extent to which ideas of fixity persist in a moving world"? Rugg, on the other hand, reacts against Dewey's obsession of the socially useful by stressing self-satisfaction in self-cultivation and self-expression, but it is only another way of urging that the new generation be practiced in the attitude of expectancy of change "including change in standards and norms of life, in standards of morality, in family life." While for Thorndike, a wholly materialistic psychologist, morality is also good social behavior and its possibility depends purely on physiological conditions. Hence he talks about selective breeding for the development of superior intelligence and the duty to improve upon nature so as to improve the social group. He would have society control the fertility of the best stocks, decrease the productivity of the poorest strains, and dictate the specialized education through which each individual should be conditioned according to his capacities as revealed by standardized tests.

Atheism, materialistic hedonism, a life ending at the grave made socially efficient through unlimited social control, such then were the offerings of our educational leaders in the first third of the twentieth century.

Since, however, we were asked to accept them in the name of a philosophy of everlasting and total change, now that the generation in which they were elaborated is passing, their advocate should be ready to admit that, on their own principles, their doctrines are in turn part of the existing thought which we should be ready to discard.

There are many signs that we are fast doing so. Even Dr. Dewey is not wholly satisfied with the existing totalitarian experiments, and Dr. Thorndike, under the pressure of other laboratory researchers is no longer so confident that the learning process is the simple S-R bond mechanism on which he based his whole doctrine. We hear again of the need of studying further the genesis of the higher mental processes.* Materialistic evolution which had such an influence on the development of naturalism is now widely discredited, as it well might be, since it did not account for origins and not even adequately for the processes of change. The works of Babbitt, More, and Foerster are available as a many-sided critique of

---

* *Cf.* Judd, Charles H., *The Education of the Higher Mental Processes* (U. of C. Press, 1937), especially the last two chapters.

naturalism. Judd, Bagley, Butler, McDougall who
early warned us against its excessive claims are being
vindicated. The emergence of younger dualistic
critics of our educational system, notably Demiashkevich, Adler, and Hutchins is most significant.
Jeans, Eddington, Carrel, even Lippmann have lately
swelled the current of important books in the same
direction. Not a few American philosophers have
become dissatisfied with monism in general, as was
revealed in connection with the joint meeting of the
American Philosophical Association and of the American Catholic Philosophical Association, itself an
indication of the felt need of conference on fundamental oppositions of thought; while the powerful
work of Gilson, widely circulating in this country,
would alone suffice to bear witness that the renova-
tion of studies on dualism in Europe has already
provided abundant material for such discussions.

The development of naturalism in American education, so thoroughly dissected by Dr. O'Connell,
is then already appearing as hopelessly onesided. If
it is true that we are living in a world of change, it
should be no less evident that we are not living in
a world of total change. Stone walls are now as im-
penetrable as in the days of Aristotle. A child continues to need protection and help for many years,
and even animal behavior points to the duty of the
parents until the young are matured; nor can a social
group survive without families of at least three children. Genuine physical science is based on the recognition of an antecedently abiding real. The
teacher may lead the child to discover facts instead
of telling them to him, but all along he knows what
they are. If he did not, the child would remain help-

less.   It can only be the same with genuine moral
science.   To intimate that the past has made no findings of permanent value in this field, that the natural
law and codes of decency it has come to recognize
as ideals of conduct may all be fanciful taboos which
the new generation can safely repudiate is the very
negation of the value of experimentalism in the name
of which it is invited to discard them.   As Irving
Babbitt expressed it: "The notion that in spite of the
enormous mass of experience that has been accumulated in both the East and the West, we are still without light as to the habits that make for moderation
and good sense and decency; and that education is
therefore still purely a matter of exploration and experiment is one that may be left to those who are
suffering from an advanced stage of naturalistic in-
toxication. From an ethical point of view, a child has
the right to be born into a cosmos, and not, as is coming to be more and more the case, pitch-forked into
chaos." *

Nor could chaos ever evolve order.   Order has to
be imposed upon chaos from without.   Man can impose order on the chaos of his contradictory impulses,
or on the conflicting interests within and between social groups, only in proportion as he establishes contact with the principle of order necessarily antecedent
to the cosmos already existing.   To deny the antecedently real is to condemn him to helpless subjectiv-
ism.   The pragmatic concept that whatever works for
our satisfaction is true and good is a fit motto for
every type of racketeer; and the instrumentalist's

---

* Babbitt, Irving, *Rousseau and Romanticism* (Houghton Mifflin, 1919), p. 388.

claim that the true is whatever works for the social good likewise begs the question, since there remains to determine what the social good should be. There can be no intelligent moral direction given to activity unless the legitimacy of a particular end is previously evident, and that legitimacy cannot be established save in terms of a transcendent universal value. To set the child against the experience and tradition of the past which might teach him such values is the worst type of obscurantism. To chain him to the experience of his own time and place and to the exclusive urges of his own desires or of those of his social group is to coerce him to remain subhuman. To betray him into believing that there is no abiding antecedent objective reality is to make him run the danger of being crushed by its consequences. What is needed is to lead him to shape changing circumstance in the light of abiding principles.

It is then but natural that many already understand that to the philosophy of total change, for which there has been such a selling campaign in the passing generation, there should be substituted a philosophy of the abiding in the changing. Change there will be, but it will be progressive only if it is guided by eternal righteousness. The founders of America understood that well. And, in spite of the progress of naturalism, their conviction is still widely instinctive. It is a matter of record that, after all, the founder of "progressive education" in the United States is not Dr. Dewey but Francis W. Parker, and Parker wrote, no farther back than 1890: "The child is the climax and culmination of all God's creation, and to answer the question 'What is the child?' is to approach nearer the still greater question 'What is the Creator and Giver of Life?' " * Parker, through Froebel, was influenced by Rousseau, but he was still in the dualistic American tradition untainted by Hegelian or by materialistic monism. In the light of that tradition, it is only too obvious that to pass from Christianity to Deism, from Deism to Pantheism, and from Pantheism to Atheism is not a progress but a devolution fraught with sinister consequences.

Because Dr. O'Connell in his objectve study has traced this devolution in detail in the works of our naturalists, and made us better understand what Irving Babbitt meant by "the naturalistic conspiracy against civilization"; * because he may well lead many to realize that to recover or to treasure the dualistic principles which built up western civilization including our own means the difference between genuine evolution and inevitable revolution, between progressive Christian democracy and regressive atheistic totalitarianism, he has rendered a distinct service not only to American educators but to all students of social questions.

Louis J. A. Mercier.

Cambridge, Mass.

---

* Parker, Francis W., *Talks on Pedagogics* (Reprinted for the Progressive Education Association. John Day Co., N. Y., 1937).
* *Op. c.*, p. 389.

ACKNOWLEDGMENTS

The author and publishers acknowledge their gratitude to the following for permission to quote from their publications:

D. Appleton-Century Company: *Education: Intellectual, Moral and Physical*, by Herbert Spencer; *Education in the United States*, by Richard G. Boon; *A History of Experimental Psychology*, by E. G. Boring; *Education and the Philosophy of Experimentalism*, by John L. Childs; *Modern Public Education*, by Isaac Doughton; *The Educational Frontier*, by W. H. Kilpatrick, Editor; *Human Learning*, by Edward Lee Thorndike; *Psychology of Wants, Interests and Attitudes*, by Edward Lee Thorndike; *Religion and the Mind of To-day*, by Joseph A. Leighton; *The American Review*: Review of "The Challenge of Humanism," by G. R. Elliott. Archabbey Press: *The Science of Education in its Sociological and Historical Aspects*, by Otto Willmann-Felix M. Kirsch. Edward Arnold & Co.: *Education: Its Data and First Principles*, by T. P. Nunn. Bureau of Publications, Teachers College, Columbia University: *A Reconstructed Theory of the Educative Process*, by William Heard Kilpatrick; *Philosophies of Education Current in the Preparation of Teachers in the United States*, by Francis Edwin Peterson; *Educational Yearbook of the International Institute*, by Isaac L. Kandel. Cambridge History of American Literature. *Commemorative Essays*, by Paul D. Schlipp. The John Day Company: *The Great Technology*, by Harold Rugg. Dodd, Mead & Company: *American Philosophy: The Early Schools*, by Woodbridge Riley. Educational Administration and Supervision: *What Teacher-Training Faculties Believe*, by Bruce R. Raup. Elementary School Journal: *A Significant Investigation of Crime in the United States*. The Forum: *President Eliot and American Education*, by Irving Babbitt. Harcourt Brace & Co., Inc.: *Culture and Education in America*, by Harold Rugg; *Psychology of Intelligence and Will*, by H. G. Wyatt. Harper & Brothers: *Humanizing Religion*, by Charles Francis Potter. Harvard University Press; *Introduction to John Dewey, The Man and His Philosophy*, by Kilpatrick, Editor. Henry Holt & Co.: *Human Nature and Conduct, An Introduction to Social Psychology*, by John Dewey; *The Conflict of the Individual and the Mass in the Modern World*, by Everett Dean Martin; *American Thought, from Puritanism to Pragmatism and Beyond*, by Woodbridge Riley; *A History of French Literature from the Earliest Times to the Present*, by William A. Nize & E. Preston Dargan; *Reconstruction in Philosophy*, by John Dewey; *Characters and Events, Popular Essays in Social and Political Philosophy*, by John Dewey; *Reconstruction in Philosophy*, by John Dewey; *Influence of Darwin on Philosophy and Other Essays in Contemporary Thought*, by John Dewey;

Creative Intelligence, by John Dewey, et al. Houghton Mifflin Company: *The Making of the Modern Mind,* by John Herman Randall, Jr.; *The History of Education,* by E. P. Cubberley; *Charles W. Eliot, President of Harvard,* by Henry James; *Education for Efficiency and the New Definition of the Cultivated Man,* by Charles W. Eliot; *The Philosophical Bases of Education,* by Robert R. Rusk; *Masters of Modern French Literary Criticism,* by Irving Babbitt. The Journal of Philosophy: *Dewey's Naturalistic Metaphysics,* by George Santayana; *Half-Hearted Naturalism,* by John Dewey; Review of John Dewey's "The Quest for Certainty," by C. I. Lewis. The Literary Digest: *The Atheists' Intolerance.* Liveright Publishing Corporation: *Education and the Social Crisis.* Longman's Green & Company: *Pragmatism,* by William James; *Religion Without God,* by Fulton J. Sheen; *Discussions and Arguments,* by John Henry Newman. John W. Luce & Co.: *Religion of the Future,* by Charles W. Eliot. The Macmillan Company: *College and University Administration,* by E. E. Lindsay and E. O. Holland; *Naturalism and Agnosticism,* by James Ward; *A Text-Book on the History of Education,* by Paul Monroe; *History of Modern Philosophy,* by Hoffding; *Liberalism and American Education in the Eighteenth Century,* by Allen Oscar Hansen; *The Rise of American Civilization,* by Charles A. and Mary A. Beard; *From Absolutism to Experimentalism,* by John Dewey; *Democracy and Education, An Introduction to the Philosophy of Education,* by John Dewey; *The Democratic Philosophy of Education,* by Herman Harrell Horne; *Education for a Changing Civilization,* by W. H. Kilpatrick, Editor; *Animal Intelligence, Experimental Studies,* by Edward Lee Thorndike; *Elementary Principles of Education,* by E. L. Thorndike and A. J. Gates; *Education: A First Book,* by Edward Lee Thorndike; *Education, Crime and Social Progress,* by William C. Bagley; *Mirage and Truth,* by M. C. D'Arcy. National Society for the Study of Education: *Seventeenth Yearbook,* Edward Lee Thorndike. *The New Era.* W. W. Norton & Company: *Experience and Nature,* by John Dewey; *The Meaning of Culture,* by John Cooper Powys. Office of Education: *Teacher Education Curricula National Survey of the Education of Teachers, Bulletin.* The Open Court Publishing Company: *Evolutionary Naturalism,* by Ray Wood Sellars. The Oxford University Press: *The Challenge of Humanism,* by Louis A. J. Mercier. The Paulist Press: *Four Great Encyclicals.* The Philosophical Review: *Contemporary American Philosophy,* by Frank Thilly. Popular Science Monthly: *The Evolution of the Human Intellect,* by Edward Lee Thorndike; *Englivics,* by Edward Lee Thorndike. The Psychological Review: *The Mental Life of Monkeys,* by Edward Lee Thorndike. G. P. Putnam's Sons: *Art as Experience,* by John Dewey; *Philosophy and Civilization,* by John Dewey; *The Quest for Certainty,* by John Dewey. School and Society: Remarks at the Unveiling of Dr. Dewey's Bust. Charles Scribner's Sons: *Types of Philosophy,* by William Ernest Hocking; *Rousseau and Naturalism in Life and Thought,* by William Henry Hudson; *Rousseau and Education According to Nature,* by Thomas Davidson; *A History of Education,* by Thomas Davidson; *Horace Mann and the Common School Revival in the United States,* by B. A. Hinsdale; *The Social Ideas of American Educators,* by Merle Curti. Sheed and Ward: *Enquiries into Religion and Culture,* by Christopher Dawson; *Religion and the Modern State,* by Christopher Dawson; *The End of Our Time,* by Nicholas Berdyaev. Sherman French & Company: *The Belief in God and Immortality,* by James H. Leuba. The Sign: *Naturalism and Education,* by Albert F. Kaiser. Simon & Schuster: *Living Philosophies. A Series of Intimate Credos,* by John Dewey. Teachers College, Columbia University: *Educational Psychology,* by Edward Lee Thorndike. Teachers College Record, Columbia University: *The mind of a Scholar.* Time Magazine. United States Government Printing Office: *Crime and Crime Control: Investigation of So-Called Rackets.* The University of California Chronicle: *Darwin's Contribution to Psychology,* by Edward Lee Thorndike. The University of North Carolina Press: *Our Educational Task,* by William Heard Kilpatrick. World's Work: *Atheism Beckons to Our Youth,* by Homer Croy. Yale University Press: *A Common Faith,* by John Dewey.

CONTENTS

INTRODUCTION

Western civilization is in the midst of a moral, social, and economic crisis. Spiritual and material distress is widespread. Peoples are discontented and statesmen tense with anxiety. It is admitted by all competent observers that the old order is dying, in fact, is already dead. Spengler's *Decline of the West,* Wust's "Crisis in the West," Berdyaev's *The End of Our Time,* Bedoyere's *The Drift of Democracy,* Dawson's *The Modern Dilemma,* Gibbs' *The Way of Escape,* to mention but a few titles, reflect the crucial situation that confronts our Western culture.

In common with other nations, America is experiencing anxious days and the prospects for the future are none too bright. George Soule's *The Coming American Revolution,* Sherwood Anderson's *Puzzled America,* Maxine Davis' *The Lost Generation,* Norman Thomas' *America's Way Out,* present us with varied aspects of our national problem and suggest varied solutions. Many are asking why it is that the movement for social and political improvement has failed to keep pace with the phenomenal growth and development of America's industrial, scientific, and material life, and why it is that our generation has actually lapsed to a distinctively lower level in the scale of moral and cultural living. Widespread political corruption, a steadily increasing divorce rate, a return to pagan standards of sex behavior, crime waves, kidnapping, juvenile delinquency: these are some of the manifestations of our "Changing Civilization." In our intellectual journals we are constantly reading articles on "Racketeers," "The New Morality," "The New Hypocrisy," "Big Business and Banditry," "Democracy and Mass Massacre," "Democracy in Question," and so on. Underlying all these phenomena we are aware of a definite decline of religious belief and a positive trend away from Christian ideals. What are the agencies that are bringing about this scheme of devolution? While it is clear that many causes have combined to produce it, some observers feel that our system of education has played, perhaps unconsciously, an important contributory rôle.

It is admitted by many social leaders and educational experts that the past achievement of American education has been a failure. This is in sharp contrast with the erection, during recent decades, of increasingly large numbers of better equipped elementary and free secondary schools, many of which are staffed with teachers trained in vastly improved teacher-training institutions. At present there are approximately one million teachers in service while our largest centers have large numbers of substitutes and long waiting lists. At the same time enlarged opportunities for college education have been made accessible to the young from all levels of society. Yet, in spite of modern buildings, more serviceable equipment, more extensive curricula of studies, and more efficient teachers, all of which have been provided by mounting educational expenditures, many are asking if education is on the right track and how far the American system is justifying the faith and the sacrifice of the American people. An increasing number

of responsible people who still believe in education
are becoming

> somewhat critical as to whether the system
> of education for which they are paying is
> justifying itself in the results which it brings
> forth, and as to whether the kind of educa-
> tion which our public institutions, both tax-
> supported and endowed, are advocating,
> makes for effectiveness, for intelligent citi-
> zenship, and for independent character to
> the extent that it has been assumed in the
> past that it did.[1]

When the results produced by a system of education are unsatisfactory, we are justified in questioning
the philosophy that underlies it. If it be true that
the philosophy of the educator determines the aims
and goals of education and, therefore, what he shall
teach and how he shall teach it, in other words, his
curriculum and his methods, it is certainly correct to
say that, allowing for the effects of heredity and the
action of other educational agencies, both formal and
informal, over which he has no control, his philosophy is responsible for the products he turns out. So
we are led today, in view of the patent failure of our
American schools to develop in their pupils that type
of social and civic efficiency which is essential to national well-being, and which they were established
to effect, we are led, I say, to question the philosophy

---

[1] Henry S. Pritchett, quoted from his biennial report (1922) as
President of the Carnegie Foundation for the Advancement of
Teaching, in *College and University Administration*, by E. E.
Lindsay and E. O. Holland (New York: The Macmillan Co., 1930),
p. 576.

of life and education professed by those who are charged with the training of our youth.

Now what is the philosophy underlying American education? Several answers to this question have been attempted. Isaac Doughton's *Modern Public Education, Its Philosophy and Background,* Merle Curti's *The Social Ideas of American Educators,* Isaac Kandel's "The Philosophy Underlying the System of Education in the United States" in the *Educational Yearbook of the International Institute of Teachers College, Columbia University, 1929,* R. Bruce Raup's "Educational Philosophies held by Faculty Members in Schools for the Professional Education of Teachers" in Volume III of the *National Survey of the Education of Teachers,* and Francis E. Peterson's *Philosophies of Education Current in the Preparation of Teachers in the United States,* furnish partial answers to this question. These works, as well as others such as Woodbridge Riley's *American Philosophy, The Early Schools,* and *American Thought, From Puritanism to Pragmatism and Beyond,* and Oscar Allen Hansen's *Liberalism and American Education in the Eighteenth Century,* indicate the several philosophical currents that have united to form the *Weltanschauung* underlying our system of public education. Among these currents is that of naturalism.

During the last three centuries, naturalism has dominated to a great extent the intellectual life of Western Europe and America. It has given rise to various theories of life such as Materialism, Positivism, Individualism, Socialism, Liberalism, and Communism. Basically, it has oriented all of these by making man continuous with nature, by confining his destiny to earth, and by eliminating the supernatural. To the naturalistic attitude of mind, the conception of Christianity with its philosophy of life directed to the here and the hereafter, is obsolete. While all the authors mentioned note the gradual spread of this naturalistic philosophy of life and education in American education, for the most part they are in sympathy with it. Many fail to realize how sinister has been its influence. Nevertheless, our examination of James H. Leuba's *Statistical Study of the Belief in a Personal God and in Personal Immortality* in the United States, an investigation of the Christian beliefs of a representative sampling of American scientists, sociologists, historians, and psychologists, recorded in Part II of his *The Belief in God and Immortality* proves that naturalism has permeated very much of the intellectual thought of our leaders.

As far as we have been able to discover, there is no comprehensive work dealing specifically with naturalism in American education. We feel that such a treatment will be of service, especially when presented from the supernatural or Christian viewpoint, since many educators who adhere to the teachings of Christianity are concerned about the naturalistic trend of our American schools. This, then, is the purpose of the present investigation.

The plan of the study is as follows: in Chapter I, naturalism in philosophy and education in general will be reviewed; in Chapters II and III, the introduction of naturalism into American education during the eighteenth and nineteenth centuries will be treated; Chapters IV, V, and VI, will be devoted to leading contemporary American exponents of natur-

alism in education; while Chapter VII will sum-
marize the findings of the studies dealing with the
philosophy taught in seventy teacher-training schools
and institutions of higher learning in America. In
Chapter VIII, some logical consequences of naturalism in philosophy and education will be set forth, in
order to show the weakness inherent in the naturalistic position as well as the extremes to which it tends.

The writer wishes to acknowledge his indebtedness
to the Rev. Doctor Edward B. Jordan, who suggested
the problem to be investigated, and under whose direction this dissertation was prepared. He desires,
also, to thank the Vice-Rector of the Catholic University of America, the Rt. Rev. Monsignor Patrick J.
McCormick, and the Rev. Doctor Felix M. Kirsch,
O.M.Cap., for generously giving of their time to the
reading of the manuscript. An expression of sincer-
est gratitude is also due to the Reverend Professor
Johnson of Catholic University, Professor Mercier of
Harvard, Professor Norman Foerster of the University of Iowa and Doctor Frazier of the Office of
Education in Washington, D. C., for their valuable
counsel. Grateful acknowledgment is given here to
his brother, the Very Reverend Doctor M. P. O'Connell, Dean of Clonliffe, Dublin, Ireland, and to his
sister Joan O'Connell, H. Dip. Ed. for their useful
criticism.

CHAPTER I

NATURALISM IN PHILOSOPHY AND EDUCATION

Naturalism is the attitude of mind characteristic of all systems of thought which deny the existence of an order transcending nature and sense-experience and confine the explanation of reality to the general viewpoint that nature contains the normal and only final answer to all philosophical problems. Even though philosophers may differ in their specific theories of life, naturalism demands that they exclude the supernatural from every hypothesis and keep within the bounds of the natural in their efforts to discover the solution of their problems.[1] Naturalism is defined by Joyce as "a system whose salient characteristic is the exclusion of whatever is spiritual, or indeed, whatever is transcendental of experience from our philosophy of nature and of man."[2] Hocking says that it is the type of philosophy "which takes Nature as the whole of reality. That is, it excludes whatever is supernatural or otherworldly. Whatever appears independent of natural law, such as human life or products of the imagination, is really a part of the scheme of nature. No doubt there is something hidden, something for which science has to search, but that hidden thing is Nature itself, not anything beyond or behind Nature."[3] And Ward

---

[1] James Mark Baldwin, *Dictionary of Philosophy and Psychology* (New York: The Macmillan Co., 1902), II, 137-138.

[2] George Hayward Joyce, *Principles of Natural Theology* (2d ed., London: Longmans Green and Company, 1924), p. 511.

[3] William Ernest Hocking, *Types of Philosophy* (New York: Charles Scribner's Sons, 1929), p. 43.

1

tells us that it is the "doctrine that separates nature from God, subordinates spirit to matter, and sets up unchangeable laws as supreme." [4]

It is an attempt to construct a theory of life from the purely scientific standpoint.[5] It excludes metaphysics in favor of the "view of the world which flows by inner necessity from the accomplishments of science" and its spirit "would seem to be one with the spirit of science itself." [6] It objects to metaphysics as an abstract, mechanical and hair-splitting exercise of the mind. It believes that metaphysics is a futile jumble of speculations unintelligible to the man in the street and resulting in no practical good. In contrast with it, it extols the physical sciences and their benefits to humanity. It fails to see that metaphysics is occupied with reality, i.e., with things as they are, with fundamental, basic notions and ideas. It will not admit that metaphysics concerns itself with incontrovertible principles, such as causality, potentiality, actuality, and the notion of change, etc., which are all directly traceable to and based upon the undeniable and evident principles of identity and contradiction.

The antithesis of supernaturalism, it holds that nature alone contains within itself uniform principles of change, the causes of all the facts of life, the knowledge of which is necessary for progressive mankind, itself a product of nature, in order to predict future events. The only method by which these principles

---

[4] James Ward, *Naturalism and Agnosticism* (New York: The Macmillan Co., 1899), I, 186.

[5] Robert R. Rusk, *The Philosophical Bases of Education* (Boston: Houghton Mifflin Co., 1929), p. 25.

[6] Roy Wood Sellars, *Evolutionary Naturalism* (Chicago: The Open Court Publishing Co., 1922), pp. 19, 5.

or causes can be discovered is the scientific method of observation, experimentation, and verification.[7]

The standard definitions of naturalism clearly indicate that it "is antithetical to supernatural religions and therefore incompatible with and consequently hostile to Christianity in its historical meaning of revealed religion." [8]

---

[7] Everett Dean Martin, *The Conflict of the Individual and the Mass in the Modern World* (New York: Henry Holt and Co., 1932), pp. 71-72. "The Naturalist is not one who is merely interested in the study of nature. He comes to that study with certain intellectual habits ... He has ... a 'prejudice' against miracles, 'mysticism' and 'superstition' ... he refuses to go outside this closed circle of the natural,—or habitually observed and quantitatively constant series of changes. The modern scientific method of course is essentially Naturalistic. Natural science has no place in its world-view for stories of Creation, or of miraculous intervention in the course of events.... All such beliefs are regarded as purely natural social phenomena,—either as ignorant attempts to account for the facts of experience, or as expressions of wish fancies. The Naturalist strives to rise above such indulgence in human frailty, to steel his heart. . . .But not everyone is capable of such achievement: and that is why Naturalism, when its tenets become popularized, becomes a serious problem in our civilization." *Ibid.*, pp. 72-73.

Writing in 1922, Sellars declares: "... we are all naturalists now. But even so, this common naturalism is of a very vague and general sort, capable of covering an immense diversity of opinion. It is an admission of a direction more than a clearly formulated belief. It is less a philosophical system than a recognition of the impressive implications of the physical and biological sciences. And, not to be outdone, psychology has swelled the chorus by pointing out the organic roots of behavior and of consciousness." *Op. cit.*, Preface vii.

[8] Louis J. A. Mercier, *The Challenge of Humanism* (New York: Oxford University Press, 1933), p. 10. In order to get a comprehensive understanding of naturalism one should study carefully this splendid work of Professor Mercier of Harvard. The author discusses the subject in its relationship to Humanism and Christianity. His basic thesis is that it has gone wrong on first principles.

Lunn says that "a philosophy in which there is no place for the supernatural or the spiritual is a philosophy in which there is no place for God. . . . 'Naturalism' is only 'atheism' in evening dress." Arnold Lunn, *The Flight From Reason* (New York: The Dial Press, Lincoln MacVeagh, 1931), p. 153. Balfour says that naturalism "numbers a formidable following, and is in reality the only system which alternately profits by any defects which Theology may sustain, or which may be counted on to flood the space from which

4   *Naturalism in American Education*

"Thus the essence of naturalism or naturism is seen to be a denial of the supernatural. From the establishment of Christianity until the eighteenth century, it was practically a minor trend in European thought; but by the middle of that century it was displacing humanism and vigorously attacking revealed religion and eventually the conception of the dualism of man's nature." [9] During the next hundred years it increased in momentum and by the middle of the nineteenth century[10] it had begun to dominate intellectual thought when scientists, fired with the spirit of the laboratory,[11] confused the scientific point of view, necessarily dealing with secondary causes, with that of philosophy concerned with first and final causes, in seeking the explanation of all reality and all truth within the realm of nature.[12] Their minds had become accustomed to scientific generalizations and to them the scientific method appeared to hold the solution of the pressing problems of mankind. Here was a theory of life inspired by the development of the physical sciences[13] using the method and spirit of science to explain everything in the universe. The millennium had arrived and the biological categories of progress began to be applied to all fields of human knowledge, to the natural sciences, and to life itself.[14]

---

[9] Mercier, *op. cit.*, p. 10.
[10] Alfred Weber and Ralph Barton Perry, *History of Philosophy* (rev. ed., New York: Charles Scribner's Sons, 1925), p. 472.
[11] Ralph Barton Perry, *Philosophy of the Recent Past* (New York: Charles Scribner's Sons, 1926), p. 2.
[12] Joyce, *Principles of Natural Theology,* p. 511.
[13] R. B. Perry, *op. cit.*, p. 2.
[14] John Herman Randall, Jr., *The Making of the Modern Mind* (Boston: Houghton Mifflin Co., 1926), pp. 454-481.

---

the tide of religion has receded." Arthur J. Balfour, *The Foundations of Belief* (New York: Longmans Green and Co., 1895), p. 6.

The progress of scientific achievement had given the naturalistic theorists the assurance that "Nature . . . the sum of things and events in space and time, subject to a single system of causal laws" was the original and ultimate end of everything, the fundamental reality within whose limits lay the adequate and natural explanation of the universe.[15]

The movement continued to gain increasing force so that William James could write in 1907:

> For a hundred and fifty years past, the progress of science has seemed to mean the enlargement of the material universe and the diminution of man's importance. The result is what one may call the growth of naturalistic or positivistic feeling. Man is no lawgiver to nature, he is an absorber. . . . The romantic spontaneity and courage are gone, the vision is materialistic and depressing. Ideals appear as inert by-products of physiology; what is higher is explained by what is lower. . . . You get, in short, a materialistic universe, in which only the tough-

---

[15] Hocking, *Types of Philosophy*, p. 43. In studying the significance of naturalism, it is highly important to note that the question at issue does not reduce itself to a quarrel with the facts which scientific investigations have given us. What is objected to is the extension of scientific principles into fields traditionally accepted as exempt from them, for naturalism arose out of "certain assumptions of 'modern science' which have led to a widespread, but more or less tacit, rejection of idealistic views of the world. These assumptions are, of course, no part of the general body of the natural sciences, but rather prepossessions that, after gradually taking shape in the minds of many absorbed in scientific studies, have entered into current thought of our time." Ward, *op. cit.*, I, Preface, v.

minded find themselves congenially at home.[16]

Natural science has made its definite impress on philosophy from the beginning of modern times. Descartes influenced philosophy through mathematics and Spinoza gave definite expression to this tendency in his geometrical methods of proof.[17] The growing importance of the new science of physics from Copernicus to Boyle challenged the sway of mathematics over philosophy through to Locke and Kant and practically maintained its dominance until Darwin's biological categories gave a fresh direction and impetus with their concepts of progress and development which Spencer's cosmic generalization applied to all human knowledge, science, and life itself. It is well to remember, however, that biology was basically influenced by the assumptions of physics.[18]

In this way, through the successive inroads of mathematics, physics, and biology into modern philosophy, did natural science gradually arrive at its position of importance. De Hovre succinctly sums up the situation as follows:

> Theoretically and practically, Natural Science occupied the center of life. Knowledge of nature was the only means of subduing the forces of nature and employing them in the service of man. In this way Natural Science came to be looked upon as the touchstone of progress. All that the previous generations had accomplished was,

---

[16] William James, *Pragmatism* (New York: Longmans Green and Co., 1925), pp. 16-17.

[17] Randall, *op. cit.*, pp. 240, 244-47.

[18] *Ibid.*, pp. 226-257, 266, 454, 440-441, 466.

so we were told, but a feeble image of that which the future held in store. The Golden Age of humanity lay ahead of us and not behind; and so the task that Natural Science had to fulfill was heralded as the sublimest hope and the loftiest ideal the human spirit had ever aspired to. Naturalism . . . recognized one domain of knowledge only, and one method of arriving at the truth, viz., by way of the physical sciences. . . . Natural Science was constituted a sort of supreme court before whose tribunal all other branches of knowledge were obliged to plead their right to recognition.[19]

Because of its pervasive tendency in modern philosophy, it is more correct to describe naturalism as an attitude of mind permeating thought, life, and society, than to present it as a coherent system of metaphysics. We find its roots in the new significance or interpretation which Francis Bacon gave to nature [20] in his attempts to build an empirical philosophy[21] on the inductive experimental method, to disregard deduction and the scholastic tradition. He has been called the author of the scientific method,[22] but it would be more exact to say that he reëmpha-

---

[19] De Hovre-Jordan, *Philosophy and Education* (New York: Benziger Brothers, 1931), p. 4.

[20] Rusk, *Philosophical Bases of Education*, p. 34.

[21] Cardinal Mercier and Professors of the Higher Institute of Philosophy, Louvain, *A Manual of Modern Scholastic Philosophy*. Authorized translation and third English edition by T. L. Parker and S. A. Parker, with a Preface by P. Coffey (London: Kegan, Paul, Trench, Trubner and Co., Ltd., 1923), II, 432-434.

[22] William Turner, *History of Philosophy* (Boston: Ginn and Co., 1929), pp. 435-438.

sized it.[23]   Due to his influence, empiricism took hold
in England whence it passed over to France in the
eighteenth century and gave impetus to the development of aesthetic materialism, the dominant philosophy of those who brought about the Revolution and
of those who succeeded them.[24]

By the middle of the nineteenth century, naturalism had spread to Germany where the reaction to
post-Kantian metaphysics was sending philosophers
to the natural sciences for a more commonsense point
of view of reality.   The result was a materialistic
monism founded on the old mechanistic theory and
the new theory of conservation.   About the same
time, Positivism arose in France, giving naturalism
a new direction.   This new tendency passed over to
England to reinforce the naturalistic evolutionism
which spread swiftly to all fields of knowledge. While
there were no outstanding thinkers of the naturalistic
turn of mind in America during the nineteenth century, it is important to note that English Naturalism
and French Positivism left their imprint on the
thought of the country.   The works of Spencer and
Darwin, Perry tells us, "exerted a powerful and
growing influence in the direction of naturalism." [25]

In our day the naturalistic influence has maintained, if not improved, its position in the thought
of the world.   Randall says pertinently:

> Present-day philosophies seem split on tech-
> nical questions, ultimately, on whether the

[23] Fulton J. Sheen, *Philosophy of Science* (Milwaukee: The Bruce
Publishing Co., 1934), p. 4.
    [24] Cardinal Mercier, *A Manual of Modern Scholastic Philosophy*,
pp. 432-440, 446.
    [25] R. B. Perry, *Philosophy of the Recent Past*, pp. 17, 5-6, 13-14.

categories and methods of the physical sciences or those of the biological sciences should be taken as fundamental. The chief problems appear to be, first, the development of an adequate philosophy of nature, in which both physics and biology can be merged in a new synthesis. . . . Secondly, there is the problem of the formation of an adequate philosophy of the new society. . . . The religious problem is still present, but in the changed form of the adjustment of the values of the personalistic philosophies to the scientific knowledge of naturalism. . . . But such problems could arise only after men had already accepted the scientific picture of the world. This was in itself a tremendous task, and its accomplishment remains the outstanding philosophic achievement of the century.[26]

While philosophers of the naturalistic bent are united in the common belief that nature contains the solution of all problems that concern men and the universe, they differ in their specific theories which present the answer to the question: What is nature and what is man? "The question of questions for mankind," says Huxley, "the problem which underlies all others, and is more deeply interesting than any other, is the ascertainment of the place which man occupies in nature and of his relation to the universe of things." [27] There are various systems of modern thought which attempt to answer this question

---

[26] Randall, *The Making of the Modern Mind*, pp. 556-557.
[27] Thomas Henry Huxley, *Evidence as to Man's Place in Nature* (London: Williams and Norgate, 1863), p. 57.

but all agree in this: they keep strictly within the limits of the natural to the definite exclusion of the supernatural.

The three main currents of naturalistic thought to which all non-theistic theories may be reduced are Materialism, Evolutionism, and Positivism.[28] Materialism maintains that, in the last analysis, everything and every event in the universe of space and time is matter in motion. Matter is the only reality, substance, and efficient cause. Nothing exists outside of it. Blind components of matter and unconscious forces have produced civilization. Thought is a function of the nervous system, itself a product of matter. Spontaneous generation produced life and blind determined law continues its development in all its higher forms. There is no teleology, no principle of finality in anything, not even in man. There is no freedom of the will, no responsibility, no immortality, and man is but a conscious automaton. The realm of nature is to be explained in terms of its physical elements. What is the essence of these elements? This question gives rise to various theories: Atomism or Mechanism, Dynamic Atomism, Energism, etc.; but whatever the decision arrived at, its consequences are the same for mankind, society, religion, ethics, and social science. Thought, action, and life are predetermined by inexorable laws and the aim of materialistic philosophy is to search for these laws in nature so that the eventual course of nature may be predicted and controlled.[29] Democri-

[28] De Hovre-Jordan, *Philosophy and Education*, p. 1.
[29] Hocking, *Types of Philosophy*, pp. 12, 43-44; John F. McCormick, *Scholastic Metaphysics*, Part I, (Chicago: Loyola University

tus, Epicurus, and Lucretius are the great pre-Christian materialists. Space will not permit a discussion of their theories, nor would such a discussion add much to our understanding of modern materialism. In considering the growth of the latter it is well to remember that Newton's formulation of the universal laws of gravitation gave considerable impetus to the mechanistic theory.[30]   Thomas Hobbes (1588-1679) is the herald of materialism in the modern era. Influenced by the Baconian principles of a materialistic naturalism in which physics, psychology, and the social sciences are dominated by mechanical necessity, the English empiricist developed the materialism of his friend.[31]

The positivistic and empirical tendency begun by Bacon and continued by Hobbes received further support in the critical and empirical philosophy of Locke (1632-1704) in the mathematical synthesis of Newton (1642-1727), and in the rational doctrines of English deism.[32]   Voltaire and Montesquieu on their return from England to France in 1729 brought back with them the ideas of the English empiricists and deists on philosophy, religion, and politics.   The result was the materialism and formalism of the Enlightenment which in turn begot the reaction of

[30] Cardinal Mercier, *A Manual of Modern Scholastic Philosophy*, II, 446.

[31] *Ibid.*, p. 434.   Philosophy, according to Hobbes, is the science of bodies, and physics is the study of the motion of atoms pulsating by mathematical and mechanical laws without any teleological purpose. *Ibid.*, p. 440.   Mind is the result of the motion of matter composing the brain. Imagination and memory are decaying sense, and reason is a train of memories. Hocking, *op. cit.*, p. 96.

[32] Randall, *op. cit.*, pp. 262-263.

Press, 1928), pp. 222-224; R. P. Phillips, *Modern Thomistic Philosophy* (London: Burns Oates and Washbourne, Ltd., 1934), I, 335-336.

Rousseau and a naturalism which spread to the masses and inspired the Revolution.[33]

The Enlightenment was materialistic, atheistic, sceptical, and rationalistic. As an intellectual revolt against the authority of the Catholic Church and the French monarchy it distinguished itself by its glorification of reason and individualism. Its aim "was to liberate the mind from the dominance of supernatural terrorism . . . to demonstrate the intellectual freedom and sufficiency of man; to destroy the terrorism over the feelings, the absolutism over thought, the tyranny over action, exercised especially by the Church, and, as supplementing the Church, the monarchy." [34]   The principal leaders were D i d e r o t,

---

[33] Harald Hoffding, *A History of Modern Philosophy*, translated by B. E. Meyer (London: The Macmillan Co., 1900), I, 456; Cardinal Mercier, *A Manual of Modern Scholastic Philosophy*, II, 446; Paul Monroe, *A Text-Book in the History of Education* (New York: The Macmillan Co., 1911), pp. 533, 538-542.

Though not a materialist, Locke prepared the way for its development in France and Germany by the aid which he gave to the critical spirit in philosophy and religion. He was opposed to scholasticism and was influenced greatly by Gassendi and Hobbes. A free-thinker in religion, he is the founder of religious rationalism. He preferred the empirical to the deductive method in philosophy, ethics, and politics. He developed the sensationalism of Hobbes, thus inspiring the idea, later developed by others, that men, born equal, become unequal through their experiences in unfavorable environment. Helvetius carried this idea further, ignoring individual differences. By analysis and deduction, Locke pictured a state of nature without civil government and then tried to discover the natural needs which necessitated government. He found certain basic natural rights—among which private property was the principal one. The Social Contract, he held, enabled each person to exercise these fundamental rights by the rule of majority and when government fails to protect these natural rights it must be superseded. The formulation of these principles aroused admiration in the minds of men like Montesquieu and Rousseau and helped to bring on the French and American Revolutions. Hoffding, *op. cit.*, I, 337-391; Randall, *op. cit.*, pp. 311-317, 341-343; Turner, *History of Philosophy*, pp. 492-496.

[34] Paul Monroe, *A Text-Book in the History of Education*, p. 538.

d'Alembert, Voltaire, Holbach, La Mettrie, Cabanis, and Montesquieu. Voltaire was a deist and outspoken in his attacks on the established order. In his *Lettres sur les Anglais* he "introduced his countrymen to a new physics, a new philosophy, and a new constitution of society. He contrasted Locke and Newton with Descartes; Socinians, Quakers, and other dissenters with Catholics; representative government with absolute monarchy. . . . These letters indicate a turning point in the history of civilization, i.e., the inoculation of English ideas on the continent." [35] His *Éléments de la philosophie de Newton* (1738) was instrumental in paving the way for the success of the new natural philosophy and the naturalism which resulted in Materialism, the dominant philosophical theory in France in the latter eighteenth century. [36]

La Mettrie opened this chapter of materialistic naturalism with *L'histoire naturelle de l'âme* (1745) and *L'homme machine* (1748). His thesis was that matter in motion is the sole reality in nature. Man is under the domination of necessary mechanical laws; consciousness is the result of the activity of the nervous system; the brain is the organ of thought; life ends with death; there is no supernatural; and the great aim of life lies in physical enjoyment. In his *Système de la nature,* Baron Holbach (1723-1789) urged the materialistic monism of La Mettrie and this became the Bible of the Materialistic school in the last decades of the century. He was a physicist and left the impress of his thought on the mind of

---

[35] Hoffding, *op. cit.,* I, 459.
[36] *Ibid.*

his time. He denied the existence of God; the freedom of the will; the immortality of the soul; and
held that Newtonian science offered a complete explanation of the universe.[37] Cabanis (1757-1808), a
physician like La Mettrie, contended that mind and
body were identical, that the brain secretes thought
as the liver secretes bile.[38] Diderot popularized and
inspired many of the naturalistic ideas of the period.
As editor of the famous *Encyclopédie, ou Diction-
naire raisonné des sciences, des arts et des métiers*
(1751-1780), his influence was tremendous. "This
work denotes a turning-point in the history of civilization for by its means knowledge and enlightenment
were conveyed to a wide circle of readers." [39] In his
Interprétation de la nature (1754) we find one of the
outstanding theoretical and naturalistic expositions
of the experimental method, which he maintains "is
a combination of perception and thought, induction
and deduction, acting and reacting on one another,
by which we pass from experience, through reason,
back to experience gain." [40] The life and intelligence
of nature are eternal. Memory and comparison result from particular sensations. The basis of right
and good is in human nature. *Tout est expérimental
en nous.* Belief in God begets absurdities and contradictions.[41] "Perhaps the chief note in his *Encyclopédie* is the way he brushed aside the traditional intellectual interests and placed emphasis upon the
mechanical arts and crafts." [42] His *Encyclopédie* con-

---

[37] Hoffding, *op. cit.*, I, 476-484.
[38] *Ibid.*, 473-475.
[39] *Ibid.*, p. 476.
[40] *Ibid.*, p. 477.
[41] *Ibid.*, pp. 476-481.
[42] Randall, *The Making of the Modern Mind*, p. 266.

tributed greatly "toward sapping the popular belief in God, in spirituality, in human liberty, and in the sacredness of the traditional ideas of morality." [43]

Voltaire and the Encyclopedists were intellectual aristocrats with little, if any, interest in the common people. They felt that the Enlightenment was not for the canaille.[44] In catering to their self-centered interest they brought on

> a period of hard and arid rationality, when the intellect reigned supreme, when the emotions were repressed or ignored. . . . Everything was seen under the chill white light of reason, and tested by the universal criterion of common sense. Cold, sceptical, cynical in its attitude towards the deeper problems of existence, the age was, at the same time, in its daily thoughts and habits, epicurean, frivolous, flippant, torpid, self-complacent. . . . The free play of passion and individuality was everywhere checked by the rigid formalism which held society in an iron grasp . . . and as was inevitable under such wholly unhealthy conditions, a widespread contempt for great moral principles was meanwhile sapping the foundations of the established order.[45]

Against this stilted and artificial outlook a reaction set in which was destined to leave its traces in modern thought and life, and Rousseau was its leader and inspirer. Despite his own paradoxical life he

---

[43] Turner, *History of Philosophy*, p. 503.
[44] Hoffding, *op. cit.*, I, 463.
[45] William Henry Hudson, *Rousseau and Naturalism in Life and Thought* (New York: Charles Scribner's Sons, 1903), p. 232.

> taught the eternal verities of a natural re-
> ligion to a society which had lost both faith
> and reverence. . . . Sentimentalist in the
> midst of the dryest rationalism and intellec-
> tuality, he did more than any other man to
> emancipate the emotions and reinstate the
> heart . . . he spoke with seductive eloquence
> of the personal freedom and the largeness of
> life which might be found beyond the
> cramping restraints of the social régime.[46]

Here was a romanticist living in the Age of Reason
but not of it, caring not at all for logic and reasoning
but living " in every fibre of his being, with a kind
of heroism, the primacy of feeling." [47]

He disagreed with the doctrines of the Enlightenment and the Encyclopedists because of their false
gentility and lack of interest in the common people,
their destructive criticism, and their materialistic
philosophy.[48] The seeds of this disagreement were
already evident in the essay which he wrote in response to the prize which the Academy of Dijon offered in 1749 for the best thesis on *Whether the resto-
ration of the sciences and arts had contributed to
purify manners.* He immediately captured the public ear with his daring reply in which he maintained
that the arts and sciences were dynamic forces in the
social corruption of civilization.[49] In 1755 he wrote
a second prize essay *On the origin of the inequality
between men.* His contention was that the substitu-

---

[46] *Ibid.*, p. 234.

[47] Jacques Maritain, *Three Reformers, Luther, Descartes, Rousseau* (New York: Charles Scribner's Sons, 1929), p. 96.

[48] William Boyd, *History of Western Education* (3d ed., London:
A. & C. Black, Ltd., 1932), p. 310 .

[49] Hoffding, *A History of Modern Philosophy*, I, 485.

tion of civilization for the state of nature was harmful, since the scarcely noticeable physical and intellectual differences of men in primitive society are not
stressed against the background of natural conditions
and hence there is no unhappiness or social inadequacy. Having only one virtue and protection, pity,
man does not know the difference between good and
evil. It is only when he begins to meditate and to
acquire property that differences in natural equipment and inequality arise and create a harmful environment which bad government perpetuates. Thus
the rich become powerful and the poor suffer.[50]

In 1762 he produced his famous *Social Contract*
which in common with the *Discourse of Inequality*
inspired the French Revolution. The basic tenet of
this treatise is liberty, and the opening sentence tells
us that: "Man is born free, and everywhere he is in
chains." This fault of civilization can be remedied
by a new pact, since man born free to follow his
natural instincts cannot now return to the state of
nature. This new compact will ensure that each
human being "shall possess the inalienable rights and
freedom with which nature has endowed him, so that
without let or hindrance he may develop his personality to the full." [51] Good government will unite
the *general will* (the ideal necessarily aiming at social
well being), and the *will of all* (the majority will).
Educated citizens will ensure that the majority can
be trusted to do the best for all concerned.[52] His

[50] *Ibid.*, p. 486.
[51] Cardinal Mercier, *A Manual of Modern Scholastic Philosophy*,
II, 449.
[52] John Morley, *Rousseau* (London: The Macmillan Co., 1891), I,
154-173.

Social Contract is the antithesis of Locke's theory of
government, for while Locke maintained that the
majority is as much to be feared as any monarch,
Rousseau defied the majority so that there remained
to no individual, rights which might not be set aside.
"Thus it is Rousseau's theory, as developed in the
French Revolution, that has formulated the basis of
the modern collectivistic state." [53]

The treatise, however, that made Rousseau famous
and the one which is the most representative of his
philosophical and educational thought is the *Émile*
or *Treatise on Education* (1762). In the opening
sentence the author lays down his basic dogma of
natural goodness. "Everything is good as it comes
from the Author of Nature; but everything degenerates in the hands of man." [54] "For a century preceding Rousseau's time," says Davidson, "educational
theories had been rife in a world awakening from the
lurid, Dantesque dreams of the Middle Age. The
old belief, that man's nature is fallen and depraved,
had gradually been replaced by a belief that it is
fundamentally sound and good; and, at the same
time, education had come to be regarded, not as a
means of eradicating vile human nature, and replac-
ing it by a new divine nature, but as a means of developing human nature itself. In England, Locke
had written a plain, commonsense treatise on education from the latter point of view, and from this
Rousseau drew his chief inspiration." [55]

---

[53] Randall, *The Making of the Modern Mind,* pp. 354-355.
[54] Jean J. Rousseau, *Émile ou de L'Education* (Paris: Garnier
Freres, n. d.), Livre I, 5.
[55] Thomas Davidson, *Rousseau and Education According to
Nature* (New York: Charles Scribner's Sons, 1898), p. 98. The title
of Locke's book was *Some Thoughts Concerning Education* (1688).

Rousseau insists on the antithesis between nature, the work of God, and civilization, the work of man. As the result of culture "All our wisdom consists in servile prejudices, all our customs are but servitude, worry and constraint. Civilized man is born, lives and dies in a state of slavery." [56]

> Our passions are the principal instruments of our conservation and it is therefore an attempt as vain as it is ridiculous to destroy them; it would be to control nature and reform the work of God. If God were to tell man to destroy the passions which He has given him, God would and would not, He would contradict Himself. But He has never given this senseless order; nothing like it is written in the human heart; and whatever God wishes a man to do He does not cause it to be told him by another man, but says it to him Himself, He writes it in the depths of his heart. [57]

Rousseau defends his thesis of the natural state in *Émile,* but it is not that of the primitive savage as maintained in the *Discourses.* Rather it is a state of the *Social Contract.* Natural rights and laws as discovered in the true nature of man are to be the basis for all development. His doctrine is one of individualism, self-love and love of goodness. The natural man is complete in himself; he is the numerical unit, the absolute whole, who is related only to himself or his fellow man. Civilized man is but a fractional unit that is dependent on its denominator, and whose value consists in its relation to the whole

---

[56] Rousseau, *op. cit.,* p. 13.
[57] *Ibid.,* p. 227.

which is the social organization. Good social institutions are those which are the best able to make man unnatural, and to take from him his absolute existence.[58] "Thus does Rousseau hold exactly the reverse of the thought of the present which conceives the natural man to be the fraction, which finds completion as the social man as a unit in the greater unity of the whole." [59] Rousseau was a deist but his deism, essentially non-rationalistic, was one of emotional expansion. His theory of religion is manifest in the Savoyard Vicar's faith.[60]

The Divinity is in every heart and, because it cannot be conceived, it cannot be subjected to reason.[61] The human will is free and to abuse this freedom is to act badly, but the Deity does not interfere in any way.[62] There is only natural religion.[63] There is no true Revelation and the Gospels contain things full of contradictions, incredible, and repugnant to reason.[64] The core of worship is that which the heart dictates.[65] Rousseau's philosophy is best gauged from his character. Davidson says:

---

[58] *Ibid.*, p. 9.

[59] Paul Monroe, *A Text-Book in the History of Education*, p. 556.

[60] Cf. Rousseau, *Émile*, IV, 295 ff. As Morley says: "The Savoyard's profession of faith was not a creed, and so has few affirmations; it was a single doctrine, melted in a glow of contemplative transport." Morley, *Rousseau*, II, 265.

[61] Morley, *op. cit.*, II, 265.

[62] Rousseau, *op. cit.*, pp. 314-315.

[63] *Ibid.*, pp. 334-335.

[64] *Ibid.*, pp. 336-337.

[65] Morley, *op. cit.*, 273. *Émile* was condemned by the Archbishop of Paris on account of its naturalistic doctrine as being contrary to the natural law, Christian religion, and the morality of the Gospels. P. J. McCormick, *History of Education*, p. 318. It was burned by the public executioner in Paris and Rousseau was expelled from the city. The Protestants of Geneva, his native city, condemned it also.

. . . the foundations of Rousseau's character were spontaneity . . . his whole life was an endeavor to give free and uncontrolled expression to this . . . his works were so many efforts to champion it, as the ideal of life, and to show how it might be preserved free from constraint and corruption. In Rousseau himself, this spontaneity, naturally very rich and strong, was fostered by an education, which leaving him at liberty to follow his momentary caprice, fired his imagination and made it ungovernable, so that he early became utterly incapable of submitting to any constraint, regulation, continuous occupation, or duty, however sacred. He lived in, and for, the present moment, seeking to draw from it the greatest amount of enjoyment, tranquil or ecstatic as his mood happened to demand, without any thought of the past, future, or claims of others.[66]

This was the man of "feeling" in which the final convergence of the tendencies of the Renaissance, the Protestant Reformation, Cartesianism, and the philosophy of the Enlightenment took place to bring on the destruction of the supernatural order in life.[67] He popularized the root principles of the rationalism of the eighteenth century. The latter had eliminated Revelation and tradition in favor of reason only to find itself in turn in the devolution whereby it was superseded by standards based on instinctive judgments, emotions, first impressions, and the dictates

---

[66] Davidson, *Rousseau and Education According to Nature*, p. 71.
[67] Maritain, *Three Reformers, Luther, Descartes, Rousseau*, p. 95.

of the heart. Feeling, not reason, henceforth was to be the basic criterion of true religion, politics and society. His view was "that man's instincts are so naturally good that without effort he can be virtuous, that he has only to let himself go, so that his analytical intellect is rather a hindrance than a help." [68] Whereas the Age of Reason held that knowledge was the essential stimulus for virtue, Jean Jacques pleaded for the full sway of the innate tendencies of human nature. His "concern was, how one might so become a citizen as yet to retain to the full the delightful liberty of a tropical savage." [69] His faith in the common man and his philosophy of life is a *via media* between the sceptical and materialistic enlightenment and the supernatural idea of the Christian ideal. Based on a natural religion of the heart, it tried to remake civilization on natural lines.

He attempted to build a philosophy of life, individual, domestic, social, economic, political, and religious on the belief that human nature was normally sound, balanced, given to no unhealthy tendencies to evil, given to no excesses to which the natural intellect and will were inclined. In this theory of his no dualism between the lower-self, with its natural intellect, will and feelings, and the higher-self with its supernatural powers, was admitted. On the contrary, he held that such an interior antagonism in man's nature had been induced by the Church's doctrine of Original Sin, which he considers

---

[68] L. A. J. Mercier, *The Challenge of Humanism*, p. 4.

[69] Joseph Rickaby, *Moral Philosophy*, (4th ed., London: Longmans Green and Co., 1923), p. 301.

to be a very blasphemy.[70] In his famous reply to Archbishop de Beaumont's condemnation of the *Émile* we find a definite expression of his belief in the natural goodness of man. He says:

> The fundamental principle of all morality, according to which I have reasoned in all my writings . . . is that man is a being naturally good, loving justice and order: that there is not any original perversity in the human heart, and that the first movements of nature are always right. I have shown that the sole passion which is born in man, that is to say, self-love, is a passion itself indifferent to good or bad; that it becomes good or bad only by accident and according to the circumstances in which it is developed. I have shown that all the vices that are imputed to the human heart are not natural to it; I have told the manner in which they are born; I have, so to say, followed their genealogy; I have shown that by the successive alteration of their original goodness, men become at last what they are.[71]

In our exposition of materialism we have inserted the Rousseauistic reaction in France. Apart from other considerations, the later development of naturalism with its profound implications for education necessitated this. We shall now consider the development of materialism in Germany, a century later. This was in substance a reaction to the extremes of idealism set forth by Fichte, Hegel, and Schelling.

---

[70] Lettre à M. de Beaumont, *Oeuvres complètes de J. J. Rousseau* (3d ed., Paris: Baudouin Frères, Editeurs, 1828), p. 55 note.

[71] *Oeuvres complètes de J. J. Rousseau,* p. 48.

Discontented with theories which failed to measure up to the dictates of common-sense in their explanations of reality, and fascinated with the success of the naturalistic sciences, the left wing of Hegelianism developed a strong materialistic trend under the leadership of David Strauss, Ludwig Feuerbach, and Karl Marx, while the work of Mayer, Joule and Helmholtz aided in popularizing the principle of conservation of matter as established by Lavoisier.[72]   The combination of the Mechanical theory of Newton with the principle of the conservation of matter begot a philosophical monism "in which nature was regarded as a fixed amount of energized matter proceeding in a ceaseless closed system, the organism being one of the forms assumed by energy." [73]   The new doctrine was set forth in Moleschott's *Circulation of Life* (1852) and Büchner's *Force and Matter* which ran into sixteen editions between 1855 and 1889. Ernst Haeckel belonged to this school for a time, but later shifted his emphasis to the theory of evolution as a result of Darwin's influence.[74]

In tracing the growth of the mechanistic explanation of the universe during the last century we must note the introduction of Mechanism into biology and the consequent application of the new viewpoint and method to the study of human nature.[75]   Whereas materialism first attempted to develop a philosophy of nature according to the categories and methods of the physical sciences, the influence of Darwin and Spencer shifted emphasis to the categories of the bio-

---

[72] Perry, *Philosophy of the Recent Past,* pp. 4-5.
[73] *Ibid.,* p. 6.
[74] *Ibid.*
[75] Randall, *The Making of the Modern Mind,* p. 461.

logical sciences which had their distinct implications in the social sciences and life in general. The century witnessed a considerable advance in scientific discovery and achievement due to a growing interest in experiment and observation. Many new facts about the structure and processes of nature were brought to light with the result that the concept of mechanistic evolution emerged as a more complete explanation of the world-machine which had grown from simple beginnings to its present complex structure. Of the two fundamental generalizations or assumptions which have dominated science in the last century, it is true that evolutionism has gained ground while the mechanistic theory has been fairly well discredited. Modern science has renounced extreme materialism and atheism in favor of evolution and agnosticism.[76]

Naturalistic method in philosophy received a definite direction and emphasis from Darwinism, the inspiration of the new trend.[77] After twenty-three years of study, Charles Robert Darwin published in 1859 his book *On the Origin of Species by Means of Natural Selection, or the Preservation of Favored Races in the Struggle for Life*. Twelve years later (1871) he gave the world his *Descent of Man*.[78] It is to be noted that he did not attempt to explain the origin of life but assumed as the basis of his hypothesis a study of the changes which produced new species including man. He broke down the line of

---

[76] Ward, *Naturalism and Agnosticism*, I, pp. 18-19.

[77] H. G. Townsend, Editor, *Studies in Philosophical Naturalism*, University of Oregon Publications, Humanities Series, vol. I, No. 1, March 1931, p. 3 (Eugene, Oregon: University Press).

[78] Perry, *op. cit.*, p. 20.

demarcation which divided the simple from the more complex forms of life.[79]   His contribution to biology was that he brought about the scientific acceptance of the general view that new species of plants and animals had a natural origin, a concession from science which Lamarck's theories failed to win.   He based this theory on a hypothesis which combined "natural selection" through the agency of fortuitous variations or "individual differences" with the struggle for existence, and the survival of the fittest, or "adaptation to environment." [80]

Darwin's evidence for Natural Selection furnished data which at least partly explained the origin of new species and he was persuaded that the more he studied the matter the more he discovered new factors which had to be considered.[81]   In his *Descent of Man,* he applied the new theory which caused a revolution in human thought.[82]   Speaking of the almost instantaneous acceptance of Darwin's doctrines, Randall says:

> Now after Darwin, however, there could be no further blinking of the fact that man was a product as well as a part of nature, that he had climbed to his present estate from lowly origins, and that all his works had been painfully acquired in the struggle against a hostile environment.   While men had long recognized that man is a rational animal, they had perhaps not unnaturally empha-

---

[79] Hocking, *Types of Philosophy,* p. 54.
[80] Perry, *op. cit.,* pp. 21-23.
[81] Arthur Kenyon Rogers, *English and American Philosophy Since 1800* (New York: The Macmillan Co., 1928), p. 132.
[82] Randall, *The Making of the Modern Mind,* pp. 473-475.

sized his distinguishing mark of rationality;
but now reason was well-nigh forgotten in
the new realization of his common animal-
ity. Man was an animal species like any
other, and he and his interests were the
proper field of biology.[83]

Evolutionistic ethics now made its appearance.
Darwin maintained that natural selection explained
moral feeling through the natural sympathy and
mutual aid for the good of the group which adaptation to environment aroused in the individual.[84]
Spencer, Huxley, and Haeckel applied the Darwinian
theory to the universe, making eternal matter the
cause of the cosmic, organic, moral, and religious
world.[85] In 1857, two years before Darwin published
his *Origin of Species,* Herbert Spencer (1820-1903)
defended the principle of evolution as a universal
law in his book: *Progress: Its Law and Cause.*[86] The
aim of his *Synthetic Philosophy* set forth after thirty
years of study,[87] was to apply the evolutionary principles to all human sciences. Beyond these there is
the unknowable which he terms force. The persis-
tence of force and its evolution extends to the non-
living, as well as to the living world.[88] Here we have
the cosmic generalization of Darwin's general law.

Ernst Haeckel (1834-1919), the outstanding leader

[83] *Ibid.,* p. 483.
[84] Cardinal Mercier, *A Manual of Modern Scholastic Philosophy,*
II, 478; Turner, *History of Philosophy,* p. 620.
[85] Cardinal Mercier, *op. cit.,* I, 234.
[86] Turner, *op. cit.,* p. 621.
[87] T. J. Walsh, *The Quest of Reality* (St. Louis: B. Herder Book
Co., 1933), p. 472.
[88] Paul Janet and Gabriel Seailles, *A History of the Problems of
Philosophy,* translated by Ada Monahan, edited by Henry Jones
(London: Macmillan and Co., Ltd., 1902), II, 142-143.

of naturalism in Germany during the latter half of
the last century, in *Die Welträtsel,* held that "consciousness has been gradually evolved from the
psychic reflex activity." [89] This was his solution of
the riddle of the gap between the inanimate and the
animate. At any rate, this is the crucial problem in
naturalistic evolution. The theories of Darwin and
Spencer and Haeckel have left the riddle unsolved
and they, in turn, have been succeeded by others. We
have, for instance, the "Mutation Theory" or abrupt
development, as well as "Emergent Evolution"—answers to the problem of how mind came about. The
difference between these new theories and the older
ones of Spencer and Haeckel lies in the fact that in
the latter the mind is ultimately reduced to matter,
while the emergent evolutionist regards it as something quite new, an addition to the elements which
produced it. [90]

The third naturalistic current of thought that we
shall consider is Positivism, the scientific and critical
philosophy of science which rejects metaphysics, final
causes, and the absolute in favor of experience and
the positive sciences. [91] It is actually a scientific method
of thinking which is preferred to *a priori* speculation.
It seeks facts and the interrelations between them and
its sole aim is to produce a systematic body of the
scientific knowledge that can stand the final test of
observation and experiment. This knowledge admits no realm but that of the sciences, and the super-

[89] Quoted in Hocking, *op. cit.,* p. 56.
[90] *Ibid.,* pp. 59-60.
[91] Janet and Seailles, *op. cit.,* pp. 161-162.

natural is absolutely beyond its scope.[92] Mental and moral processes are, in the last analysis, categories of the natural sciences.[93] In a word, what falls under the observation of the senses is the sole objective of the sciences and the ultimate aim is to reduce to simplification the connection between discovered laws. The scientist may then predict the outcome in various life situations both for man and for society, and thus enable science to formulate laws for the good life. Logic, ethics, aesthetics, religion, and sociology fall within the competency of this positivistic philosophy of life, and in this way it allies itself with Empiricism.[94] The outstanding representatives of Positivism in France in the nineteenth century are Comte, Renan, Claude Bernard, Taine, Littré, and Le Dantec.[95]

In conclusion, it may be said that Deism, by its rejection of revealed Christianity, definitely prepared the way for naturalism in its extreme form. However this religion of reason still distinguished "human nature from the rest of nature by reason of the existence in man of a spiritual principle which [had] its own laws. . . . It still asserted . . . the spirituality and immortality of the soul, the freedom of the will, 'a law for man' in nature distinct from 'the law for the thing.' " [96] Voltaire and Rousseau, each after his own fashion helped to infuse thought and life with this doctrine, but it was Materialism, Positivism, and

---

[92] Cardinal Mercier, *A Manual of Modern Scholastic Philosophy,* I, 251.

[93] Baldwin, *Dictionary of Philosophy and Psychology,* II, 137.

[94] Cardinal Mercier, *op. cit.,* II, 475-476; Janet and Seailles, *op. cit.,* II, 142.

[95] De Hovre-Jordan, *Philosophy and Education,* p. 4.

[96] L. A. J. Mercier, *The Challenge of Humanism,* p. 11.

Evolutionism which finally completed the cleavage between the supernatural and the natural. Evolution, the final and extreme stage of naturalism, claimed that it afforded a complete explanation of nature, from inanimate to animate and organic. Man, the highest stage in the evolutionary process, was the result of successive transformations from the simple to the complex. A product of nature, he stood at the summit of nature's economy because of his intelligence and reason. This introduced the question of his mind. What is it? How did it come about? Naturalism, relying on the principle that all truth was to be found in natural sciences, answered in no uncertain terms maintaining that mind was purely "a function of the brain, an organ in an organism, and subject like the rest of the body to the laws of cause and effect which include that body in the circuits of physical nature." [97] Denying the soul, it explained away the dualism between mind and body by reducing mental functions to physiological processes. Hence consciousness and intelligence were simply forms of adaptation to environment acquired through chance and preserved because of utility in the struggle for existence. Feeling, reason, volition were in the last analysis processes of the great mechanism by which organisms adapted themselves to life after having emerged by degrees in response to vital needs. In a word, man and all that he is were products of nature in which purpose and plan did not exist. [98]

Hence the naturalistic system, confining its attention to this world and indifferent to, or at least unin-

---

[97] Hocking, *op. cit.*, p. 61.
[98] Hocking, *Types of Philosophy*, p. 45.

formed about, the hereafter, is not interested in the existence of an omnipresent Deity or of an eternal law. In applying the theories of science to the problems of philosophy, naturalism denies the existence of a First Cause or at least relegates the question to the Unknowable.[99] It is confident that the day will come when Science will supplant Religion. Meanwhile under the naturalistic aegis, reason challenges faith, knowledge attacks superstition, evolution opposes revelation, scepticism takes the place of dogma, lay morality supplants religious morality, and science throws down the gauntlet to religion.[100] The central question of all philosophies, that concerning man and his destiny, is decided in the solvent of naturalism which excludes the Christian idea of an immortal soul distinct from corporeal nature. Moral sentiment is really an adaptation to environment, a social instinct developed in connection with the survival of the fittest. The Darwinian theory tended to substitute mechanical for teleological causation in the organic world and the Spencerian cosmic generalizations, extending this to all life, inanimate, animate and social, found supernatural categories superfluous. Naturalism is simply concerned with society and man. Physical nature was to be examined and brought under control. Instincts together with experiences gained through the interaction of the individual and his environment were to indicate rules of conduct. Conscience and will became obsolete terms. Hedonism and the discipline of natural consequences were all-embracing and all-sufficing factors

---

[99] *Ibid.,* p. 45.
[100] Benjamin Kidd, *Social Evolution* (New York: The Macmillan Co., 1894), pp. 97-98.

for the future happiness of mankind.[101] A new science of human conduct was introduced in which the theory of relativity was applied to morality. Evolution had introduced categories of growth; and the idea of an absolute, unchanging, unconditional moral law was found to be unscientific. In fine, man's intellectual and volitional faculties, his philosophy of life, character and conduct were all to be explained as the product of physical and social heredity. They were evolved through the agency of natural selection by the process of adaptation to environment. All action became reaction while creation was really transformation. Initiative was explained in terms of imitation. Internal and personal activity was denied. Man became merely a perfected animal.[102]

The devolution from the supernaturalistic to the naturalistic attitude of mind in philosophy was gradually reflected in educational theory and practice. As long as Christendom was united in one Faith, "the religious element was the core of Christian education," [103] and education was really a preparation for life here and hereafter. The Christian ideal aimed unreservedly at "the complete changing of the personality," [104] in preference to its harmonious and general development.[105] The Renaissance, however, reviving the ancient classics and ancient ideals intro-

---

[101] Rusk, *The Philosophical Bases of Education,* p. 37.

[102] De Hovre-Jordan, *op. cit.,* p. 9.

[103] Willmann-Kirsch, *The Science of Education,* I, 171.

[104] *Ibid.,* p. 173.

[105] Willmann tells us that: "Religion occupies the central place in the soul life of the Middle Ages and also determines the spirit and tendency of medieval education. Studies, science, knowledge, intellectual development are not valued for their own sake, but as means for attaining Christian perfection." *Ibid.,* p. 234.

duced "many elements . . . that were by their nature antagonistic to Christian educational principles." [106] Thus the domination of the "other-worldly" ideal was gradually replaced by interest in this world and human affairs. Humanism, with its emphasis on the literature and culture of the classical peoples, began to draw its intellectual food from Latin and Greek which entered into the schools and profoundly affected educational practice.[107] The knowledge of words and formal training took precedence over a knowledge of things. Grammar, dialectic and rhetoric were emphasized.[108] The Protestant Reformation of the sixteenth century reinforced the ideals of Humanism, and at the same time made state-control of schools an actuality.[109] This is a cardinal factor in subsequent naturalistic education; secularization was its final result.

As the era of Humanism began to wane, that of naturalism set in and realism and sense-realism began to pave the way for naturalistic education. New discoveries and inventions now led the Sense-Realists to look upon nature as the source of knowledge and upon education as a natural rather than an artificial development. Wolfgang Ratke and John Amos Comenius began to apply the Baconian principle pertaining to the investigation of truth in education.[110] But

---

[106] *Ibid.*, p. 246.

[107] Frank Pierrepont Graves, *A History of Education During the Middle Ages and the Transition to Modern Times* (New York: The Macmillan Co., 1910), p. 108.

[108] Willmann-Kirsch, *op. cit.*, pp. 251, 255.

[109] *Ibid.*, p. 273.

[110] Patrick J. McCormick, *History of Education* (Washington, D. C.: The Catholic Education Press, 1915), pp. 269-282. Cf. Thomas Davidson, *A History of Education* (New York: Charles Scribner's Sons, 1901), p. 196.

it is with John Locke, empiricist and free-thinker in religion, that we notice more definite tendencies toward naturalism in education.[111]

The outstanding philosophers of naturalistic education, however, until the close of the nineteenth century are Rousseau and Spencer. Though neither is an original thinker in this field, both synthesized the tendencies of their times and prepared the way for modern non-supernatural education. The importance of Rousseau lies in his revolutionary influence.[112] Just as he rebelled against the formalism, artificiality, and hypocrisy of the Enlightenment in its religious, social, and political life, thus launching the back-to-nature movement and sounding the call for the recognition of human freedom, so too, he be-

---

[111] Mary Louise Cuff, *The Limitations of the Educational Theory of John Locke Especially for the Christian Teacher*, Ph. D. dissertation (Washington, D. C.: Catholic University of America, 1920), pp. 43 ff., 131 ff. While Locke has something in common with the Humanists and the Disciplinarians, there is much to classify him with the Realists, the Sense-Realists and the Naturalists. The educational theory in his *Thoughts Concerning Education* supplemented by his *Conduct of the Human Understanding* shows his antagonism to the education of his time and represents an influential force in the direction of naturalistic education. Monroe says: "In a sense, Locke is the founder of the naturalistic movement in education, for in many respects Rousseau freely acknowledges indebtedness to him." Paul Monroe, *A Text-Book in the History of Education*, p. 522. There is a wide difference, it is true, between Rousseau and himself in so far as he held the purpose of education to be the control of the natural tendencies of the child by the discipline of reason. John Locke, *Some Thoughts Concerning Education*, with introduction and notes by the Rev. R. H. Quick (new edition, Cambridge: University Press, 1892), p. 21. However, "The sensationalism of Locke became the philosophical basis of the naturalism of Rousseau so far as it sought one in the nature of knowledge." Monroe, *op. cit.*, p. 522. Like Rousseau, Locke believed that the primary basis of education was a sound body, a training in sense-perception. While learning was minimized, moral education by natural consequences was stressed, and reason substituted for authority.

[112] H. A. Taine, *The Ancient Regime*, (New York: Henry Holt and Co., 1896), p. 273.

lieved that reform was urgently needed in education. The first principles of his social philosophy formed the basis of his pedagogy. In order to rebuild society on natural lines conformable to human nature as he conceived it, the men and women of tomorrow were to be allowed to develop naturally instead of being educated artificially. To this end he wrote the *Émile*, his most important work. Its keynote is found in the opening sentence: "Everything is good as it comes from the hands of the author of nature, but everything degenerates in the hands of man." [113]

Rousseau is not so much an educational reformer as he is an educational revolutionary. In place of the traditional system of education with its aesthetic, cultural, and moral objectives, he tried to introduce a natural, emotional, and utilitarian formation, stripped of the teachings of Christianity. The historical significance of *Émile* lies in its definite protest against the educational practices of the eighteenth century. Education must be based on the cardinal principle that the child is by nature innately good; and, since evil is the work of man, the teacher's task is to prevent his pupil from coming into contact with *society until he is developed*.[114] Nature will dictate

---

[113] Jean J. Rousseau, *Émile ou de L'Education* (Paris: Garnier Frères, no date), Livre I, 5. This is the master thought of his *Discourses on the Sciences and the Arts* (1750), the *Discourse on Inequality* (1754), and the *Social Contract* (1762). *Émile* was published in 1762. It is not an abstract treatise but an educational romance, the case-history of an imaginary orphan child chosen for experiment. It is divided into five parts, Émile's infancy, childhood, boyhood, adolescence, and the training of his wife Sophie. "Émile ... is humanity personified, in the natural condition of childhood; a tutor teaches the child of nature naturally." H. Barnard, "Jean Jacques Rousseau," *Barnard's Journal of Education*, V, 463.

[114] Cf. *Émile*, pp. 7, 18.

this development, the natural aims of which are freedom, individualism, and emotionalism. The future
must surrender to the present. The original nature
of the child is the fundamental question. Thus, according as the child's faculties mature, we see him
growing first like an animal, between two and twelve
years of age, undifferentiated in feeling, his mentality
dominated by the senses.[115] He lacks all reasoning
activity and is oblivious to morality,[116] knowing only
the law of physical necessity. During the pre-ado-
lescent period he begins to regulate his activity from
the utilitarian standpoint.[117] His conscience counts
for very little. During adolescence the sex passions
assert themselves, the soul takes its place beside the
senses and intelligence, virtue becomes an aim and
conscience is given its place in a naturalistic religious
setting.[118]

In the principle of "following nature" in education
Rousseau heralded the break with the past and the
traditional school curriculum.[119] His negative education had its moral implications—the doctrine of
natural consequences. The child's physical being
and individual welfare were his only consideration.
Authority, tradition, and Christianity were to be set
aside.[120]

---

[115] *Ibid.*, pp. 39, 76.

[116] *Ibid.*, pp. 72, 74, 234.

[117] *Ibid.*, p. 118.

[118] *Ibid.*, pp. 256-257, 192, 285-289.

[119] Cf. Hudson, *Rousseau and Naturalism in Life and Thought,*
p. 205.

[120] Monroe sums up Rousseau's doctrine in the following words:
"... education is a natural, not an artificial process ... it is development from within, not an accretion from without . . . it comes
through the working of natural instincts and interests and not
through response to external force ... it is an expansion of natural
powers, not an acquisition of information . . . it is life itself, not

Rousseau introduced the critical spirit of inquiry and investigation into the work of instruction in science. Children were to discover and not merely learn facts. Such training was to initiate an abiding interest in science. He stressed the doctrine of interest to the neglect of effort.[121]

His theory of education is based on sentimentalism, freedom, abhorrence of discipline, and negation of the Christian past. The study of the child becomes the focal point in education, not the imparting of knowledge.[122] Freedom from restraint, the arts of being ignorant and doing nothing are the starting points of his method. Training the senses, development of the animal side of the child's nature, delayal of the intellectual, ignoring of the spiritual and the moral—these were the new aims.[123]

Before the nineteenth century the religious theory of education had controlled the elementary schools. These schools remained conservative in the tradition of the past. With Rousseau's *Émile* as the inspirational theory, however, and Pestalozzi, Basedow, and leading statesmen desirous of translating it in its essential into practice, a new elementary school—the secular national elementary school of the nineteenth

---

[121] "Present interest," he says, "is the grand motive power, the only one which leads with certainty to great results." *Émile*, p. 107.
[122] Cf. Robert Herbert Quick, *Essays on Educational Reformers* (New York: D. Appleton and Co., 1899), pp. 245-246.
[123] *Ibid.*, p. 264.

---

preparation for a future state remote in interests and character from the life of childhood." Paul Monroe, *A Text-Book in the History of Education*, p. 566.

century—came into being; and naturalism penetrated to the very heart of education—the child.[124]

The next outstanding educational naturalist previous to the twentieth century is Spencer. His philosophy of life is, as we have seen, naturalistic.[125] He lived in a period when the development of the natural sciences and the secular spirit were gaining momentum. He stands out as the one who caught the spirit of the age and gave to education a new synthesis based completely on naturalism.[126] In 1859, Spencer's essay, *What Knowledge is of Most Worth?* brought the question of the new scientific studies into the limelight. He challenged the existing classical curriculum and by implication the faculty theory on which it rested. This essay is the most important one of the four included in his *Education.*[127] In it we note that he judges all human knowledge and education by the standards of nature and science. Since life is limited to this earth, education has for its aim and purpose earthly life. The greatest good is to live it well. Hence, "To prepare us for complete living

---

[124] Samuel Chester Parker, *A Textbook in the History of Modern Elementary Education* (Boston: Ginn & Co., 1912), pp. 205, 208; cf. Chapter X.

[125] Cf. Weber and Perry, *History of Philosophy* (revised ed., New York: Charles Scribner's Sons, 1925), pp. 482-483.

[126] Rusk says that: "Naturalism in Education is coincident . . . with the introduction of the scientific conception in education, and Herbert Spencer's work *On Education* is typical of the naturalistic school." Robert R. Rusk, *The Philosophical Bases of Education* (Boston: Houghton-Mifflin Co., 1929), p. 35.

[127] The four chapters of this work had already appeared in British reviews with a view to republication in book form. At the invitation of American admirers, he revised these articles and published them in America in 1860. Cf. Herbert Spencer, *Education: Intellectual, Moral and Physical* (New York: D. Appleton Co., 1890), preface, pp. 17-18.

is the function which education has to discharge." [128]
To this end knowledge of science is essential. Some
knowledge of physiology is required to maintain
health and life. Mathematics, physics, chemistry,
biology, and sociology are essential for indirect self-
preservation. The political, economic, and social
implications of history are required to fit men for
citizenship.[129] Physiology, mechanics, and psychology
are the basic requirements for the leisure part of life,
for sculpture, painting, music, and poetry.[130] A knowledge of science, therefore, is the most useful for life
and consequently of most worth.[131] Spencer views
life as a biologist and therefore gives physical life the
priority. The life of the spirit and that which separates man from brute creation are in the class of desirable but dispensable luxuries.[132] The basic principle of Spencer's method of education is that

> The education of the child must accord
> both in mode and arrangement with the
> education of mankind as considered his-
> torically; or in other words, the genesis of
> knowledge in the individual must follow
> the same course as the genesis of knowledge
> in the race.[133]

This theory of recapitulation is based on a biological
analogy and assumes the transmission of acquired
characteristics.

---

[128] *Ibid.*, p. 31.
[129] *Ibid.*, pp. 32-33.
[130] *Ibid.*, p. 84.
[131] *Ibid.*, p. 93.
[132] *Ibid.*, p. 103.
[133] *Ibid.*, p. 122. "His main principle of method, Spencer derives
from animal development." Rusk, *op. cit.*, pp. 35-36.

In his essay on Moral Education, Spencer is purely naturalistic. Just as Rousseau held that moral training ought to be the result of permitting the child to suffer the natural consequences of his actions, so Spencer stresses the same doctrine as the essential of moral training. He is hedonistic.[134] The basis of the moral education of the child is the principle of punishing through natural consequences.[135]

To sum up briefly, Spencer maintains that man is a natural being, the product of the forces of nature. Hence biological well-being is his main purpose in life. The means to this utilitarian end is the knowledge and use of natural science. This is to take precedence over the social sciences and the cultural subjects of the curriculum, for to be a good animal is the basis of all education.[136] A moral act has the same worth as a biological act, otherwise there is no external moral law. Spencer is the modern leader of naturalistic education. De Hovre says, "He may be called the leading educator of Naturalism. In the words of Spencer especially we find the cult of natural science carried almost to the point of fanaticism." [137] The value of knowledge is over-emphasized as a preparation for life. The critical tendency and the scientific method alone are the criteria of all standards and values. The main question is how mankind must live, not why. There is no absolute aim or purpose in education. Everything is relative. Nature, not man, is the essential basis of life. He asserts "the superiority of the knowledge which the in-

---

[134] Cf. *Ibid.*, pp. 173-174. Cf. Rusk, *op. cit.*, p. 37
[135] *Ibid.*, pp. 172-173, 176.
[136] *Ibid.*, p. 103.
[137] De Hovre-Jordan, *op. cit.*, I, 16.

dividual can verify for himself and use to solve the problems of his own life, as compared with the knowledge which rests on tradition and makes no direct call on personal judgment." [138] His "preparation for complete living consists, first in the acquisition of knowledge that is best adapted for the development of the individual and social life; and, secondly, in the development of the power to use this knowledge. What knowledge is of most worth becomes, as with Rousseau and with Bacon, the chief question of educational importance." [139]

Thus we have seen that naturalistic education is based on a theory of life that is not concerned with the world to come. We have traced briefly the devolution from the supernaturalistic education of the Middle Ages down through the Renaissance ideal, on to the Realism, the Sense-Realism, and the Naturalism of modern times. With Locke as the inspirer of Rousseau, who in turn summed up the educational needs of a society artificial and weary within itself, we find education emphasized as the means for the re-creation of the life of the world. Religion in the supernatural sense no longer is an essential part of the curriculum, much less its core. True, a diluted religion, naturalistic religion, is mentioned in a vague fashion by Locke, and as an emotional factor by Rousseau, but with the advent of Spencer it is no longer required. Science is its successor. Education through science is to beget preparation for this life; the afterlife will take care of itself, if there is one. The primary concern is to train good animals who may

---

[138] W. Boyd, *The History of Western Education*, p. 393.
[139] Paul Monroe, *op. cit.*, p. 686.

enjoy life to the full and develop according to the evolutionary tendencies of their nature. Relativity in morals, in ethics, and in educational aims is a cardinal principle. There is no abiding definite revealed religious or moral law. Utility, pleasure, freedom, rather than self sacrifice, effort, and authority are the ends of life. Natural instincts, impulses, and feelings must be free from repression. Nature is sound and well balanced. The child must develop harmoniously therefore and not be changed interiorly. Experience rather than positive instruction must be his teacher. Intellectually, the natural curiosity of the child must be aroused. Morally, he must be guided by natural consequences. There is a biological predestination in human nature and hence adaptation to an ever-changing environment is imperative. Man is a superior animal and his training must be devised accordingly.

CHAPTER II

Introduction of Naturalism Into American Education

I. THE EIGHTEENTH CENTURY

The purpose of this chapter is to trace the infiltration of naturalism into American thought and educational theory. It is a fact that dominant philosophies invariably influence educational theory and practice, and it is a fundamental law of education that every system is based on a philosophy of life.[1] So intimately are theories of education dependent on the philosophies which produced them that "without the latter they are meaningless and as purposeless as a limb detached from the body to which it belongs."[2] Litt expresses this forcibly when he tells us that: "Not only are education and philosophy connected with one another by the logical bond of cause and effect, but there is a vital solidarity between them such as is found in two branches springing from the same trunk."[3] We shall see, in the course of this chapter, that these basic principles are true of American philosophy and education.

The New World from colonial times until the days of Emerson was the natural haven of the dominant

---

[1] De Hovre-Jordan, *Catholicism in Education*, p. 3.
[2] *Ibid.*
[3] Theodor Litt, *Die Philosophie der Gegenwart und ihr Einfluss auf das Bildungsideal* (Leipzig: Teubner, 1925), p. 12.

European philosophies.[4]   This constant influence
upon American thought, coming simultaneously with
the conquest of the frontier and the triumphant
scientific invasion of industry, could not be without
its effect upon political thinking and educational
theory.   The history of America's intellectual and
political evolution is summarized in the transition
which took place from the absolutism of theocracy to
the freedom of democracy, from Puritanism to Deism
and free-thinking.

> Developing side by side, the one influencing
> the other, the philosophical and political
> movements passed through the same
> changes.   In the seventeenth century, we
> find men's interest chiefly centered about
> God.   In the eighteenth century that inter-
> est is twofold: it concerns itself with nature,
> as well as with God.   In the nineteenth cen-
> tury the interest has transferred itself mainly
> to nature.   The same transfer of thought
> takes place in politics.[5]

Logically this development is reflected in due time in
educational thought, though its reduction to practice
follows later.   During the early colonial period, the
dominant system was Puritanism introduced from
England and maintaining "a metaphysical monopoly
for almost two centuries.   From the landing of the
Pilgrims to the appearance of Emerson the prevalent

---

[4] Woodbridge Riley, *American Philosophy, The Early Schools*
(New York: Dodd, Mead and Company, 1907), p. 4.
[5] Woodbridge Riley, *American Thought, from Puritanism to
Pragmatism and Beyond* (New York: Henry Holt and Company,
1915), p. 2.

faith of the colonists and their descendants was Calvinism." [6]

The early colonial settlers who came to the New World in the seventeenth century were Anglicans, Lutherans, Presbyterians, Calvinists, Catholics—English, Scotch, Dutch, and German. Deeply imbued with religion and a philosophy of life flowing from it, they transplanted their ideas of education to such an extent that: "The original object aimed at in American education had been to make good Christians rather than good citizens." [7] It is important to bear this fact in mind for had these ideas prevailed naturalism would not have gained the foothold it has today. The scene presented in those early colonial

---

[6] *Ibid.*, p. 6. Calvinism was a clear-cut system of thought. It had its definite solutions for the debates of the Renaissance and the Reformation on human nature, free-will, authority, revelation, and God. It held that human nature was essentially corrupt and that free-will existed solely in the absolute Deity. Within the limits of a foreordained predestination, all mankind was caught up. Some were chosen to be the elect, to be happy forever hereafter, while the rest lay under the ban of an irrevocable damnation. Determinism existed in the physical, religious, and ethical orders of Calvinism. *Catholic Encyclopedia*, III, 198-204. Riley gives a complete account of Puritanism in Chapter I of his *American Philosophy, The Early Schools.* Puritanism was a result of the Renaissance. The question which it answered was the fundamental one of human nature which it considered weak and depraved. "François Rabelais and Jean Calvin are respectively the positive and negative poles of the Renaissance. Drawing their inspiration from the newly discovered classics, with an equal opposition to medieval pedantry, they yet represent the parting of the ways in their conflicting ideals: Rabelais, the exuberant apostle of freedom, and Calvin, the rigid disciplinarian. To the one, human nature appeared essentially healthy and hence trustworthy; to the other it appeared totally depraved and therefore in pressing need of renewed contact with the Deity." William A. Nitze and E. Preston Dargan, *A History of French Literature from the Earliest Times to the Present* (Rev. Ed., New York: Henry Holt and Co., 1927) p. 145.

[7] J. T. Adams, *The March of Democracy, The Rise of the Union* (New York: Chas. Scribner's Sons, 1933), I, 69.

times is adequately described by Cubberley, who informs us that:

> Children were constantly surrounded week days and Sundays, by the somber Calvinistic religious atmosphere in New England, and by the careful religious oversight of the pastors and the elders in the colonies where the parochial-school system was the ruling plan for education. . . . Religious matter constituted the only reading matter, outside the instruction in Latin in the grammar schools. The Catechism was taught and the Bible read and expounded. . . . This insistence on the religious element was more prominent in Calvinistic New England than in the colonies to the south, but everywhere the religious purpose was dominant.[8]

While this state of affairs continued until the nineteenth century, a definite change had begun to manifest itself earlier in educational and religious thought. By the middle of the eighteenth century, "the change in religious thinking in America had become quite marked."[9] Several factors contributed to this. The challenge of the frontier begot a new spirit of freedom quite opposed to the conventions and traditions of the Atlantic coast settlements, apart altogether from the discontent of the colonists with English domination.

This new freedom was a logical stimulus to the new doctrine of the indefinite perfectibility of man

---

[8] E. T. Cubberley, *The History of Education* (Boston: Houghton Mifflin Company, 1920), p. 375.
[9] *Ibid.*, p. 519

and social life. Theocratic Calvinism, with its fundamental dogmas of the total depravity of human nature and determinism, began to receive a definite challenge from Arminianism and Deism or free-thought, so that by "1750, it might almost be said, a large part of the population had already been prepared by the actual conditions of living to welcome the doctrines of the French Enlightenment and the theories that were inherent in the French Revolution." [10] A new trend of evolutionary development in American thought and life had made its appearance; the philosophy of democracy with its slogan of equality, freedom, and fraternity had found fertile ground in this period of change; while new inventions as well as the continuing spirit of the Renaissance, the Reformation, the Copernican Revolution, and of the ideas of Bacon, Hobbes, Descartes, and Locke stimulated the questioning and critical attitude gradually supplanting the age-old acceptance of tradition and authority. By the middle of the century "the critical spirit was fully aroused and resulted on the one hand in Deism and on the other in a rationalism strongly influenced by French thought," [11]

---

[10] I. L. Kandel, "The Philosophy Underlying the System of Education in the United States," *Education Yearbook, 1929* (New York: International Institute of Teachers College, Columbia University, 1930), p. 467.

[11] *Ibid.*, pp. 469-470. "Deism was a product of eighteenth century rationalism, an attempt of the Enlightenment to reduce religion to ethics, revelation to a spiritual law in the natural world." Riley, *American Philosophy, The Early Schools*, p. 191. Deism spread from England to France. Montesquieu and Voltaire had spent considerable time in England and imbibed there the deistical attitude and brought it to France. The Encyclopedists adopted it and based their criticisms of the existing religious order in France upon its principles. A considerable proportion of the leaders of the Enlightenment became openly naturalistic. Cf. Riley, *American Thought*, pp. 9-10. Deism was common in England towards the end of the

Deism appeared in colonial America through the influence of English thought. Besides, Americans went to France and England and brought back with them the new ideas. Benjamin Franklin and Thomas Paine represent the deistic movement. This early American deism was really, at bottom, a movement against Calvinism and revealed religion. As Riley says: ". . . the dogmas of an unnatural religion were giving way to the principles of natural religion, and rationalism had at last a chance to assert itself. Here deism constituted the moving cause and the colonial college the vehicle in the transaction." [12]

Deism or free-thinking challenged the monopoly of Calvinism in America and resulted in scepticism. It was decidedly an English importation. It represented the gradual withdrawal from a supernatural revealed religion to one that was natural and based on reason. It denied the immanence of God and unduly stressed His transcendence, denying providence, miracles, revelation, and the supernatural. God is not interested in the world. Prayers are superfluous. It was a re-

[12] Riley, *American Thought*, pp. 56-57. Ethan Allen was one of the first determined opponents of Calvinism in America. He did not conceal his contempt for Christianity and was brave enough to say what many others silently felt. He argued against the depravation of mankind and denied miracles and prophecies. As Riley puts it: ". . . his work furnishes a good example of the popular recoil from Puritanism on the part of one who wished to pursue the 'natural road of ratiocination.' " *American Thought*, p. 13. Allen wrote *Oracles of Reason* in 1784.

seventeenth century. It arose in a spirit of criticism against the traditional authority and beliefs of the Church. It substituted instead a rationalistic naturalism. Deism is a comprehensive name for many individualistic views which agree basically in desiring to eliminate authority in religious teaching. John Herman Randall, *The Making of the Modern Mind* (Boston: Houghton Mifflin Company, 1926), pp. 285, 291.

action against the gloomy doctrine of predestination. Some deists went so far as to deny existence after death and consequently rewards and punishments because man was too unimportant.

Hence the eighteenth century in America is one of transition from supernaturalism to naturalism. Through the influence of deism, philosophy becomes independent of theology and the tone of religious life diminishes to a considerable degree.[13] Scepticism, atheism, and materialism are distinctive among the leading lesser thinkers of this period "many of whom are in the colleges and therefore influencing the rising generation." [14] Theocracy gives way before the movement from supernaturalism to science, revelation to reason. "From England come Locke's *Inquiry on Human Understanding*, and Hartley's *Observations on Man;* from France Condorcet's *Progress of the Human Spirit* and La Mettrie's *Man a Machine;* from Scotland come the similar humanistic treatises of Hume, Reid and Stewart." [15]

Materialism in America

> was an orderly reproduction of the European movement—deriving its mechanical notions from Newton, its psychological from Hobbes, its physical from Hartley and Darwin, and, as the last step in the historic succession, approaching the sensualistic philosophy of the French schools. Nevertheless,

---

[13] Howard Mumford Jones, *America and French Culture, 1750-1848* (Chapel Hill: The University of North Carolina Press, 1927), p. 375.

[14] *Ibid.*, p. 376; Cf. Riley, *American Philosophy, The Early Schools*, pp. 10-11.

[15] Riley, *op cit.*, p. 17.

besides these larger historical connections, American materialism had a double national significance, first, as a form of naturalism and in marked contrast to the austere idealism of the North, it prevailed in sections other than New England, Philadelphia being its radiating centre and the south the chief sphere of influence; secondly, as a scientific movement, it was not the clergy but the medical profession which sought to reduce mental activities to a physiology of the nerves and to combine therewith the study of pathology and of the psychology of infants and of animals.[16]

Cadwallader Colden, Joseph Buchanan, Joseph Priestley, Thomas Cooper, and Benjamin Rush were the prominent materialists.

The colleges were affected by all this. Harvard, strongly imbued with Calvinism from its foundation, was already showing signs of the liberalistic trend by the beginning of the eighteenth century.[17] The Congregationalist monopoly of control there was decisively defeated when Cotton Mather failed of election to the presidency and the liberals won out.[18] The influx of deism brought about a toleration of all sects

---

[16] *Ibid.*, pp. 20-21.

[17] When Governor Bellemont at the end of the seventeenth century advised Harvard College that an address should be sent to the king requesting a royal charter for itself, the representatives of the assembly asked for the introduction of a clause restricting the right to hold office in the college to Presbyterians, Congregationalists and followers of traditional orthodox policy, so necessary was it to preserve the sectarianism of Harvard amid the changing currents of New England thought, but the Governor "refused to accept any bill containing a religious restriction. . . ." Kenneth Ballard Murdock, *Increase Mather; The Foremost American Puritan* (Cambridge, Mass.: Harvard University Press, 1925), pp. 353-354.

[18] Paul Monroe, Ed., *A Cyclopedia of Education*, III, 227.

in the various colleges.[19]   The College of New Jersey, later Princeton, in 1746; King's College, later Columbia, 1754; and the University of Georgia, in 1785 make this clear in their charters.[20]   Ten colleges were in existence prior to 1776 and of these all, with the exception of Franklin's Academy at Philadelphia, had been founded on sectarian principles.   The following two decades saw the establishment of fourteen more.   Only four of these, two in New England and two outside it, were sectarian.

COLLEGES FOUNDED PRIOR TO 1800 [21]

1. Harvard	Massachusetts	1637	Congregationalist
2. William & Mary	Virginia	1693	Episcopal
3. Yale	Connecticut	1701	Congregationalist
4. Princeton	New Jersey	1746	Presbyterian
5. U. of Penn.*	Pennsylvania	1749	Non-sectarian
6. Columbia	New York	1754	Episcopal
7. Brown	Rhode Island	1764	Baptist
8. Dartmouth	New Hampshire	1769	Congregationalist
9. Queen's (Rutgers)	New Jersey	1770	Reformed
10. Hampden-Sydney	Virginia	1776	Presbyterian
11. Wash. & Lee	Virginia	1782	Non-sectarian
12. Washington U.	Maryland	1782	Non-sectarian
13. Dickinson	Pennsylvania	1783	Meth.-Episcopal
14. St. John's	Maryland	1784	Non-sectarian
15. Nashville*	Tennessee	1785	Non-sectarian
16. Georgetown	D. C.	1789	Roman Catholic
17. U. of N. Car.*	N. C.	1789	Non-sectarian
18. U. of Vermont*	Vermont	1791	Non-sectarian

* State

---

[19] "In examining the books of the early colleges and the thoughts of representative men, there have been found numberless signs of colonial free-thinking, of mental independency before political independence."   Riley, *American Thought*, p. 86.

[20] John Maclean, *History of the College of New Jersey from Its Origin in 1746 to the Commencement of 1854* (Philadelphia: J. B. Lippincott & Co., 1877), I, 51, 61; Brander Matthews, and others, *History of Columbia University, 1754-1904.* Published in commemoration of the one hundred-fiftieth anniversary of the founding of King's College (New York: The Macmillan Co., 1904), pp. 5-6, 7; Augustus L. Hull, *A Historical Sketch of the University of Georgia* (Atlanta: The Foote and Davies Co., 1894), p. 7.

[21] Richard G. Boone, *Education in the United States; Its History*

19. U. of E. Tenn.	Tennessee	1792 Non-sectarian
20. Williams	Massachusetts	1793 Congregationalist
21. Bowdoin	Maine	1794 Non-sectarian
22. Union	New York	1795 Non-sectarian
23. Middlebury	Vermont	1795 Congregationalist
24. Frederick Coll.	Maryland	1796 Non-sectarian

Prior to the arrival of Dr. Thomas Coke at Cambridge on December 5, 1784, no religious services had been held for some years and the church had been used to house cattle and hogs.[22] The situation at Yale was not much better before Dwight became president in 1795. In his *Autobiography*, Lyman Beecher states that the college was "in a most ungodly state. The college church was almost extinct. Most of the students were skeptical, and rowdies were plenty. . . . Most of the class before me were infidels, and called each other Voltaire, Rousseau, D'Alembert, etc." [23] Free-thought, under the inspiration of Thomas Paine and Thomas Jefferson, was prevalent.[24] In 1782 the student body at Princeton counted only two Christians.[25] Columbia embraced deism under the leadership of Samuel Johnson and William Livingston.[26] Griswold says that atheists were "comparatively much more numerous and more dignified in talents and positions" in Washing-

---

[22] Drew, *op. cit.*, p. 94.
[23] Leonard Woolsey Bacon, *A History of American Christianity,* American Church History Series, XIII (New York: The Christian Literature Co., 1897), 231.
[24] Riley, *American Thought*, p. 66.
[25] Bacon, *op. cit.*, p. 230.
[26] Riley, *American Thought*, p. 66.

---

from the Earliest Settlements (New York: D. Appleton & Co., 1902), p. 77. Cokesbury College, near Baltimore, is to be added to this list. It was Methodist. *Ibid.* Cf. Samuel Drew, *The Life of the Rev. Thomas Coke, LL.D.* (New York: J. Soule & T. Mason, 1818), pp. 120-127.

ton's day than since then.[27] Riley tells us in his *American Philosophy* that: "It was the slow encroachment of rationalism, by way of the colleges, that brought about the disintegration of Calvinism. Here the most potent solvent was deism." [28] The president of Transylvania University was suspected of teaching naturalism.[29]

Benjamin Franklin was a deist and a free-thinker.[30] "It was due to his influence as founder that the University of Pennsylvania became noteworthy for requiring no religious test of its instructors, and for being so unprejudiced as to bestow an honorary degree even upon Thomas Paine." [31] Through his leadership, Philadelphia became noted for naturalistic scientific spirit. He died in 1790.[32] Thomas

[27] Rufus Wilmot Griswold, *The Republican Court, or American Society in the Days of Washington* (New York: D. Appleton & Co., 1864), p. 290. Quoted by Jones, *op. cit.*, p. 379.

[28] Riley, *American Philosophy, The Early Schools*, p. 15.

[29] Jones, *American and French Culture*, p. 382; Riley, *American Philosophy, The Early Schools*, p. 306.

[30] In 1723 he was forced because of his radical opinions to leave Boston. He was seventeen years old at this time and had already read Locke's *Essay on the Human Understanding*. At nineteen he wrote a deistic pamphlet in London entitled *A Dissertation on Liberty and Necessity, Pleasure and Pain* (1725). Three years later he composed his *Articles and Acts of Religion* in which, among other things, he enumerates his First Principles. He is probably one of the ablest Americans as he surely is the greatest diplomat and scientist of his day in the New World. He was well acquainted with the French Encyclopedists and received many letters from them. He knew Voltaire, Condorcet, and Hume. In France he was considered a naturalistic philosopher. He was the organizer of the American Philosophical Society. Riley, *American Thought*, pp. 68-76; Charles A. and Mary A. Beard, *The Rise of American Civilization* (New York: The Macmillan Co., 1930), I, 157-159. Franklin's Library Company was founded in 1731 and its catalogue had "the largest collection of rationalistic literature in the country" at that time. Riley, *American Philosophy; The Early Schools*, p. 243.

[31] Riley, *American Thought*, p. 76.

[32] Beard, *op. cit.*, I, 157-159.

Jefferson held the same views as Franklin. He was a
noted deist and free-thinker.[33] As events proved, he
was to become the dominant force in higher education in his section of the South,[34] and he saw to it that
the French ideas on education which he had imbibed
abroad should be incorporated as far as possible in
the University of Virginia. The agnostic naturalism
which underlay the University's system of education
for many years was due to Jefferson.[35] Jefferson insisted that religion should be excluded from the University.[36]

Reisner tells us that the naturalism inherent in the
eighteenth century French and English liberalism

[33] In his twentieth year he could read Latin, Greek, and French
fluently and he also knew Spanish, Italian, and Anglo-Saxon. He
was familiar with higher mathematics and, particularly, chemistry.
In 1767 after five years of law he was admitted to the bar. He
went to France as American minister for five years before the out-
break of the Revolution. His sojourn there gave him "an insight
into the possibilities of materialism when carried to a logical
conclusion." Riley, *American Thought*, p. 80. Riley states pertinently that "when on different occasions Jefferson exclaimed: 'I am
an Epicurean'; 'I am a Materialist'; 'I am a sect by myself,' there
was discoverable beneath these various disguises the strut and swag-
ger of the Age of Reason." *Ibid.* While in France he met many
of the Encyclopedists and was influenced by the doctrines of the
French Revolution. He founded the University of Virginia at
Charlottesville. The following motto is inscribed on his tomb:
"Author of the Declaration of American Independence, of the
Statute of Virginia for Religious Freedom, and the Father of the
University of Virginia." *Ibid.*, p. 77. Riley says further that "the
College of William and Mary had a marked influence on Jefferson's
mind. In addition to the liberty of philosophizing advocated in its
charter the scientific spirit prevailed in the place. . . . In regard to
the proposed University of Virginia [he said]: 'The Gothic idea
that we are to look backwards instead of forwards for the improvement of the human mind is not an idea which this country will
endure.'" *Ibid.*, pp. 77-78. Cf. Frederick Eby and Charles Flinn
Arrowood, *The Development of Modern Education* (New York:
Prentice-Hall, Inc., 1934), pp. 544-547.
[34] Jones, *op. cit.*, p. 479.
[35] *Ibid.*, p. 384.
[36] *Ibid.*

had considerable influence on the educational theo-
rizing of the formative period of the American Republic.[37] Locke had prepared the ground by his *Two
Treatises of Government, Letters Concerning Toleration,* and an *Essay Concerning Human Understanding.* He was recognized as an authority in the colleges.[38] Due, however, to natural prejudice against
England and things English on the part of Americans,
the doctrines of the French Enlightenment, inspired
likewise by Locke, dominated the American mind
from 1760 to 1820.[39] Townsend states the case thus:
". . . the French thinkers influenced the leaders of the
American Revolution greatly; for even though they
did not originate, they at least disseminated the doctrines so characteristic of the period. Washington,
Jefferson, and Franklin found kindred spirits among
French men of letters and did not bother to inquire
into the more remote sources of their common opinions."[40] Richard Price and Thomas Paine introduced
the doctrines of Rousseau[41] and thus the ideas of the
Social Contract made their way into the Declaration
of Independence and the American Constitution.[42]
Rousseau's slogan that "man is born free, and yet is
universally enslaved"[43] made a strong impression in

---

[37] G. E. Reisner, Introduction, p. ix in Allen Oscar Hansen,
Liberalism and American Education in the 18th Century (New
York: The Macmillan Co., 1926).

[38] H. G. Townsend, *Philosophical Ideas in the United States* (New
York: American Book Co., Copyright, 1934), p. 19. Used by permission of the publishers.

[39] *Ibid.*, p. 64. [40] *Ibid.*

[41] Hansen, *op. cit.*, p. 5.

[42] Paul Monroe, *A Text-Book in the History of Education* (New
York: The Macmillan Co., 1908), p. 547.

[43] J. J. Rousseau, *A Dissertation on Political Economy to which
is Added a Treatise on the Social Compact or the Principles of*

the colonies just when they were developing a national self-consciousness. "Here the economic and
political influences of the frontier freedom had already made themselves felt. Of all lands here was
the one which had less of the old to destroy before it
could begin to build the new, and what of the new
had already developed was showing signs of the excellence which brave minds of Europe aspired to for the
older society." [44] "As the crown, and religion, and
property lost favor as foundations of government,
nature came to be the obvious parent of democracy." [45]

From 1760 to 1820, French influence is important in
America. As we have seen, the leading men of the
Revolutionary movement were in touch with the
French preachers of the new order, those prolific
writers and pamphleteers who had adapted English
thought to suit their own peculiar needs.[46] The an-

---

[44] Reisner, in Hansen, *op. cit.*, Introduction, p. x.

[45] Frederic L. Paxon, *History of the American Frontier 1763-1893*
(Boston: Houghton Mifflin Co., 1924), p. 101.

[46] Van Becelaire says that French radical influence in the Revolu-
tion was comparatively small and that Otis in 1761 had anticipated
Rousseau's *Social Contract* published a year later. L. Van Becelaire,
*La Philosophie en Amerique, Depuis les Origines Jusqu' à Nos
Jours (1607-1900)* (New York: The Eclectic Publishing Co., 1904),
Sec. 11. Nevertheless, Hayes holds that the philosophy underlying
the Declaration of Independence was that of the radical thinkers of
the time and the same as that which later inspired the French
Revolution. C. J. H. Hayes, *A Political and Social History of
Modern Europe* (New York: The Macmillan Co., 1917), I, 332.
Beard, speaking of the Constitution says: "Its preamble did not
invoke the blessings of Almighty God or announce any interest in
promoting the propaganda of religion. Instead, it declared purposes that were earthly and in keeping with the progressive trend
of the age—'to form a more perfect union, establish justice, insure
domestic tranquillity, provide for the common defense, promote

---

Politic Law (The first American edition, Albany: Barber and
Southwick, 1797), p. 4.

tagonism toward England concealed from American leaders the fact that the French Enlightenment had its roots in English philosophy and was burgeoning a century before Rousseau appeared. Most of the leaders of the Revolution in America were, as we have noted, imbued with naturalism, Paine, Franklin, Jefferson, Rush, Cooper, and others being among them.[47] In order to understand the influence, especially of Rousseau, on American thought, we must remember that Rousseau's ideas were inspired by Locke.[48] *An Essay Concerning Human Understanding, Two Treatises of Government,* and *Letters Concerning Toleration,* the same books that were Rousseau's sources, were also read in America. "It was well beyond the beginning of the eighteenth century before Locke was accepted among the orthodox leaders, but once established in the colleges he became the oracle of wisdom." [49] There is no doubt that Locke had

---

[47] Townsend, *op. cit.,* p. 65.

[48] Thomas Davidson, *A History of Education* (New York: Charles Scribner's Sons, 1901), pp. 218; 209-214; William Henry Hudson, *Rousseau and Naturalism in Life and Thought* (New York: Charles Scribner's Sons, 1903), p. 129.

[49] Townsend, *op. cit.,* p. 19. To get a good idea of this consult C. E. Merriam, *A History of American Political Theories* (New York: The Macmillan Co., 1928), p. 90. Merriam holds that colonial political thought finds its source in Milton, Locke, Sydney and Montesquieu. *Ibid.,* 89-92. Jones says that the influence of the Geneva theologians is important. Jones, *America and French Culture, 1750-1848,* p. 369 (note). See also Riley, *American Philosophy, The Early Schools,* pp. 10 ff.; Carl L. Becker, *The Declaration of Independence, A Study in the History of Political Ideas* (New York: Harcourt, Brace and Co., 1922); F. Emory Aldrich, "John Locke and the Influence of His Works in America," *Proceedings of the*

---

the general welfare and secure the blessings of liberty to ourselves and our posterity.' " Beard, *The Rise of American Civilization,* I, 439. President Washington permitted it to be said that "the government of the United States is not in any sense founded upon the Christian religion." *Ibid.*

considerable influence in America,[50] and was the principal source of the tendencies which resulted in deism. Rousseau's influence in the political order is not important in so far as the actual Revolution goes. Otis, as has been noted, had given expression to many of the ideas of the *Social Contract* one year before it was published. With regard to Rousseau's influence on the Declaration of Independence, Hudson holds that: ". . . his indirect influence can hardly be doubted. The document is conceived wholly in his spirit, and in places his very accent is unmistakable." [51] Davidson says that "the formulas in which the Declaration of Independence was couched were largely drawn from Rousseau. When its framers demanded 'life, liberty, and the pursuit of happiness,' for every citizen, they were speaking in his language." [52] The effects of his influence were felt also in religion.[53] The most recent work on education in the eighteenth century in America says significantly that: "The political documents and tracts of the period gave abundant evidence of Rousseau's influence." [54] Thomas Paine and Richard Price intro-

---

[50] Jones, *op. cit.*, p. 366.

[51] Hudson, *op. cit.*, p. 152.

[52] Davidson, *Rousseau and Education According to Nature*, p. 233.

[53] Edward Frank Humphrey, *Nationalism and Religion in America, 1774-1789* (Boston: Chipman Law Publishing Co., 1924), p. 14.

[54] Hansen, *Liberalism and American Education in the Eighteenth Century* (New York: The Macmillian Co., 1926), p. 26. "The ideas of the French philosophers were in the air, and there is plenty of evidence in the colonial newspapers for 15 or 20 years before the Revolution that the French influence was increasing. Even during the French and Indian War, booksellers advertised French texts, grammars, and dictionaries in the papers, while courses in

American Antiquarian Society (April, 1879), pp. 23-39. Henry Adams, *History of the United States of America* (New York: Charles Scribner's Sons, 1889), I, 124; Beard, *op. cit.*, I, 187.

duced Rousseau's theories into America. Paine was
the great popularizer of French naturalism between
1774 and 1800.[55] Influenced by the French writer, he
held that while society was natural, government
hitherto unnatural should be adapted to agreement
with nature.[56]

The principles advocated by Tom Paine
and others led many at the close of the Revolution to think that some social instrument
must be invented whereby this liberal
philosophy could become a permanent part
in determining the thought in the new republic and in fashioning institutions in harmony with these principles. Chief among
the means sought was a system of national
education that would promote such a na-

---

[55]Hansen, *op. cit.*, pp. 5, 22, 27; also see note on p. 22.
[56] Thomas Paine, *Common Sense;* Addressed to the Inhabitants
of America (Philadelphia, printed; London, reprinted, J. Almon,
1776), Introduction, pp. v-vi, 2-14; cf. Hansen, *op. cit.*, p. 27.

French were often announced. Before the close of the war we find
The Boston Gazette printing extracts from Montesquieu's *The
Spirit of Laws*, with an apology and the repressed hope that it may
not be 'political heresy' to suppose that 'a Frenchman may have
juster Notions of Civil Liberty than some among ourselves!' After
1760 all the important works of Rousseau, Montesquieu and the
Encyclopedists as well as many other French books were advertised
for sale in the colonial press. Such advertisements indicate the
taste of the reading public more accurately than do catalogues of
private libraries, which represent individual preferences. Voltaire
had long been known in the colonies, Rousseau's *Social Contract*
was advertised as a *Treatise on the Social Compact,* or *the Principles of Political Law.* He himself is referred to again and again
as 'the ingenious Rousseau' or 'the celebrated Rousseau.' And
Émile and *La Nouvelle Héloise* were evidently in demand.…
Reports of French interest in America inclined the colonists still
more to the French philosophy of government." *Cambridge History
of American Literature,* I, 119.

tional culture as would be an expression of
these principles.[57]

When independence had been won, the intellectual
leaders of the new republic showed a marked interest in education as the instrument to ensure the new
democracy. The remarkable number of articles,
pamphlets, and books on the subject command attention for their advanced views. Beard states a pertinent fact when he writes: "Though most of the
tracts and pamphlets lie buried in the dust of libraries, their influence still lives in American educational theory." [58]   Leaders like Washington, Jefferson,
Benjamin Rush, Noah Webster, James Sullivan,
Robert Coram, Nathaniel Chipman, Samuel Knox,
and Samuel Harrison Smith gave their serious attention to the question.[59]   The general theory maintained was that there should be a national system of
education from the elementary school to the university, open to all and supported by general taxation.[60]
"Such a national system was not impracticable.   It

[57] Hansen, *op. cit.*, p. 45. Paine was invited to come to America
by Franklin. Born in England in 1737, he died here in 1809. He
wrote the *Age of Reason* (1794-95) in which he popularized the
deism of the seventeenth and eighteenth centuries. His philosophy
is "Follow Nature" and "Investigate Truth Objectively." Reason
was to take place of tradition and authority. His thesis was the
humanitarian one. He was not a Christian. His *Age of Reason*
is in line with Rousseau and the Encyclopedist tradition. The
Bible is a book of lies and Revelation is detestable. He believes in a
Creator. "Among the secular writers, Tom Paine was the most
trenchant and influential," according to Beard, *op. cit.*, I, 260. One
hundred thousand copies of first pamphlet for independence were
immediately sold. *Ibid.*, 183, 238, 446-447; see Townsend, *op. cit.*,
p. 69; Hansen, *op. cit.*, p. 40.

[58] Beard, *op. cit.*, I, 486.

[59] *Ibid.*

[60] *Ibid*, p. 487.

could be created as easily and be as efficient as a national system of justice, and, in the end, the expense of education would be less and the service more efficient." [61] The scientific method should dominate the curriculum:

> there should be an objective, impartial attitude created by the schools through science and experimentation. Until obsolete customs and institutions were destroyed and scientific control substituted, human progress would be very limited. It was the business of the nation to create an effective national system of education that would stimulate the greatest progress of civilization. [62]

The American Philosophical Society for Promoting Useful Knowledge, presided over by Franklin from its foundation in 1769 to his death in 1790, then by David Rittenhouse for six years, and next by Jefferson, who remained president for nineteen years, became active in behalf of a system of education. This interest is important because the Society was most representative of American spirit at that time. [63] Before 1800 it included in its membership 650 of the greatest minds in America. It was the means of further spreading French influence in the new nation. Buffon, Condorcet, Cabanis, Du Pont de Nemours, Du Ponceau, and Linnaeus, prominent French materialists and physiocrats, were members. "There can

[61] Hansen, *Liberalism and American Education in the 18th Century,* p. 261.
[62] *Ibid.*
[63] *Ibid.,* p. 145.

be no doubt that the American Philosophical Society was one of the instruments that helped to give America the philosophy of the Revolution." [64] The Society, wishing to advance the new national government after the Revolution, offered a prize for "the best system of liberal Education and literary instruction, adapted to the genius of the Gov. of the U. S.; comprehending also a plan for instituting and conducting public schools in this country, on the principles of the most extensive utility." [65]   Many contended for the premium which was divided between Samuel Knox and Samuel Harrison Smith, both of whose essays maintained that American education should be nationalistic and humanitarian.   Knox was opposed to private schools because of their lack of equal opportunity, the tendency to establish double standards, and class distinctions. [66]   His essay stood clearly for separation of church and state in education.   "It is a happy circumstance peculiarly favorable to a uniform plan of public education, that this country hath excluded ecclesiastical from civil policy, and emancipated the human mind from the tyranny of church authority; and church establishments." [67]   Knox recommends the philosophy of Locke and Bacon and in particular "Locke's admirable *Essay on human understanding* and Bacon's *Novum Organum*" [68] for the courses of study in the state college.   In a word, the school was to be a national instrument in which

---

[64] *Ibid.*, p. 109.

[65] Samuel Knox, *An Essay on the Best System of Liberal Education Adapted to the Genius of the Government of the United States* (Baltimore: Warner and Hanna, 1799), p. 45.

[66] Hansen, *op. cit.*, p. 119.

[67] Knox, *op. cit.*, p. 78.

[68] *Ibid.*, p. 142.

science was to replace prejudice and superstition, and religious domination was to be excluded.[69] Smith's plan was a national system free from local, racial, and religious prejudices in which "the scientific attitude should be the chief aim."[70] He admired Rousseau and was influenced by him. He said: "The mind of Rousseau was, without doubt, a good one; it emitted as copiously as genius or fancy could desire, the sparks of a noble intellect, which dared to disdain the shackles of prejudice, and break the chains of ignorance."[71]

In all the plans presented for a system of national education there is "a strong emphasis . . . placed upon a mind free from prejudice and one that comprehends the real meaning of objective scientific procedure."[72] For instance, Benjamin Rush, of Philadelphia, convinced as he was that the security of the Republic lay in education, wrote *Thoughts upon the Mode of Education Proper in a Republic* in 1786. He stated that universal education was an essential, Greek and Latin were to be excluded in favor of a new education which would not be limited to the few.[73] "The rejection of the Latin and Greek languages from our schools, would produce a revolution in science, and in human affairs. . . . The nation which shall first shake off the fetters of those ancient languages, will advance further in knowledge, and

---

[69] Hansen, *op. cit.,* pp. 138-139.

[70] *Ibid.,* p. 166.

[71] Samuel Harrison Smith, *Remarks on Education: Illustrating the Close Connection Between Virtue and Wisdom. To Which is Annexed a System of Liberal Education.* (Philadelphia: Printed for John Omrod, 1798), p. 32.

[72] Hansen, *op. cit.,* p. 47.

[73] Benjamin Rush, *Essays, Literary, Moral and Philosophical* (Philadelphia: Thomas and Samuel F. Bradford, 1798), p. 25.

in happiness, in twenty years, than any nation in
Europe has done in a hundred." [74] "Rousseau," he
said, "has asserted that the secret of education consists in 'wasting the time of children profitably.' " [75]
Robert Coram in 1791 issued his Plan for the General Establishment of Schools throughout the United
States.   To preserve the revolutionary principles
there should be a nationalistic system of education.
The "education of children should be provided for
in the constitution of every state. . . . Education then
ought to be secured by government to every class of
citizen, to every child in the state.   The citizen
should be instructed in the sciences by public
schools." [76] In the same year that Coram wrote, James
Sullivan issued his Plan for a National System of
Education.   Holding that the conditions of colonial
life were suitable for the growth of the ideals of the
Enlightenment and the democratic ideals of the eighteenth century, not least of which was the absence of
religious regulations, he held that Americans were
free in thought and action. [77] "Prejudices in politics
insert themselves into the human mind, in the same
manner as they are seen in matters of religion and
morals." [78]

[74] *Ibid.*, p. 43.

[75] Benjamin Rush, *Thoughts upon Female Education, Accommodated to the Present State of Society, Manners, and Government in
the United States of America* (Philadelphia: Prichard and Hall,
1798), p. 79.

[76] Robert Coram, *Political Inquiries: To Which is Added, a Plan
for the General Establishment of Schools Throughout the United
States* (Wilmington, Del.: Andrews and Brynberg, 1791), p. 57.

[77] Hansen, *Liberalism and American Education in the Eighteenth
Century,* pp. 79-83.

[78] James Sullivan, *An Impartial Review of the Causes and Principles of the French Revolution. By an American* (Boston: Benjamin Edes, 1798), p. 21; *quoted in* Hansen, *op. cit.,* p. 87.

In common with the leaders of American thought
after the American Revolution, "Education appeared
to them as well as to many of the eighteenth century
philosophers to be an almost omnipotent instrument
for determining human conduct." [79] The rule of reason must be substituted for superstitious prejudice.
Between 1770 and 1800 Noah Webster was the great
leader of the movement working for educational reconstruction.   Living in a period of change when
the scientific method was being applied to all fields
of knowledge, when the French and American Revolutions were begotten in a new political philosophy,
"he was a pragmatist in his conception of morals, and
held a critical attitude toward religion" up to 1800.[80]
Up to that time he advocated investigation and experimentation.   After 1800 he adopted a conservative attitude toward religious and political dogmas
which was in marked contrast with his previous experimental bent.   His *History of the French Revolution* shows a general acquaintance with the French
philosophers.   "He seems to have digested such writers as Ascham, Montesquieu and Rousseau. Webster
had read Rousseau's *Émile* and *Le Contrat Social.*"
He knew Paine of whom he said: "The Continent
was electrified by his writings—the minds of the
people were prepared for the great event." [81] He was
in communication with Priestley. In 1800 he wrote
the latter saying: "The theories of Helvetius, Rousseau, Condorcet, Turgot, Godwin and others, are
founded on artificial reasoning, not on the nature of
man; not on fact and experience. . . . Between these

[79] Hansen, *op. cit.,* p. 87.
[80] *Ibid.,* p. 201.
[81] *Ibid.,* pp. 203, 204.

theories and the old corrupt establishments, there is
a *mean,* which probably is the true point of freedom
and national happiness." [82]   Earlier he believed in
Rousseau, but the French Revolution begot a reaction about 1793.   The following is significant in
view of what has been said concerning French influence in America.   Writing to Priestley, Webster said:
". . . the bulk of the people in America, in the
strength of their prepossessions for a Republican government, and in their honest credulity, continued to
think well of the view of the French Reformers, until two or three years later." [83]

Nevertheless, despite the reaction which set in to
sober the democratic outlook at the turn of the eighteenth century due to the excesses of the French Revolution,[84] the stage had been set for the development
of naturalism in thought and education in America.
We shall endeavor to show in the next chapter how
this was realized during the nineteenth century.

The evidence which has been adduced in this chapter proves that English and French naturalism gradually permeated intellectual, political, and educational thought in America during the eighteenth century.   The challenge of the expanding frontier with
its demand for social and economic freedom prepared
the way for the spread of democracy.   The naturalistic philosophy of the French Enlightenment and the
liberalism of Rousseau's *Social Contract* exerted considerable influence in the development of the new

---

[82] Noah Webster, *Ten Letters to Dr. Priestley in Answer to His
Letters to the Inhabitants of Northumberland,* (New Haven: Read
and Morse, 1800), p. 21.
[83] Webster, *op cit.,* p. 5.
[84] Hansen, *op. cit.,* p. 47.

social order in which equality of opportunity for all and the indefinite perfectibility of man by natural means were fundamental principles. Side by side with the growth of the democratic ideal went the growth of irreligion, rationalism, atheism, and materialism in the minds of the outstanding thinkers and leaders of the transition. The scientific temper and attitude of mind believing "that the continuous development of the human race through scientific control was the only valid function of institutions" [85] gripped the imagination of the molders of public opinion. The higher institutions of learning were variously affected by the naturalism of the times, a fact which is important in the future development of American life and ideals. Noted Americans began to formulate manifestly naturalistic theories of education on the basis that education was the exclusive function of the democratic state. Thus were sown the seeds of a system of public state-controlled education. Whereas the religious ideal dominated the schools of the colonial period, the introduction of the State theory made its appearance during the last decades of the eighteenth century. Gradually the new states assimilated the current theory into their laws. "Though a number of writers contributed to the change, the one book that did more than any other to sap the foundations of the old religious theory of education was the *Émile* (1762) . . . of Rousseau." [86] Naturalism had definitely entered into American education.

---

[85] *Ibid.*, Preface, p. v.
[86] E. T. Cubberley, *Introduction to the Study of Education* (Boston: Houghton Mifflin Co., 1925), p. 152.

CHAPTER III

INTRODUCTION OF NATURALISM INTO AMERICAN EDUCATION

II.   THE NINETEENTH CENTURY

From what has been said thus far it is clear that the naturalistic theory of life and education was unduly influential in the formative stage of the Republic.   In direct proportion to the transition from theocracy to democracy, it was in due time reflected in the spiritual, intellectual, political, and economic life of the people.   According to Beard: "The colonies were from the first hospitable to the spirit of science," and "By the secularizing political process and the march of scientific skepticism, still deeper inroads were made into the sovereignty of theology and mysticism, especially among the educated classes." [1] Gradually the schools reflect the changes in national thinking.   The last decades of the eighteenth and the first half of the nineteenth century produced a definite transition in the field of education in striking contrast to the previous transplantation of European ideals.   This is true especially in the case of the new Academy with its curriculum adapted to secular interests of a commercial and scientific nature, as opposed to the classical curriculum of the Latin Gram-

---

[1] Charles A. and Mary A. Beard, *The Rise of American Civilization*, I, 156; 447.

mar school. The latter gradually gave way to the more practical institution. Dexter tells us that: "From about the time of the Revolution until the middle of the nineteenth century, it was the undisputed leader in secondary education."[2] And Cubberley gives the reason when he says: "A study of real things rather than words about things, and a new emphasis on the native English and on science were prominent features of their work."[3] Two important features of many of these schools were coeducation and the absence of sectarianism.[4] Meanwhile, from the middle of the eighteenth century, parochial and elementary schools were diminishing in number and education continued to lose ground, due in great measure to the unrest of the times, the advent of new sects, and the expansion of population on the frontier. American democracy was not able yet to take over the schools.[5]

The advent of Independence marked a step forward in the field of educational policy. The Federal Constitution (1787) by implication permitted education to be regarded as a State concern.[6] This was a definite naturalistic trend. As Davidson puts it, "In proportion as education has passed into the hands of the State and the laity, it has more and more, turned its attention to nature, and life in nature."[7] In time

[2] Edwin Grant Dexter, *A History of Education in the United States* (New York: The Macmillan Co., 1904), p. 90.
[3] Cubberley, *The History of Education*, p. 464.
[4] Edgar W. Knight, *Education in the United States* (Boston: Ginn & Co., 1929), p. 374.
[5] Cubberley, *op. cit.*, pp. 439; 653-658.
[6] Knight, *op. cit.*, p. 282.
[7] Thomas Davidson, *A History of Education* (New York: Charles Scribner's Sons, 1901), p. 226.

the principle that education was a state function, and not a Church matter, gained force. Congress began to give national land to new states for state schools and a state university. "We thus see, in the new United States, the theories of the French revolutionary thinkers and statesmen actually being realized in practice. The constitutional provisions and even the legislation . . . mark the evolution in America of a clearly defined state theory as to education, and the recognition of a need for general education in a government whose actions were so largely influenced by the force of public opinion." [8] The history of secularism in American education may be traced in the legislative enactments in the various states.[9] From the arrival of the first colonists until the early nineteenth century, it had been accepted that the education of the young was a Church function. In some instances the state recognized this by giving state aid for such schools which continued until the middle of the nineteenth century. Even when state schools were organized it was not unusual for the state to take over and aid private and church schools. But the state aims gradually excluded the otherworldly aims until secularization became a fact. Then education for citizenship and life became the dominant aim.[10]

After 1812 we enter the period of outstanding organizers and administrators in state educational sys-

[8] Cubberley, *op. cit.*, p. 524.

[9] Burton Confrey, *Secularism in American Education, Its History* (Washington, D. C.: The Catholic University of America, 1931), Ph. D. Dissertation, Chapter III, 47-125.

[10] Ellwood P. Cubberley, *An Introduction to the Study of Education and Teaching* (Boston: Houghton Mifflin Co., 1925), pp. 691-692.

tems. It is a commonplace to say that Horace Mann, "the father of the common school," was the great herald of the new ideal "with instruction adapted to democratic and natural rather than religious ends." [11] Because of his tremendous influence on American education, it is important to point out the main principles of his philosophy of education which may be readily deduced from his philosophy of life. Reared in strict Calvinism, he early rebelled against its gloomy tenets. His biographer, Hinsdale, tells us significantly that: "To him Christianity was rather a system of exalted ethics rather than an evangelical message or gospel; he built more upon Nature than upon Revelation; he held that the power of natural religion had scarcely begun to be understood or appreciated." [12]   Evidently he did not accept Christianity as a revealed religion.[13] This is important in

---

[11] *Ibid.*, p. 692. Cubberley says: He "will always be regarded as perhaps the greatest of the 'founders' of our American system of free public schools. No one did more than he to establish in the minds of the American people the conception that education should be universal, non-sectarian, and free and that its aims should be social efficiency, civic virtue and character." *History of Education*, p. 690. Cf. Knight, *op. cit.*, pp. 210-218, in which there will be found an excellent account of Mann's influence and work. In 1870 there were 26 superintendents of public schools. In 1890 there were over 2900. See *United States Commissioner of Education Report, 1889-1890* (Washington, D. C.: U. S. Bureau of Education), p. 614.

[12] B. A. Hinsdale, *Horace Mann and the Common School Revival in the United States* (New York: Charles Scribner's Sons, 1898), p. 84.

[13] When Mann was twelve years old, his brother was drowned. At the funeral service, Dr. Emmons, his pastor and a rigid Calvinist, preached such a sermon on the perils of dying unreconciled that the widowed mother's groan of despair made "his soul rise in rebellion and there immediately ensued a crisis in his life." *Ibid.*, p.83. He recoiled from Christianity under the form of Calvinism. The sensitive and impressionistic youth had early read many of the books in the town library donated by Benjamin Franklin. Edwin E. Slosson, *The American Spirit in Education* (New Haven: Yale

any evaluation of his work in the public school. Since he did not believe in a supernatural and revealed religion, it was only natural that his reforms should be found to compromise easily on the question of dogmatic religious instruction in the schools. A decade before he became the secretary of the newly-appointed State Board of Education in Massachusetts a law had been passed (1827) excluding from the school, books which were sectarian.[14] In view of what we know of his later reforms, this is seen in line with his own ideas on the subject. He did say that the Bible could be read without comment in the schools. The consequences of such a use of the Holy Book need not be urged here. While Mann tried to outline a plan for moral and religious education which would be consistent with the law,[15] he was charged with "reducing teaching to natural religion and morality—the lowest form of Unitarianism."[16]   This

[14] George H. Martin, *Evolution of the Massachusetts Public School System* (New York: D. Appleton & Co., 1894), pp. 92, 229; cf. Confrey, *op. cit.,* p. 74.

[15] Ellwood P. Cubberley, *Public Education in the United States* (Boston: Houghton Mifflin Co., 1919), p. 175.

[16] *Ibid.*

University Press, 1921), p. 124. Later when he went to college he assimiliated the deism of Cicero from the classics. He tutored Latin and Greek and acted as librarian at Brown University for two years and arrived at the conclusion that the modern sciences were superior to the classics. "His valuation of scientific studies was far in advance of the time and he longed to pursue them further." Hinsdale, *op. cit.,* p. 88. Later he became a Unitarian. Unitarianism rejects belief in the Trinity, in Christ as a divine person, in Hell, in the Atonement of Christ. It rejects all theological doctrine. It rests on principles based on natural reason and its rationalism results "in a keen intellectualism, strong natural virtue and simple piety." *The Catholic Encyclopedia Dictionary,* Donald Attwater, ed. (New York: The Macmillan Co., 1931), p. 537. See T. L. Bouscaren, "Horace Mann and the Public School," *America,* 30 (Oct. 27, 1923), 46-47.

is not difficult to understand since he did have a definite anti-orthodox complex from sermons heard in his youth.[17] Due to objections against particular dogmas, Mann finally came to the position "that the state was justified in excluding all religious teaching; but the indispensable moral instruction and training must be supplied. Other states imitated the procedure in Massachusetts, and as result, at the N.E.A. in Boston (July, 1903), the U. S. Commissioner of Education, Dr. Harris, could say that necessarily the public schools cultivated thinking 'hostile and skeptical in its attitude towards religious truth.' " [18] It may be said, therefore, that Mann's solution of the religious question was definitely conducive to secularization of the public school system.

Had Mann been non-naturalistic and strongly imbued with supernaturalism, he could never have arrived at the solution he did arrive at in this instance. Why was it not possible for the children in the schools to receive religious instruction according to their respective faiths as did the children in Prussia? But we have definite proof that this very fact displeased him during his visit to Prussian Schools.[19] The fact is that he was not a Christian, believing in Revelation, but a rationalist, trusting in human nature as good in itself and infinitely improvable. He overstressed intellectual training and in this he was

[17] Raymond B. Culver, *Horace Mann and Religion in the Massachusetts Public Schools* (New Haven: Yale University Press, 1929), pp. 244 ff.

[18] Confrey, *Secularism in American Education, Its History*, p. 137.

[19] Cf. Horace Mann's *Seventh Annual Report to the Board of Education in Massachusetts*, an extract from which entitled "Bible History and Bible Knowledge in the Prussian Schools" is printed in Henry Barnard, *National Education in Europe* (2d ed., New York: Charles B. Norton, 1854), pp. 73-74.

a naturalist.   His aim was to train good citizens.[20]
His biographer says that: ". . . his great theme was
the relation of intellectual and moral knowledge to
human well-being, individual and social. . . . In no
other name did he trust for the safety of society.   A
confirmed rationalist, he looked with supreme confidence to the healing power of popular intelligence
and virtue." [21]   His theory of education demanded
that science and the scientific method should dominate the curriculum.   He approved strongly of Pestalozzianism and its methods of induction from nature,
and he disapproved as strongly of authority.[22]   Mann's
belief in the phrenology and its interpretation of human nature as held by George Combe, his friend, the
Scottish philosopher, is another indication of his
naturalism.   As a result, he stressed the use of the
sciences and physiology in education.   Knowledge of
nature was to be the solution of all man's difficulties,
and the source of his perfection.   As Hinsdale puts
it:

> It would not be difficult to show that Mr.
> Mann, like all men of his habit and mind,
> overestimated the efficiency of knowledge
> and teaching, and so of schools and educa-
> tion as leading to the amelioration of man's
> estate.   He no doubt failed to appreciate
> how much still remains to be done when a
> man has been taught the way of life more
> perfectly: he must be induced or moved to
> walk in that way.   Mr. Mann did not justly

---

[20] Hinsdale, *Horace Mann and the Common School Revival in
the United States,* pp. 112-114.

[21] *Ibid.,* p. 274.

[22] Davidson, *A History of Education,* pp. 252-253.

measure those elements of character and life
that transcend the understanding. He did
not make sufficient allowance for the power
of heredity, conservative habit, inertia, custom, or for the play of feeling and will. He,
therefore, expected results to flow from rational causes that human experience has
never justified.[23]

In view of his naturalistic philosophy of education, it
cannot be denied that Mann had much to do with
advancing the cause of naturalism in American education.

Pestalozzianism is one of the currents by which
naturalism in American education was spread extensively. Inspired by Rousseau, it helped to establish
realism and education according to nature in the new
world. While Rousseau's spirit was, as we have seen,
manifest among the radical influences of the Revolution and gave rise to the theory that every one has a
right to education, it was Pestalozzianism which enabled this theory to be put into practice.[24] Burton says
that, "From 1800 on, increasingly after 1850-1860, Pes-

---

[23] Hinsdale, *op. cit.*, pp. 103-104.
[24] Monroe, *A Text-Book in the History of Education*, p. 572.
Graves has this to say about Rousseau's influence on American
education. His "revolutionary thought would seem to have had
much to do with causing the unrest that gradually resulted in
upsetting the aristocratic and formal training of the young and in
secularizing and universalizing the public school system." Frank
Pierrepont Graves, *A Student's History of Education* (New York:
The Macmillan Co., 1921), p. 222. While Messenger says: "The
French influence came chiefly from Rousseau. . . . Rousseau had
furnished a part of the spirit and content of our Declaration of
Independence. He had said that education is the right of every
child and that it is the duty of the state to provide it for him."
James F. Messenger, *Interpretative History of Education* (New
York: Thomas Y. Crowell, 1931), p. 281.

76 *Naturalism in American Education*

talozzianism stressed the need for study of the physical
environment, of real things."[25]   It was introduced

---

[25] William H. Burton, *Introduction to Education* (New York:
D. Appleton-Century Co., Inc., 1934), p. 426. Pestalozzi (1746-1827)
dedicated his life to naturalistic education as a result of reading
the *Émile*. In common with the majority of later secular educa-
tionalists, he felt that education was the principal means for the
reformation of society. *Émile* suggested the plan which he followed.
He wanted *every* child to have an education. In this he was the
herald of education for the masses. As a young man he was profoundly influenced by Rousseau. After rejecting the law and the
ministry he turned to farming and began to put the doctrines of
Émile to the test in the education of his own son, named after
Rousseau, Jacques. "So far as his general view of the nature and
aim of education went Pestalozzi was in all essential respects a
disciple of Rousseau." William Boyd, *The History of Western
Education* (3d ed., London: A. & C. Black, Ltd., 1932), p. 341.
Like Rousseau, he believed that nature is good and that the unperverted impulses of the child are towards good. This is clear from
what he says in *Gertrude Teaches Her Children:* "Sound education
stands before me symbolized by a tree. . . . Man is similar to the
tree. In the new-born child are hidden those faculties which are
to unfold during life. . . . It is not the educator who puts new
powers and faculties into man. . . . He only takes care that no
untoward influence shall disturb nature's march of development.
The moral, intellectual and practical powers of man must be nur-
tured within himself and not from artificial substitutes." Quoted
in Paul Monroe, *A Text-Book in the History of Education*, pp.
611-612. Cubberley says: "The greatest contribution of Pestalozzi
lay in that following the lead of Rousseau, he rejected the religious
aim and the teaching of mere words and facts . . . and tried instead
to reduce the educational process to a well-organized routine, based
on the natural and orderly development of the instincts, capacities,
and powers of the growing child. Taking Rousseau's idea of a
return to nature, he tried to apply it to the education of children.
This led to the rejection of what he called the 'empty chattering
of mere words' and 'outward show' in the instruction in reading
and the catechism, and the introduction in their places of real
studies, based on observation, experimentation, and reasoning.
'Sense expression' became his watchword." Cubberley, *History of
Education*, p. 541. It is true that "in place of an elementary education based on reading, a little writing and spelling, and the catechism, all of a memoriter type and with religious ends in view, a
new primary school, essentially secular in character, was created by
the work of Pestalozzi." *Ibid.*, p. 544. Pestalozzi emphasized the
civic aims of education to the neglect of the supernatural. Experimentation replaced tradition and the tested truths of the old education. Willmann-Kirsch, *The Science of Education* (Beatty, Pa.:

from abroad in various ways. William McClure, a
retired merchant of Philadelphia, with definite lean-

Archabbey Press, 1921), I, 42. When he maintained that the child
was like the sapling he failed to recognize that some trees grow
well and some do not. His thesis was sound if human nature had
no evil tendencies. Caroline Frye, reviewing one of Pestalozzi's
books, said: "If there be a people between the Alps in the bosom
of whose offspring there is an innate principle of faith and love,
that needs only to be cultivated and cherished by the sacred power
of innocence, to produce pure morality and exalted devotion, this
book belongs to them. It need not have been put into English, or
any language into which the word of God has been translated;
for it belies it utterly. We have no such children to educate, and
therefore the book is useless to us." Quoted in Paul Monroe, *op.
cit.*, p. 589. His vitalized observation makes no provision for faith
or religion. Experimentation is correct within limits but some
things cannot be experimented on and religion is one. The defect of his system was that it took no account of significant
things like tradition, obedience, discipline, and the Christian virtues. His stressing of interest to the neglect of effort gave impetus to the work of other secular educators. The Pestalozzian
movement by its insistence on observation and experimentation
prepared the way for scientific movement with its emphasis on
the natural sciences. *Ibid.*, pp. 606; 678. His "system is pat-
terned all too closely after the intellectualism and the worship of
method so characteristic of the Enlightenment." Willmann-Kirsch,
op. cit., I, 316. Not what the child must know but what he can
know is his doctrine as it was Rousseau's. Boyd, *op. cit.*, p. 344.
He forgot that there are certain things the child cannot know as a
child, things which supernatural training alone can give. There
are good activities and bad activities in child nature left to itself.
As Nunn says: ". . . the tragic history of the human conscience, and
the sad story of what man had made of man, show how doubtful
is the search [after the good] and how often it ends in disaster.
While, then, the unperverted impulses of childhood may have a
biological bias towards the good, it is too much to expect them
to solve unaided the problems of life which have baffled some of
the best intentioned minds and most highly gifted races of mankind." T. P. Nunn, *Education: Its Data and First Principles* (10th
impression, London: Edward Arnold & Co., 1926), p. 99. In the
preface of Joseph Neef's book, printed in 1808 at Philadelphia
entitled: *Sketch of a Plan and Method of Education Founded on
the Analysis of the Human Faculties and Natural Reason, Fitted
for the Offspring of a Free People and of All Rational Beings*
(Joseph Neef, formerly a coadjutor of Pestalozzi at his school near
Berne, Switzerland), the author indicates clearly the naturalism of
his master when he writes: "Considering that man is born neither
good nor bad, but that the disposition to become either good or

ings toward naturalism, visited Pestalozzi at Yverdun twice, in 1804 and in 1805, and during his last visit invited the reformer to take over a school at Philadelphia. The latter was then almost sixty years old and recommended in his stead one of his former Burgdorf teachers, Joseph Neef, who was conducting a Pestalozzian school at Paris. Neef accepted the offer and arrived at Philadelphia in 1806, where he taught for three years. Later he founded schools in Louisville, Kentucky and elsewhere. He died in 1854.[26] McClure, by his writings, articles, and financial support did much to make the principles of Pestalozzianism known in the United States. Barnard says that he was the first to introduce these views by an article in the *National Intelligencer,* Washington, June 6, 1806, and in the same month he wrote two further articles on Pestalozzi's method based on the French work of D. A. Chavannes.[27] A voluminous literature

---

[26] Neef, an Alsatian, studied for the priesthood but at twenty-one "experienced profound changes in his religious views," W. S. Monroe, *op. cit.,* p. 61, and became a soldier in Napoleon's army and was wounded during the campaign in Italy. Retired from the army and admiring Pestalozzi's works, he served as one of his teachers at Burgdorf in 1800. He was "not a believer in dogmatic religious instruction in the schools." *Ibid.,* p. 88. He held that education should develop the instincts of the child because "the citizens of the animal world are very near relations of ours." Quoted *Ibid.,* p. 90. He was a liberal in religion and was charged with teaching atheism to his pupils in America. Monroe says this charge was false. *Ibid.,* p. 107.

[27] Henry Barnard, *American Journal of Education,* 30 (1880), 561. McClure, born at Ayr, Scotland in 1763, became a successful mer-

---

bad is intimately interwoven with his organization, he [Pestalozzi] became soon convinced that our education is the only cause of our becoming either good, useful, intelligent, rational, moral and virtuous beings, or wicked, . . . ignorant, senseless, superstitious and therefore miserable creatures." W. S. Monroe, *History of the Pestalozzi Movement in the United States* (Syracuse: C. W. Bardeen, 1907), pp. 78-80.

on Pestalozzianism came into being in America between 1820-1860. *The American Journal of Education*, edited by William Russell, 1826-1830, and *The
American Annals of Education*, edited by William C.
Woodbridge, 1831-1839, contain several articles dealing with Pestalozzianism, including accounts of personal observations of the system at work in Europe.[28]
Henry Barnard wrote articles in favor of the movement in his *Journal* (1855-1881). He spent two years
in Europe (1835-1837), examining especially Pestalozzian schools. On his return, as a member of the
legislature of Connecticut, he was influential in getting the law of 1839 passed. This law set up a State
Board of Commissioners for Common Schools similar
to the Massachusetts Board. He was the first Secretary of this Board, continuing in office until the
Board was abolished in 1842. The next year he was
invited to examine the schools in Rhode Island and
was State Commissioner of Public Schools there from
1845 to 1849. From 1851 to 1855 he was Secretary
of the Connecticut State Board of Education and
head of the new state normal school. His work for
state education is second only to Mann's in its influ-

---

[28] Woodbridge, writing in his journal, March, 1827, speaks of the
Pestalozzian school at New Harmony, Indiana, in these words:
"The system is the improved Pestalozzian; and of course they never
attempt to teach children what they cannot comprehend. In consequence, all kinds of dogmas of every sect and persuasion are banished from the schools." Quoted in W. S. Monroe, *op. cit.*, p. 120.

---

chant in the new world. In his youth he manifested his opposition
to the traditional education in favor of natural history. He had
much influence in furthering the scientific studies in Philadelphia
and was one of the leaders in founding the Academy of Natural
Sciences, June, 1812. He became president of the scientific society
in 1817 and remained in office until his death—a period of twenty-
three years. W. S. Monroe, *op. cit.*, pp. 40; 47. He was tolerant in
religious matters and opposed to sectarian instruction. *Ibid.*, p. 53.

ence on American state educational theory.[29] He published a work entitled *Pestalozzi and Pestalozzianism*
in 1858 which later was revised under the title of
Pestalozzi and His Educational System.

In 1819 Professor John Griscom of New York, published a work in two volumes entitled *A Year in
Europe.* This was the account of a sojourn in
Europe which he spent examining educational institutions. He called at Yverdun and Burgdorf and
was definitely impressed by what he saw. His work
played an important part in the spreading of Pestalozzianism in America.[30]

During this second quarter of the nineteenth century, official reports on European schools, especially
German, were decidedly influential in molding the
American educational mind. The translation of Vic-
tor Cousin's *Report on the State of Public Instruction in Prussia,* Professor Calvin E. Stowe's report on
Elementary Education in Europe, the *Report on Education in Europe* by President Bache of Girard College, Philadelphia, and the *Seventh Report of Horace
Mann to the Massachusetts Board of Education,* giving his impressions of what he himself saw in European education—all of these helped to develop a powerful trend in American education in favor of strong
state systems, teacher training, Pestalozzianism in
theory and methods, and schools of manual arts.
Barnard published important extracts from all of
these reports in his volume *National Education in*

---

[29] Cubberley, *A History of Education,* pp. 690-691.
[30] Samuel C. Parker, *The History of Modern Elementary Education* (Boston: Ginn & Co., 1912), p. 299.

Europe.[31] Cubberley says that Pestalozzian ideas after 1860 "resulted in a thoroughgoing reorganization of American elementary education." [32]

Just as Rousseau's *Émile* suggested to Pestalozzi, a psychologized universal, secular education for the masses, so too it prepared the way for the introduction of the natural sciences into the curriculum. The emphasis on preparation for life and state secular theories of education gradually focussed attention on the scientific method until the nineteenth century found "its ideals, methods, and results . . . patent in every department of human knowledge." [33] Added to the opposition against the doctrine of formal discipline which Pestalozzi, Herbart, and Froebel had waged, was the further opposition to the exclusive study of the Classics. The argument was that they did not offer educational equipment for life in a rapidly changing industrial civilization. Here we have a definite advance in naturalistic educational theory. More and more this life becomes the crucial issue. The anxieties about a future life and preparation for it have lessened with the domination of the scientific method, evolutionism, and agnosticism.

During the latter half of the nineteenth century, naturalistic philosophy was dominant in America. One of its main sources lay in the theories of evolutionism. Perry is clear on this when he states that "the teaching of Darwin, combined with that of Spencer, whose works were read in America almost as

[31] (New York: Chas B. Norton, 1854); Parker, *op. cit.*, p. 299; Frank Pierrepont Graves, *A History of Education in Modern Times* (New York: The Macmillan Co., 1917), pp. 148-162; *Educational Yearbook*, 1929, pp. 493-495.
[32] Cubberley, *op. cit.*, p. 546.
[33] Graves, *A History of Education in Modern Times*, p. 321.

promptly and as widely as in England, exerted a powerful and growing influence in the direction of naturalism." [34]   The Civil War had hardly passed when the
Descent of Man began to challenge discussion in the
universities and among the intellectuals.   Ingersoll
became the new Paine.   Huxley entered into combat
with the theologians; and Spencer's philosophy with
its evolutionary ideas on ethics, politics, economics,
and education became a greater challenge still in the
uncharted vistas it opened out.[35]

> Certainly nowhere in the world was Spen-
> cer's work more cordially received than in
> the United States.   Admirers in America
> gave him several thousand dollars in 1866
> to help in the prosecution of his studies;
> the sale of his books was larger here than in
> England; and the Popular Science Monthly,
> founded by E. L. Youmans, afforded the
> English philosopher an audience that was
> astounding in its range and enthusiasm.
> Suffused with the optimism dominant in
> New World life, Spencer's theories were em-
> ployed to fortify at every point the idea of
> progress that had been so potent in earlier
> years.[36]

The Universities and the scientists felt the reverbera-
tions of all this.   The "probationary period" between
1859 and 1873 went by.   Agassiz, unflinching in his
opposition to the new ideas, died, and Asa Grey, professor of biology and botany at Harvard, James

---

[34] R. B. Perry, *Philosophy of the Recent Past* (New York: Chas.
Scribner's Sons, 1925), p. 17.
[35] Beard, *The Rise of American Civilization,* II, 406.
[36] *Ibid.,* 407.

Dwight Dana of Yale, and McCosh of Princeton, began to compromise. It remained for John Fiske (1812-1901) of Harvard to put the finishing touches to the popular acceptance. His *Outlines of Cosmic Philosophy,* which went through many editions, and his lectures, were potent in establishing the new doctrines.[37] These and lesser men aided in the secularizing process. Theological traditions were being surrendered so that during the closing decades of the century it could be claimed that "there were few thinkers in higher university groves, who accepted without fatal reservations the simple epic made immortal by Milton. Indeed science was so enthroned in America that it became a kind of dogmatic religion itself whose votaries often behaved in the manner of theologians, pretending to possess the one true key to the riddle of the universe." [38] During the time that evolutionism was winning its way into American minds and the natural sciences were being rapidly developed, a change of attitude was taking place on the part of American educators with regard to the content of the curriculum and the idea of a liberal education. The scientific tendency in life was bound to be reflected in the schools. The industrial, technical, and professional training which the material development of the industrial age demanded opened up the opportunity for the advent of sciences into the secondary and higher fields of education. Spencer interpreted in his brilliant way the spirit of the times in his *Essays on Education.* He claimed that not only

---

[37] Riley, *American Thought,* pp. 191; 201; 215.
[38] Beard, *op. cit.,* II, 416.

were the sciences[39] the most useful and therefore the
most worthwhile for preparation for complete living
in this life, but he also insisted on them on the score
of formal discipline. The aim of his education, however, is not wholly material or utilitarian since his
idea of "science" is to improve conduct, to conduce
to a more pleasant and more potent life, something
that the old humanistic classical studies failed to do.[40]
As the outstanding philosopher of the nineteenth century, his educational writings had a powerful influence on his age.[41] Now just at the period when the
ideas of the liberal theorists and politicians of the
formative period of the Republic were bearing considerable fruit, at least in state systems of public education, the influence of Spencer's scientific tendency
could not fail to make its impact in view of the popular acceptance of his ideas about life and a liberal
education. The times were propitious too. The new
civilization demanded industrial, technical, and professional training for its future citizens. Hence we
note that, "After 1870 the character of these (high)
schools was vastly improved, their number increased,

---

[39] It is to be noted that he used the word "science" in the sense
of social, political and moral, as well as physical and biological
science, thereby including matter that more correctly should be
denominated "humanities." See Frank Pierrepont Graves, *Great
Educators of Three Centuries, Their Work and its Influence on
Modern Education* (New York: The Macmillan Co., 1912), p. 280.

[40] *Ibid.,* p. 281.

[41] *Ibid.,* p. 283. He based his argument for scientific studies on an
individualistic outlook, quite the opposite of the educational leaders
of the Enlightenment, excepting Rousseau, who insisted on a
curriculum of scientific studies in the interests of national education. Spencer, therefore, is onesided in his claims in contrast to
John Tyndall and Thomas Huxley and all those who held for a
state theory of education. See Boyd, *The History of Western Education,* pp. 394-395.

and the work in science was expanded to include physics, chemistry, botany, and zoology, in well-organized courses." [42] In the elementary school curriculum, physiology and geography were present from the fourth decade of the nineteenth century. Horace Mann's influence was mainly responsible for the introduction of the former. The study of nature and object teaching had come with Pestalozzianism.[43] The colleges taught science from the earliest times.[44]

---

[42] Paul Monroe, *A Text-Book in the History of Education,* p. 700. The Academies in America distinguished themselves by stressing the sciences, astronomy and natural philosophy, geography and very often chemistry. In 1807 Harvard required geography in its entrance examinations and in 1870 physical geography also, while physics was required in 1872. See *Ibid.,* pp. 699-700. In the early high schools, free academies, city colleges, English classical schools, there was a definite tendency to the sciences in the curriculum. *Ibid.* The educational philosophy was, however, less radical than the ones which were emphasized later and especially that of Spencer's.

[43] Paul Monroe, *op. cit.,* p. 702.

[44] Harvard taught astronomy in 1642. The colleges established after it followed the same example. About 1690 Harvard taught physics or natural philosophy. Yale taught the sciences early in the eighteenth century. King's College (Columbia) in 1754 and the University of Pennsylvania in 1755, which were not under denominational control, initiated a new attitude while the Classics continued to be the core of the curriculum; theology was absent from the studies. In King's College, Surveying, Navigation, Husbandry, Commerce, Government, and "the knowledge of *all Nature* . . . and of everything *useful* for the Comfort, the Convenience, and Elegance of Life . . ." were included. *Ibid.,* p. 694. This is taken from the advertisement for King's College, May, 1754, 5th section. In 1762 the scope of this ambitious plan was limited and very little progress in introducing the sciences was made until after the Revolution. *Ibid.* At Pennsylvania in 1756, natural philosophy, applied mathematics, astronomy, natural history, chemistry, and agriculture are listed. In 1779, due to Jefferson, the same general plan existed at William and Mary. And gradually more scientific studies entered into the curriculum of the various universities as required subjects but the disciplinary idea of education definitely continued until the middle of the nineteenth century when the motive of interest began to command attention. In 1825, however, the University of Virginia was founded on the elective system. Much freedom in studies was allowed in Harvard from 1845. Eliot established the elective system there in 1869. Cornell in 1867 was organized

86   *Naturalism in American Education*

The various naturalistic trends which we have thus
far seen introduced into America find their best expression and synthesis, as far as the final decades of
the nineteenth century and the first of the twentieth
are concerned, in the work of Charles W. Eliot. In
1929 Irving Babbitt said, "Most of the heads of our
institutions of learning, great and small, have been
content for a generation and more to follow in the
wake of President Eliot," [45] and Henry James tells us
that "in the field of higher education at any rate,
Eliot stood head and shoulders above his contempo-
raries for forty years. . . . He was one of the men with
whom the student of American history in the nineteenth century will have to reckon." [46]

[45] Irving Babbitt, "President Eliot and American Education,"
Forum, LXXXI (January, 1929), 9.
[46] Henry James, *Charles W. Eliot, President of Harvard, 1869-
1909* (Boston: Houghton Mifflin Co., 1930) Prefatory Notes, I, vii.
In editing Eliot's *Education for Efficiency and the New Definition
of the Cultivated Man* (Boston: Houghton Mifflin Co., 1909), Henry
Suzzallo, at that time professor of the philosophy of education at
Teachers' College, Columbia University, said of him: "For forty
years president of America's oldest and greatest university, for more
than a quarter of a century an active leader in the reform of our
lower schools, and for the same period of time a distinguished
leader in our national life, no one is better fitted than he to suggest standards for the guidance of those who will teach our citizens."
Ibid., vii. Rugg notes that 1859 is a premonitory year in the history
of the concept of evolutionary growth. Charles Peirce graduated
from Harvard, William James commenced his scientific studies in
chemistry with Eliot, Darwin published the *Origin of Species*, and
Dewey was born. Harold Rugg, *Culture and Education in America*
(New York: Harcourt Brace and Co., 1931), pp. 99-100. Cf. Townsend, *Philosophical Ideas in the United States*, p. 136.

on the same principle "with a strong bias in favor of the scientific
and technical subjects." Harvard in 1847 and Yale in 1860 founded
special schools of science. "With the elective system came the general ascendancy of the scientific studies." *Ibid.*, p. 696. Nor must
we forget the Morill Land Grant Act (1862). Congress set aside
13 million acres for the support of a college in each state whose
chief aim was studies in agriculture and the mechanic arts. *Ibid.*
See also Graves, *History of Education in Modern Times*, pp. 346-351.

It is important, therefore, to examine briefly Eliot's religious, philosophical, and educational ideas. Eliot's religious views give us the background for his philosophical outlook. A Unitarian by preference, he did not believe in Christianity as a revealed religion. At the close of the Eleventh Session of the Harvard Summer School of Theology, 1909, he delivered a lecture entitled *The Religion of the Future*,[47] in which he affirmed his belief that "in the future religion there will be nothing 'supernatural' . . . religion, like all else must conform to natural law so far as the range of law has been determined. In this sense the religion of the future will be a natural religion." [48] Recalling the fact that his intellectual life had observed and covered the extraordinary period which embraced Darwin's *Voyage on the Beagle,* Spencer's development of the theory of evolution, the higher Biblical criticism and the industrial revolution, he goes on to state that, "The religion of the future will not be based on authority, either spiritual or temporal." [49] Neither will it be fixed but chang-

---

[47] Charles W. Eliot, *op. cit.,* (Boston: John W. Luce and Co., 1909).

[48] *Ibid.,* p. 29. He held that this new religion would be completely natural in quality. "In all its theory and all its practice it will be completely natural. It will place no reliance on any sort of magic, or miracle, or other violation of, or exception to, the laws of nature." *Ibid.,* pp. 29-30.

[49] *Ibid.,* p. 8. He tells us that "it is evident that the authority both of the most authoritative churches and of the Bible as a verbally inspired guide is already greatly impaired, and that the tendency towards liberty is progressive, and among educated men irresistible." *Ibid.,* p. 9. Henry James informs us that temperamentally a non-conformist with a preference to Unitarianism, "Catholicism, the Church of England, and the American Episcopal Church excited in him an almost instinctive antipathy." James, *op. cit.,* I, 370.

ing from century to century,[50] "not bound to any
dogma, creed, book, or institution." [51]   The chief
tenet of this new religion "is the doctrine of a sub-
lime unity of substance, force, and spirit, and its chief
precept is, Be Serviceable." [52]   Hence it will urge "its
disciples to believe that as the best and happiest man
is he who loves best and serves, so the soul of the universe finds its perfect bliss and efficiency in supreme
and universal love and service." [53]   The fundamental
precept, therefore, of religion, according to Eliot, lies
in service.[54]   Its primary object is not "the personal
welfare or safety of the individual in this world or
any other . . . but . . . service to others, and contributions to the common good." [55]   To this end it must
be built on the actual experience of man and of society,[56] using the scientific method to attain its aims.[57]
Eliot's religion is naturalistic.   His conception of
God is pantheistic.   He does not believe in the Ten

[50] Eliot, *op. cit.,* p. 4.

[51] *Ibid.,* p. 52.   Christianity in its institutional form he views as
"A paganized Hebrew-Christianity." *Ibid.,* p. 45. "The love of nature mounts and spreads," he says, "while faith in fairies, imps,
nymphs, demons and angels declines and fades away." *Ibid.,* p. 10.

[52]*Ibid.,* p. 57.

[53]*Ibid.,* p. 42.   He declared that he found evidence in the moral
history of the human race that an immanent and loving God ruled
the world. *Ibid.,* p. 60. "To my thinking," he wrote, "no one needs
to find God; because in Him we live and move and have our being,
literally, completely, and now." Quoted by James, *op. cit.,* II, 302.

[54] Eliot, *The Religion of the Future,* p. 52. Its discipline is that
of cooperative good will.   Its aim is to carry men out of their individual selves in order to show mutual regard for each other and
social and industrial cooperation. *Ibid.,* pp. 54-55.

[55] *Ibid.,* p. 14.

[56] *Ibid.,* p. 61.

[57] Charles W. Eliot, *Education for Efficiency and the New Definition of the Cultivated Man* (Boston: Houghton Mifflin Co., 1909),
p. 36.

Commandments nor in an unchanging moral law and eternal sanctions.[58]

His philosophy of humanitarian idealism and pragmatism flows directly from his naturalistic religion. In fact the two are identical. His outlook on life is based on a belief in altruism and utilitarianism. He exhibits in his philosophical and educational outlook a synthesis of naturalistic strains flowing from Montaigne, Locke, Milton, Rousseau, Spencer, and Emerson, all of whom influenced him.[59] Writing of Spencer in his Introduction for the Everyman's Edition of the *Essays on Education,* he says "Through him, the thoughts on education of Comenius, Montaigne, Locke, Milton, Rousseau, Pestalozzi, and other noted writers . . . are winning their way in practice." [60]

Eliot's educational ideal embraces two fundamental aims, personal culture and social efficiency. The essentials of culture which education must provide are scientific method and a knowledge of natural science, as well as training in bodily excellence, manual skill, and habitual contact with the world of man

---

[58] Eliot, *The Religion of the Future,* p. 60. "The fear of hell," he tells us, "has not proved effective to deter man from wrong-doing, and heaven has never yet been described in terms very attractive to the average man or woman. Both are indeed unimaginable." *Ibid.,* pp. 60-61. "The modern man," he continues, "would hardly feel any appreciable loss of motive-power towards good or away from evil if heaven were burnt and hell quenched. The prevailing Christian conceptions of heaven and hell have hardly any more influence with educated people in these days than Olympus and Hades have." *Ibid.,* p. 61.

[59] James, *Charles W. Eliot, President of Harvard,* I, 349-351.

[60] *Spencer's Essays on Education,* Introduction, "Everyman's Library," (London: J. M. Dent and Sons, 1911) (New York: E. P. Dutton & Co.), p. viii.

and of nature.[61] Hence education must inculcate the
scientific temper of mind with its passion for truth
based on fact. Human powers "must be exerted in
accordance with the natural and moral law, or, in
other words, in accordance with the facts of the
world." [62]

Education is for social efficiency. By efficiency he
means "effective power for work and service during a
healthy and active life." [63] Education, therefore,
whose goal is training for the power of work and service in this world, must provide pupils with "the elements of a considerable variety of subjects, such as
language, mathematics, history, natural science, sani-
tation, and economics . . . in order that they may
sample several kinds of knowledge, initiate the mental processes and habits appropriate to each, and have
a chance to determine wisely in what direction their
own individual mental powers can be best applied." [64]
This is the first proposition regarding the selection
of studies which, he feels, commands almost universal acceptance. "The second is that training for
power of work and service should be the prime object
of education throughout life, no matter in what line
the trained powers of the individual may be applied." [65]

Since Eliot contends that no single element or kind
of culture is essential,[66] naturally his educational

---

[61] Eliot, *Education for Efficiency*, pp. 36-38. The scientific method,
he believes, "has become indispensable in all fields of inquiry,
including psychology, philanthropy, and religion." *Ibid.*, p. 36.

[62] *Ibid.*, p. 24.

[63] *Ibid.*, p. 1.

[64] *Ibid.*, p. 5.

[65] *Ibid.*

[66] *Ibid.*, p. 55.

theory will not be built on or oriented by revealed religion, the essence of supernatural education. Neither will it provide for instruction in eternal moral law and unchanging ethics. The only moral elements of the new education according to him "are individual choice of studies and careers, early responsibility accompanying this freedom of choice, love of truth, now that truth may be directly sought through rational inquiry, and an omnipresent sense of social obligation. These moral elements are so strong that the new forms of culture are likely to prove themselves quite as productive of morality, highmindedness, and idealism as the old." [67] From this we conclude that he is entirely motivated by purely naturalistic motives which he desires to infuse into universal education.

A cursory study of Eliot's theory of education for power and service proves to what an extent the materialistic and sentimental spirit of the times was reflected in him. Nowhere does he manifest any concern for preparation for an immortal destiny. Everywhere the interests of this life dominate his outlook. In his educational philosophy the individual personality is neglected in favor of the common good. Education is no longer character formation but preparation for community service. Probably no educational institution felt this new spirit to the extent that the college did and herein especially lies the significance of Eliot, the most influential spokesman of these newer naturalistic trends in the New World. [68] At the same time we must not forget that his ideas per-

---

[67] *Ibid.*

[68] Cf. Norman Foerster, "The College, the Individual, and Society," *The American Review*, IV, n. 2 (December, 1934), 129-146.

vaded American education in general. His influence practically speaking lies in the loosening of rigid requirements for entrance into college and the substitution of elective studies in place of the prescribed traditional course. What Jefferson had failed to do at Virginia, Eliot, "a chemist with radical ideas in education," did during his time as president of Harvard, and his example was followed in time by practically all other American colleges.[69] In extending the elective system and in emphasizing modern subjects in the curriculum of school and college, Eliot rendered exceptional services to the sciences and scientific thought,[70] Eliot's educational theory, viewing the natural man as good by nature, reflects the tendency of his age. He refuses to consider man as he is and any educational system based on a philosophical misconception of the nature of man must of necessity be warped and one-sided. Openly espousing the naturalistic philosophy in education, he rejects the philosophy of education which draws its nourishment from Revelation and from unchanging principles and standards. His humanitarian doctrine is based on faith in human progress through science and altruism. Babbitt believes that: "President Eliot deserves to rank as our chief humanitarian idealist in the educational field, not because of any novelty in his views, but because of the consistency and unwavering conviction with which he applied them." [71] In his views we find no suggestion that the natural self in man needs discipline and restraint under the guidance of an eternal abiding law.

---

[69] Slosson, *The American Spirit in Education*, p. 280.
[70] Graves, *A History of Education in Modern Times*, p. 333.
[71] Babbitt, *loc. cit.*, p. 2.

There is no principle of control over natural impulses or desires and therefore no compelling motive for the exercise of will power and effort. The problems of character formation and the inner life are completely neglected in favor of altruism and service and worldly interest. The purpose of education is not service of God but service of man, not preparation for immortality but preparation for this life. Happiness lies in humanitarian service, not in doing God's will. Hence his educational ideal is training for service and power. Original sin and its educational implications are rejected in favor of belief in the essential goodness of mankind. Thus the traditional curriculum of the school with its underlying supernaturalistic and idealistic philosophy of education is abandoned. For the prescribed curriculum with its accepted disciplinary values he substitutes the elective system with its emphasis on science and inborn aptitudes to the neglect of general cultural education. Furthermore, his system is utilitarian and therefore leads to specialization with the result that education becomes solely informational. Finally, he derives his standards of education exclusively from the physical and social sciences instead of basing them on the Christian ideal. The result is that man is caught in the naturalistic stream of life instead of surmounting it. We conclude therefore that he is exclusively and decidedly non-supernaturalistic in his outlook on life as well as in his educational theory.[72]

The introduction of the sciences into the curricula of educational institutions, especially in the nine-

[72] *Ibid.*, pp. 1-10.

teenth century, is closely related to the psychological
tendency in education.   Apart altogether from the
contention that a knowledge of nature was essential
to modern life in lieu of the Classics, the doctrine of
formal discipline hitherto advanced as an argument
for the Classics was taken over by some educators and
used as an argument for the sciences which were held
as potent in training the general powers of the mind.
Spencer, Combe, Youmans, and others held this
view.[73]   This idea did not survive, however.   The
"methods of the sciences, enforcing both inductive
and deductive reasoning," gradually affected the psychology of education and method as well as content.[74]
Before speaking of the last important factor in the
introduction of naturalism into America, it is fitting
to insert the opinion of an important English educator on what he saw in American education.   In 1865,
the Rev. James Fraser, a graduate of Oxford and an
enthusiastic advocate of national education in England, visited American schools and made a scholarly
report on what he saw.   His judgment is of more
than passing interest because of his eminent qualifica-
tions.   This is what he says in part:

> If I were to compare them [the results of the
> American system] with the results of the best
> education at home, I should say that an
> American pupil probably leaves school with
> more special knowledge, but with less gen-
> eral development.   He would have more

---

[73] Graves, *A History of Education in Modern Times*, p. 334 ff.
[74] *Ibid.*, p. 352; Paul Monroe, *A Text-Book in the History of Education*, pp. 702-703.

acquaintance (not very profound, though) with certain branches of physical science, perhaps more . . . with mathematics. . . . The mistake that is commonly made in America is . . . a confusion of thought between the processes that convey knowledge and the processes that develop mental power, and a tendency to confine the work of the school too exclusively to the former . . . the inevitable tendency of an age of material prosperity and utilitarian ideas.[75]

He emphasizes here "the presentation" of *facts* in American education, at the time, to the neglect of the development and training of the *faculties*. He found too exclusive devotion to observation and memory and much less attention to the discipline of reason and the cultivation of taste.[76]

The tone [he says] of an American school . . . is yet incomplete. . . . The intellectual tone is high; the moral tone, though perhaps a little too self-conscious, is not unhealthy; but another tone, which can only be vaguely described in words, but of which one feels oneself in the presence of when it is really there, and which for want of a better name, I must call the 'religious' tone, one misses and misses with regret. . . . I do not like to call the American system of education . . . *irreligious*. It is perhaps even

---

[75] Report of Rev. James Fraser on American Schools, *Barnard's American Journal of Education*, 19, (1870), 579.
[76] *Ibid.*

going too far to say that it is *non-religious* or purely secular."[77]

When Woodworth stated that: "First psychology lost its soul, then it lost its mind, then it lost consciousness; it still has behavior of a kind,"[78] he described pithily what has happened to the science of human personality under the influence of naturalism in America. The influence of the new psychology, naturalistic in theory and method, has been such a definite factor in modern educational theory and practice that it may be said to color the educational thought of the leading American educators. This new psychology "inherited its physical body from German experimentalism, but it got its mind from Darwin."[79]   At the beginning of the nineteenth century psychology was an essential part of philosophy; but through the influence of Herbart, who broke definitely with the scholastic faculty theory, the way was prepared for psychology to become a natural science. Weber, Fechner, and Wundt were the pioneers in this new experimental psychology. William James, the greatest American psychologist, by his influence and writings, focussed American attention on the experimental physiological psychology which Wundt was developing in his laboratory at Leipzig.[80]   Wundt, who may be said to have inaugu-

---

[77] *Ibid.*, p. 580. Rev. James Fraser was a minister of the Established Church of England, a graduate of the Public Grammar School and of Oxford, an assistant commissioner of education at one time, and later Bishop of Manchester. *Ibid.*

[78] Robert S. Woodworth, *Psychology, A Study of the Mental Life* (New York: Henry Holt & Co., 1928), p. 2. Footnote.

[79] E. G. Boring, *A History of Experimental Psychology* (New York: The Century Co., 1929), p. 494.

[80] *Ibid.* James, in his *Principles of Psychology* (New York: London: Macmillan and Co., 2 vols., 1890), rejected the scholastic psy-

rated the anti-metaphysical tradition, contending that psychology was an independent science and emphasizing the method of experiment,[81] attracted American students like Stanley Hall.[82] J. McKeen Cattell, Frank

---

[81] He did not consider experimentation the only psychological method. Boring, *op. cit.*, p. 315.

[82] Granville Stanley Hall (1844-1924) was attracted to the new psychology when Wundt's *Physiologische Psychologie* was published in 1874. Having taken his doctorate at Harvard under James—the first in the new psychology in 1878 in America—he went at once to Berlin and then to Leipzig, becoming Wundt's first American student. After two years he returned to America, lectured in education at Harvard, and in 1882 received a lectureship at Johns Hopkins where John Dewey, Cattell, Sanford, Burnham, and Jastrow were studying. He established the first psychological laboratory in the New World there in 1883. In 1887 he started the *American Journal of Psychology*, the first of its kind in America. In 1888 he became the first president of Clark University where he held the chair of psychology while Sanford came to take over the laboratory and Burnham later became head of the new department of pedagogy. He became the first president of the American Psychological Association in 1892. In 1915 he established the *Journal of Applied Psychology*. By this time there were fifteen psychological journals in the country. Boring, *op cit.*, pp. 505-508.

---

chological theory of the faculties in favor of the biological psychology that man is a behaving organism. He compared consciousness to a flowing stream due to sense-experience. He thought of it "as if it were an organ with a function in the psychological economy." Boring, *op. cit.*, p. 501. He denied "the need of an abiding mind as the thinking subject." Louis J. A. Mercier, *The Challenge of Humanism*, p. 54. James said: "The passing thought is itself the thinker. . . . Each thought is born an owner and dies owned, transmitting whatever it realized as its self to its later proprietor." James, *op. cit.*, I, 401; 338-339. He was opposed alike to materialism, mechanism and super-naturalism and may be called a naturalistic spiritualist. Perry, *Philosophy of the Recent Past*, p. 186. His idea of reality is experience. His theory of knowledge reduces "relations, substances, activities and other transcendent elements to the continuities of sense experience." *Ibid.*, p. 189. He stressed the categories of interest and practice. Late in life he wrote, "For twenty years past I have mistrusted consciousness as an entity; for seven or eight years past I have suggested its non-existence to my students. . . . It seems to me that the hour is ripe for it to be openly and universally discarded. . . ." In his essay, "Does Consciousness Exist?" posthumously published. Quoted by Eliott Park Frost in "Cannot Psychology Dispense with Consciousness?" *Psychological Review*, XXI, No. 3 (May, 1914), 204.

Angell, Edward Bradford Titchener, Charles H. Judd, and others. Hall, while at Williams College (1863-1867) became very much interested in the philosophy of John Stuart Mill and in evolution, "an attitude that is one of the unifying threads of his varied intellectual life." [83] Wundt's *Physiologische Psychologie* saved the day for him just as he was beginning to think that philosophical speculation was impractical. He learned the scientific technique of the new psychology which he felt was the true approach to philosophy. "Within philosophy he also assimilated the doctrine of evolution, and thus his psychology was always an evolutionary psychology, or as he called it 'genetic psychology.' " [84] In time this psychology led to child psychology, to pedagogy, and later to the study of adolescence. [85] Inclined to some of the theories of Freud as well as applying the evolutionary theory to psychology, he did much to foster the belief that education should be founded on psychology. As Boring says, his contribution is "mostly to educational psychology." [86] For a period, while at Hopkins and later at Clark, he was looked upon as a

---

[83] Boring, *op. cit.*, p. 505.

[84] *Ibid.*, p. 508.

[85] His *Adolescence: Its Psychology, and Its Relations to Physiology, Anthropology, Sociology, Sex, Crime, Religion, and Education*, published in 1904, came to light at the crucial moment in the life of the new psychology and commanded very much attention. He continued his interest in child study, concentrating his attention on growth, imagination and play. Both his own studies and those of his students relied too much on the questionnaire in gathering statistical data to the neglect of observation and experimentation; but his efforts to found a Child Institute failed. This defect of method and his interpretation of original tendencies, his belief in the culture epoch and recapitulation theory subjected him to considerable criticism. *Ibid.*, p. 509; Knight, *Education in the United States*, pp. 526-527.

[86] Boring, *A History of Experimental Psychology*, p. 510.

leader by the majority of the American psychologists.[87] From all of this we may conclude, especially in view of his opposition to the scholastic psychology[88] and his basic philosophy of evolution, that his influence in propagating naturalistic psychology was considerable.

George Trumbull Ladd (1842-1921) is one of the triumvirate of which James and Hall were the other members, all pioneers in the introduction of experimental psychology into this country in the eighties. A functional psychologist, he is noted for his textbooks on physiological psychology. He uses Wundt's works as a guide. He conceives of the mind as a useful organ. Consciousness for him meant the activity of the "self" and its function was to solve problems.[89] While he held the soul to be a real entity distinct from the body, he maintained that its essence was conscious activity.[90]

James Mark Baldwin (1861-　) is an important leader in this new psychological tendency. His psychology was influenced by evolution. His attraction

---

[87] *Ibid.*

[88] Knight, *op. cit.,* p. 526.

[89] Boring, *op. cit.,* pp. 512-513.

[90] He says: ". . . the origin of every mind . . . must be at the exact point of time when the mind begins to *act* (consciously); its origin is *in* and *of* these past conscious activities. Before this first (conscious) activity the mind is not. But even thus it cannot be admitted that any mind springs into full being at a leap, as it were." "For the origin of every mind is in a process of development." George Trumbull Ladd, *Philosophy of Mind,* pp. 363, 364, quoted by Michael Maher, *Psychology, Empirical and Rational* (London: Longmans, Green and Co., 1902), p. 576. This was contrary, of course, to the scholastic teaching which holds that "in the origin of the new human being the creative action is exerted according to the universal law prescribed by divine wisdom, in the act and at the instant in which the incipient vital principle is evoked in the germinating cell." Maher, *op. cit.,* p. 577. According to Ladd's theory the infant is without a soul. *Ibid.*

to Wundt introduced him to the psychology of experimentalism. His two books, *Mental Development
in the Child and the Race* (1895), and *Social and
Ethical Interpretations in Mental Development*
(1897), written while he was at Princeton, "present
clearly and forcibly the evolutionary principle in
psychology, and even seek to modify Darwin's theory
by the conception . . . called 'organic selection.' "[91]
The evolutionary theory was his great thesis.[92] He
maintained that psychology should study individual
differences.[93]

James McKeen Cattell (1860-   ) may be said to
have advanced naturalistic psychology in America
because of his influence in preparing the way for behaviorism. He taught psychology for twenty-six
years at Columbia and thus exerted a greater influence on students of psychology than perhaps any
other American, an influence which was extended by
his editorship of six important psychological journals. He is an evolutionist and is representative of
the trend in American psychology. His main interest
lies in the psychology of individual differences,[94]

[91] Boring, *op. cit.,* p. 518.

[92] His doctoral dissertation written at Princeton was a refutation
of materialism. In 1893-1903 he was professor of psychology at
Princeton where he organized a new laboratory. In 1903 he began
to infuse new life into the laboratory at Johns Hopkins. He wrote
a *History of Psychology* (1913), a *Handbook of Psychology, The
Story of the Mind,* etc. He cooperated in founding the *Psychological Review* (1894), the *Psychological Index, Psychological Mono-
graphs,* and the *Dictionary of Philosophy and Psychology.* Experimentation, however, was not his forte—he preferred philosophy.

[93] "The influence of Darwin upon psychology has always been to
favor the study of individual differences, as we have seen with
Galton, and as was equally true with Hall and Baldwin." Boring
op. cit., p. 519.

[94] In 1880-1882 he studied in Europe under Lotze and Wundt.
He studied for a semester under Hall at Johns Hopkins and in

which he began to diagnose by mental tests. Through his influence in developing mental tests, reaction time experiments and statistical method with objective results as against introspection, Columbia developed a psychology of human *capacity*. It is a functional psychology though Boring says "it is perhaps not wise to give so unphilosophic a movement this formal systematic name. Nevertheless, it is important to realize the significance of the movement, because it, more than any other 'school,' has been typical of the American trend." [95]

From all this it is clear that a new attitude, based on and inspired by the evolutionary hypothesis, was being developed in American psychology during the last decades of the nineteenth century and the first decades of the twentieth. The technique of the scientific method in psychology had its beginnings in German experimental psychology but the theory back of it was the Darwinian theory of evolution. Through the impressive influence of James, Hall, Baldwin, and Cattell, not to mention the many lesser men, education was given a completely new direction. Since,

---

[95] *Ibid.*, p. 527.

1883 was back at Leipzig where he became the self-appointed and first assistant to his professor. He spent three years there working on his own problem, individual differences and reaction time. He took his doctorate, and in 1887 lectured in psychology at the University of Pennsylvania and at Bryn Mawr College. In 1888 he taught at Cambridge and met Galton who was interested also in individual differences. From 1888 to 1891 he was professor of psychology at Pennsylvania. He introduced the use of statistical method in psychology and the concept of the probable error idea. Then he went to Columbia and founded a laboratory there just as he had done in Pennsylvania. He remained there for twenty-six years until 1917. He was elected president of the Ninth International Congress of Psychology in 1929. He was not a philosopher like James, Hall, and Baldwin. Boring, *op. cit.*, pp. 520-528.

according to the functional psychology, consciousness was a developmental process, while the substance or essence psychology of the scholastics with its belief in the faculties or powers of the mind, like observation, memory, imagination, judgment, and reason, was considered obsolete, it was only natural that, as the new psychology entered education, a new aim would emerge as against the old one of formal discipline.   And so it happened that as a result of Rousseau's insistence that education should follow nature, Pestalozzi's desire that it should be the "natural, progressive, and harmonious development of all the powers and capacities of the human being," Herbart's doctrine of interest, apperception and the five formal steps, the conviction came about that the child's capacity for learning is the central fact in education. Thus it was that psychology became interested in the nature of the learning process, laws of learning, and the vocational capacities of children. The triumphant progress of the theory of evolution was acclaimed in the field of psychology and the evolutionary idea manifested itself distinctly in the study of the child's mental development inaugurated, in America, by G. Stanley Hall.[96]   Gradually there developed an educational psychology fingering off from the parent stem, using the scientific method of objective observation, and interesting itself in the study of behavior through the administration of certain types of tests. This educational psychology in America was influenced considerably both by the methods and categories of the biological sciences and in the extreme

---

[96] Cf. G. S. Hall, *Life and Confessions of a Psychologist* (New York: D. Appleton & Co., 1923).

form it became behavioristic, i.e., an objective, experimental branch of natural science, having its roots
in psychology. This extreme form of educational
psychology was not interested in consciousness which
it considered indefinable and useless as a concept for
scientific investigation.[97] And so one more extraordinary factor in naturalism entered into the theory
and practice of American education, already definitely modified by the spread of secularism and the
advance of naturalistic science, and thus began, under the influence of leading educators who were definitely agnostic in their religious views that period
of educational development in the New World which,
aiming to create a new civilization of ever changing
standards and purposes, has completely broken with
the past and its traditions.

---

[97] Cf. John B. Watson, *Behaviorism* (Revised edition, New York:
W. W. Norton and Co., 1930); *ibid.*, *Psychology from the Standpoint of a Behaviorist* (Chicago: Lippincott Co., 1929).

CHAPTER IV

DEWEY AS AN EXPONENT OF NATURALISM IN EDUCATION

Having defined naturalism and explained its relation to philosophy and education, we gave an account of its entrance into the American scene. The factors which nourished and encouraged its growth and the logical development of its influence in education being demonstrated, it is now proposed to investigate its bearing on the educational thought of four recognized leaders in America. It is not difficult to select such a list; for the names of Dewey, Kilpatrick, Rugg, and Thorndike represent American educational endeavor in a highly significant manner. The positions of importance which they have held and are holding in American universities, the numerous influential treatises on education which they have published, and the encomiums of superlative praise which they continually receive from American teachers are all indications of their status in American education. Let us examine, therefore, what philosophies of life underlie their theories of education and what are the educational implications of these doctrines.

In this chapter, we shall consider Professor John Dewey. All educators who discuss him agree that he is *the* outstanding and most influential thinker in American educational theory and practice.[1] Let us,

---

[1] Paul Arthur Schilpp, *Commemorative Essays,* 1859-1929 (Stockton, Calif.: Privately published, 1930), p. 41, where we read that of

therefore, examine his philosophy of life, his philosophy of religion, and his philosophy of education. It
is important to bear in mind during this exposition
the factors which have motivated his outlook on life,
and in the first instance what is implied when he tells
us that: "Upon the whole, the forces that have influenced me have come from persons and from situa-

the many illustrious sons of the United States who have had "tremendous influence" upon her progress and destiny none "has so
profoundly and in so many areas of human endeavor influenced and
determined his own age as . . . America's dean of philosophers:
John Dewey." Horne thinks that: "Dr. Dewey has exerted a great
influence on education both at home and abroad," his text *Democracy and Education* being one of the two "most widely used in our
country in the field of educational philosophy." Herman Harrell
Horne, *The Democratic Philosophy of Education* (New York: The
Macmillan Co., 1933), p. ix. A former pupil, himself an important
leader in American education, Ernest C. Moore, Director of the
University of California at Los Angeles, says: "We think of Professor Dewey as the most profound and understanding thinker on
education that the world has yet known." "John Dewey's Contribution to Educational Theory," in *John Dewey, the Man and His
Philosophy* (Cambridge: Harvard University Press, 1930), p. 7.
Merle Curti tells us that: "John Dewey's work covers a range much
broader than that . . . of any . . . psychologist or educator . . .
vast . . . impressive in extent." *The Social Ideas of American Educators* (New York: Charles Scribner's Sons, 1935), p. 499. Godfrey
H. Thomson, Professor of Education at the University of Edinburgh,
a leader in British educational circles, feels that Dewey's "influence
on the schools of America has been enormous." *A Modern Philosophy of Education* (New York: Longmans Green and Co., 1929), p.
77. Harvey Gates Townsend, Professor of Philosophy at the University of Oregon, is persuaded that Dewey has to a "very unusual
degree . . . been able to affect the cultural habits and the intellectual outlook of a whole generation." *Philosophical Ideas in the
United States* (New York: American Book Co., Copyright, 1934),
p. 234. Used by permission of the publishers. Cf. also Michael Demiashkevich, *An Introduction to the Philosophy of Education* (New
York: American Book Co., 1935), p. 112. Isaac Doughton, *Modern
Public Education, Its Philosophy and Background* (New York: D.
Appleton-Century Co., Inc., 1935), pp. 88ff. Quincy A. Kuehner, *A
Philosophy of Education* (New York: Prentice-Hall, Inc., 1935), p.
xiii. Normal Woelfel, *Molders of the American Mind* (New York:
Columbia University Press, 1933), p. 119.

tions more than from books," [2] that "the sense of
divisions and separations that were . . . borne in upon
me as a consequence of a heritage of New England
culture, divisions by way of isolation of self from the
world, of soul from body, of nature from God brought
a painful oppression—or, rather, they were an inward
laceration." [3]   These statements enable us to understand more readily how he might conclude that, "the
task of future philosophy is to clarify men's ideas as
to the social and moral strifes of their own day," [4] and
that, "there is probably . . . no historic philosophy
which is not in some measure a reflection, an idealiza-
tion, a justification of some of the tendencies of its
own age." [5]   Certainly this is eminently true of his
own philosophy of life, religion, and education.

Born in Burlington, Vermont, in 1859, the year
that Darwin's *Origin of Species* appeared, raised "in
a conventionally evangelical atmosphere of the more
'liberal' sort," [6] he proceeded in due time to the University of Vermont, where several influences sowed
the seeds of future thought.   Butler's *Analogy*, used
as a text in the philosophy of religion, strangely
enough, "with its cold logic and acute analysis was
. . . in a reversed way, a factor in developing 'scepticism,' " [7] whereas a naturalistic book of Huxley, the

[2] John Dewey, "From Absolutism to Experimentalism," in *Contem-
porary American Philosophy, Personal Statements*, edited by George
P. Adams and William Pepperell Montague (New York: The Mac-
millan Company, 1930), II, 22.
    [3] *Ibid.*, p. 19.
    [4] John Dewey, *Reconstruction in Philosophy* (New York: Henry
Holt and Company, 1920), p. 26.
    [5] John Dewey,. *Characters and Events, Popular Essays in Social and
Political Philosophy*, edited by Joseph Ratner (New York: Henry
Holt and Company, 1929), II, 437.
    [6] "From Absolutism to Experimentalism," p. 15.
    [7] *Ibid.*, p. 16.

text in a non-laboratory course of physiology, aroused in him "a sense of interdependence and interrelated unity that gave form to intellectual stirrings that had been previously inchoate, and created a type or model of a view of things to which material in any field ought to conform." "Subconsciously, at least," he tells us, "I was led to desire a world and a life that would have the same properties as had the human organism in the picture of it derived from study of Huxley's treatment." [8]

Thus his philosophic interest was awakened and directed along naturalistic lines. At the same time he read Francis Bacon and Harriet Martineau's work on Comte, the French positivist, with deep interest. Later he went to Johns Hopkins for graduate studies where his admiration for Hegel increased. He confesses that: "Hegel's synthesis of subject and object, matter and spirit, the divine and human, was . . . no mere intellectual formula; it operated as an immense release, a liberation. Hegel's treatment of human culture, of institutions and the arts, involved the . . . dissolution of hard and fast dividing walls." [9]   It is

---

[8] *Ibid.,* p. 13.

[9] *Ibid.,* p. 19. Cf. William Taft Feldman, *The Philosophy of John Dewey, A Critical Analysis,* Ph.D. dissertation, (Baltimore: Johns Hopkins Press, 1934), Chapter 1 of which is devoted to the organismic logic in Dewey's philosophy, showing the Hegelian source of many of his ideas. These were at first plainly orthodox Hegelianism. He believed in God, Absolute Reality, Perfect Will. In the nineties his philosophy shifts to the problem of reflective experience in human life, retaining his organismic logic, newly interpreted. Intelligence functions now in particular situations in experience, wherein problems demanding planned action arise. Metaphysics is ignored, ontological speculation held invalid. This latter position is surrendered when *Experience and Nature* appears in 1925. The difference between his positions in 1886 and 1925 is that, whereas at the former time he believed it possible to attain to the absolute, now he holds it is impossible. Hence the title of

important to note that social interests and problems
attracted him from an early period, having the appeal
for him which others usually find in religious questions.[10] As we shall see, social emphasis distinguishes
his thought in its fullest growth. During the fifteen
years after he graduated from Johns Hopkins in 1884,
he drifted imperceptibly from Hegelianism, but
acquaintance with Hegel left a permanent deposit
in his thinking.[11]

There are four important points in the development of his outlook on life. His great interest in the
theory and practice of education fused together his
interests in psychology, social institutions, and social
life. He became persuaded "that philosophizing
should focus about education as the supreme human
interest in which, moreover, other problems, cosmo-
logical, moral, logical, come to a head."[12] Then the
dualism between science and morals, which he ab-
horred, made him greatly desire a logic, a method of
effective enquiry, which would maintain the continuity between them and supply what he felt was
the greatest practical need. Instrumentalism was the
result. Added to these two factors was the influence
of the biological strain in William James' Psychology
which had "its roots in a return to the earlier biological conception of the *psyche*, but a return possessed
of a new force and value due to the immense progress
made by biology since the time of Aristotle. . . . It
worked its way more and more into all [his] ideas

---

[10] "From Absolutism to Experimentalism," p. 20.
[11] *Ibid.*, p. 21.
[12] *Ibid.*, p. 23.

Dewey's essay, "From Absolutism to Experimentalism," in *Contemporary American Philosophy*. Personal Statements, II.

and acted as a ferment to transform old beliefs." [13] This evolutionistic, biological, approach to psychology suggested a similar treatment of social problems with emphasis on communication and participation, and from this angle he endeavored to build a philosophy of life on the principles of modern science in its relation to the problems of education, morals, and religion. [14]

Invariably, it would seem, naturalistic writers attracted him. The inspiration of Francis Bacon, Locke, Hume, Lamarck, Huxley, Darwin, Spencer, the laboratory-mind attitude of Peirce, the theory of evolution, the advance of the sciences, the naturalistic biological psychology of James, all contributed powerfully towards the modification of his thought [15] and shared in bringing about the transition from Hegelianism to Experimentalism.

Evolutionary and biological concepts are the basis of Dewey's philosophy of life. There is nothing closed, permanent, or planned in the universe. It is not constant in change but a constant order of change; "change is omnipresent," constant in function, not constant in existence, without final ends and

---

[13] *Ibid.*, p. 24. "I doubt," he says, "if we have as yet begun to realize all that is due to William James for the introduction and use of this idea." *Ibid.*, p. 24. Cf. John Dewey, *Philosophy and Civilization* (New York: Minton, Balch and Company, 1931), p. 28, where he refers to this biological aspect of *Principles of Psychology* by James in its relation to Instrumentalism.

[14] "From Absolutism to Experimentalism," pp. 25-26.

[15] Curti suggests in this connection that "the socially conservative philosophy of the master Hegelian in America, William F. Harris," antagonized Dewey's democratic tendencies. Added to this fact was the growing challenge to democratic ideals brought about by the transition from an agrarian to an industrial civilization. This made him dislike the *laissez faire* implicit in Hegelianism. Curti, *The Social Ideas of American Educators*, p. 504.

forms.[16] Within it man finds his home. He is continuous with nature. The human organism, in-
dividually and collectively, in continuous interaction
with environment, finds itself in need of favorable
adjustments, controls, and reconstructions in order
to preserve its own well-being and satisfaction. When
problems of maladjustment arise and desires and ap-
petites are obstructed, thought is provoked and solutions arrived at under the guidance of experimental
method. The correct responses which solve these
difficulties become habits of the organism, which continues its growth, meeting and solving situations in
experience. Hence there is no thinking without a
problem, no thought except in a problem in experience. Thinking is limited to experience, never transcending it, since there are no realms of the unexperi-
enced and unexperienceable. In a word, there is no
transcendent world, no supernatural universe with
which man is in any way concerned.[17]

---

[16] Dewey, *Reconstruction in Philosophy*, pp. 61, 69. "The world
of modern science is an open world, a world varying indefinitely
without possibility of assignable limit in its internal make-up, a
world stretching beyond any assignable bounds externally." *Ibid.*,
p. 54.

[17] John Dewey, *Experience and Nature*, (New York: W. W. Norton and Company, Inc., 1929), p. 282. Living as an empirical affair
"is not something which goes on below the skin-surface of an organism: it is always an inclusive affair involving connection, interaction
of what is within the organic body and what lies outside in space
and time." *Ibid.* "Man's home is nature: his purposes and aims
are dependent for execution upon natural conditions. Separated
from such conditions, they become empty dreams and idle indul-
gences of fancy. This philosophy is vouched for by the doctrine of
biological development which shows that man is continuous with
nature, not an alien entering her processes from without." John
Dewey, *Democracy and Education, An Introduction to the Philosophy of Education*, (New York: The Macmillan Company, 1933),
p. 333. Cf. John Dewey, *The Quest for Certainty: A Study of the
Relation of Knowledge and Action*, (New York: Minton, Balch

Thus Dewey's philosophy, originating in the conflicts and difficulties of social life, and concerning itself with problems of the relationship between mind and matter, body and soul, humanity and physical nature, individual and social, theory and practice, is not defined by subject matter envisioning finality and completeness. "The very nature of experience as an ongoing changing process forbids" it.[18]

"The true 'stuff' of experience is recognized to be adaptive courses of action, habits, active functions, connections of doing and undergoing; sensori-motor coördinations."[19] And its "method of empirical naturalism . . . provides . . . the only way . . . by which one can freely accept the standpoint and conclusions of modern science: the way by which we can be genuinely naturalistic. . . . The naturalistic method . . . destroys many things once cherished; but it destroys them by revealing their inconsistency with the nature of things . . . it inspires the mind with courage and vitality to create new ideals and

---

[18] *Democracy and Education*, p. 379. Cf. John Dewey, "The Need for a Recovery in Philosophy" in *Creative Intelligence* (New York: Henry Holt and Company, 1917), pp. 10-11; *Quest for Certainty*, pp. 214-215.

[19] *Reconstruction in Philosophy*, p. 91.

---

and Company, 1929), p. 246. Cf. John Dewey, *Art as Experience*, (New York: Minton, Balch and Company, 1934), pp. 22-23, where we read that: "Full recognition . . . of the continuity of the organs, needs and basic impulses of the human creature with his animal forbears, implies no necessary reduction of man to the level of the brutes . . . what is distinctive in man makes it possible for him to sink below the level of the beasts. It also makes it possible for him to carry to new and unprecedented heights that unity of sense and impulse, of brain and eye and ear, that is exemplified in animal life, saturating it with the conscious meanings derived from communication and deliberate expression."

values in the face of the perplexities of a new world." [20]

Here is an experimental naturalism which, excluding the superempirical and supernatural, finds itself motivated by the progress of science, industry, and democracy, and builds its system solely on an experimental epistemology and a social ethics. The world in which man has been begotten, which science has discovered, is the human inheritance. It is human destiny to reconstruct the individual and social organism through the instrumentality of achieved intelligence under the aegis of the scientific method to the end that social progress without fixed ends or preconceived goals may keep on advancing in evolutionary progress for the betterment of mankind.

Dewey's Instrumentalism is defined by himself as: "an attempt to establish a precise logical theory of concepts, of judgments and inferences in their various forms, by considering primarily how thought functions in the experimental determinations of future consequences." [21]   Evolutionism is its basis as well as the inspiration of its theory of knowledge and mind.[22]

---

[20] *Experience and Nature*, pp. II-III.

[21] *Philosophy and Civilization*, p. 26. It contains varying and at times conflicting strains of thought due to the temperament of its author who abhors confining himself to anything fixed once and for all. Cf. Virgil Michel, "Some Thoughts on Professor Dewey" in *The New Scholasticism*, II, No. 4, (October, 1928), pp. 327-341. Cf. Feldman, *The Philosophy of John Dewey*, wherein is found the discrimination and classification of the factors in the varying strains of Dewey's thought.

[22] Theodore and Grace Andrus De Laguna, *Dogmatism and Evolution* (New York: The Macmillan Company, 1910), Part III, Chapters 1, 2, 5,. On page 123 we read that: "Pragmatism is the first whole-hearted attempt at an appreciation of the significance of Darwinism for logical theory." See p. 122 for reference to Dewey in this respect.

It is a philosophy in terms of struggle and survival, adaptation, and adjustment. Knowing is nothing more than the act of a participant, himself a product of, and continuous with, nature inside its natural and social scene. The sole true object of knowledge lies in the consequences of directed action within that scene.[23]

Since experience consists of the mutual interaction of the organism and its environment, knowledge is a biological function. Evolution determines the intellect as the organ in the struggle for existence. This is the sole justification of mind. Thinking "is something that *happens* to experience under certain definable conditions."[24]

Reason, the *nous* of the Greeks, the *intellectus* of the Scholastics, which once signified "an inherent immutable order of nature, superempirical in character, and the organ of mind by which this universal order is grasped,"[25] has surrendered to naturalized intelligence which "is associated with *judgment:* that is with selection and arrangement of means to effect consequences and with choice of what we take as our ends . . . the knowing which occurs within nature involves possibility of direction of change. This conclusion gives intelligence a foothold within nature which 'reason' never possessed. That which acts outside of nature and is a mere spectator of it is, by definition, not a participator in its changes. Therefore it is debarred from taking part in directing them."[26]

---

[23] Dewey, *The Quest for Certainty*, p. 196.
[24] Arthur Kenyon Rogers, *English and American Philosophy Since 1800, A Critical Survey* (New York: The Macmillan Company, 1923), p. 390.
[25] Dewey, *The Quest for Certainty*, p. 212.
[26] *Ibid.*, p. 213.

Intelligence, therefore, is "domesticated" within nature. It is simply the interaction which directs the course of change in nature's own continuing inter-actions which, without it, would be undirected, hav-ing only effects not consequences.[27] "The intelligent activity of man is not something brought to bear upon nature from without: it is nature realizing its own potentialities in behalf of a fuller and richer issue of events."[28] Knowledge, therefore, is *instru-mental,* the *only* means of regulation and direction in experience.[29]

Man possesses no soul, mind, or reason in the supernaturalistic meaning of these words. There is no spiritual substance, the substantial form of the body, the principle of immanency of life. The doc-trine of organic development has eliminated the dualism of soul and body.[30]

---

[27] *Ibid.,* p. 214.

[28] *Ibid.,* pp. 214-215.

[29] *Ibid.,* pp. 218-219. Hocking observes in this regard that: "Build-ing on this biological view of mind, Professor Dewey calls this type of Pragmatism 'Instrumentalism,' that is, thought is to be con-sidered simply as an instrument for promoting life, not an organ for reaching a knowledge of things as they are in themselves." Hocking, *Types of Philosophy,* pp. 155-156.

[30] Dewey rejects the idea of the soul because "The independently existing soul restricts and degrades individuality making of it a separate thing outside of the full flow of things, alien to things experienced and consequently in either mechanical or miraculous relations to them." John Dewey, *Influence of Darwin on Philos-ophy and Other Essays in Contemporary Thought* (New York: Henry Holt and Company, 1910), p. 268, footnote. Cf. *Democracy and Education,* pp. 391-393. "The conception of mind as a purely isolated possession of the self," he says, "is at the very antipodes of truth. The self *achieves* mind in the degree in which knowledge of things is incarnate in the life about (man)." *Ibid.,* p. 344. There is no such thing as mind existing "with mental states and opera-tions that exist independently." Such a conception is "mythical," since "Mind appears in experience as ability to respond to present stimuli on the basis of anticipation of future possible consequences

Now the human organism in its natural environment needs security through certainty of knowledge transcending belief. This can be accomplished in only one way, i.e., by the scientific method. Hence experimental inquiry, which has begotten a new attitude to the natural occurrences and interactions of experience, must be utilized to make improved changes in the environment and man's relation to it.[31] "Henceforth the quest for certainty becomes the search for methods of control; that is, regulation of conditions of change with respect to their consequences. Theoretical certitude is assimilated to practical certainty; to *security*, trustworthiness of instrumental operations."[32] In this philosophy of life, ideas have an empirical status, that of acts to be performed. They always arise in the conditions of prior experience which begets them by supplying obstacles to the desired goal as well as supplying the means to be used to reach it. Ideas and the end in view are in a continual process of creation and re-creation, i.e., as often as those in habitual use manifest defects or values. They have no predetermined course to follow. "Ideas . . . are plans of operations to be performed . . . integral factors in actions which change the face of the world . . . ideas are statements not of what is or has been but of acts to be performed."[33] Hence they are just hypotheses, not finalities, to be

---

[31] *The Quest for Certainty*, pp. 22, 79, 85, 86.
[32] *Ibid.*, p. 128.
[33] *Ibid.*, p. 138. Cf. 111-112.

---

and with a view to controlling the kind of consequences that are to take place." *Ibid.*, p. 153. Cf. "The Naturalization of Intelligence," Chapter VIII, *The Quest for Certainty;* Cf. "Nature, Life and Body—Mind," Chapter VII, *Experience and Nature.*

tested by the consequences of operations to be carried out by the experimental method. They are not to be judged by something existing prior to them.[34] Ideas and thought are productive and constructive in the sense that they are experimental. Experimental knowing begets the monistic pattern of mind and its organs, removing the dualistic separation of theory and practice. It shows knowing as a kind of action which alone safely and progressively gives natural existence realized meanings. The concern of philosophy is with immediate human problems calling for solution by the experimental method, which consequently must be applied to all fields within human experience. All traditions, beliefs, institutions are to be tested continually by their capacity to meet the tests of scientific method when immediate needs and difficulties demand such action. Thus "Human experience consciously guided by ideas evolves its own standards and measures and each new experience constructed by their means is an opportunity for new ideas and ideals." [35]

From all this it is evident that the traditional doctrines of soul, body, mind, intelligence, reason, ideas, and nature are meaningless. Knowledge is not an act performed by a person who seeks to know reality

---

[34] *Ibid.*, p. 167.

[35] *Ibid.*.Cf. p. 168. Cf. John L. Childs, *Education and The Philosophy of Experimentalism* (New York: The Century Company, 1931), Preface IX. The motive underlying Dewey's anti-metaphysical philosophy, according to Schilpp, "is the attempt to furnish an intellectual basis, justification, and method for biological and social progress. His primary interest, is and evidently always has been, in the betterment of human life and of its environment for the sake of human advancement (i. e., the biological development of the human species). The practical interest has been foremost in Dewey's life and work." *Commemorative Essays*, p. 42.

outside of himself through the medium of his percep-
tions, thoughts, and ideas. No dualism exists between the knowing thought and the object known,
since experience does not belong to the knower in
any sense. Knowledge is a functional part of experience, not a finished logical system. What was once
known as reason is actually intelligence in the sense
of experimental judgment, i.e., what happens to experience scientifically controlled. This intelligence
is only "the purposeful energetic reshaper of those
phases of nature and life that obstruct social well-
being." [36]

When Santayana, himself an avowed naturalist and
materialist,[37] reviewing Dewey's *Experience and Nature,* termed its author's mode of thinking half-
hearted naturalism,[38] a characterization which Thilly,
an idealist, approved,[39] Dewey felt himself con-
strained to object against any charges of half-hearted-

---

[36] *Reconstruction in Philosophy,* p. 51. Cf. Rogers, *op. cit.,* pp.
388-390.

[37] Cf. Townsend, *Philosophical Ideas in the United States,* pp.
250-251. Cf. Santayana's, *Scepticism and Animal Faith,* 1923, *The
Realm of Matter,* 1930.

[38] George Santayana, "Dewey's Naturalistic Metaphysics," in *The
Journal of Philosophy,* XXII, No. 25 (December 3, 1925), 673-688.
He says: "In reviewing it, I may . . . be excused from attempting to
sum up his chief contentions in his own language, considering especially that his language, as he himself says, is the chief or only
obstacle to understanding him." (p. 673).

[39] Frank Thilly, "Contemporary American Philosophy," in *The
Philosophical Review,* XXXV, No. 6. (November, 1926), 522-538.
He says: "Santayana's judgment that Dewey is an 'inveterate
naturalist' would . . . seem to be well founded. . . . We must not
forget that Dewey the naturalist is also a sincere and ardent social
idealist. . . . The fact is that Dewey does not carry naturalism to
its logical, naturalistic conclusion because he has an abiding faith
in human nature. This is what Santayana must mean when he
characterizes his naturalism as 'half-hearted and short-winded,' and
defines his attitude as 'essentially a moral attitude or lay religion'
. . ." *Ibid.,* p. 532.

ness in the matter at all and vindicated his position by an article entitled "Half-Hearted Naturalism."[40] This clarification of his position makes it very certain that he is and wishes to be known as a "whole-hearted" naturalist.[41] While this is evident from a careful study of his numerous works, it is particularly pertinent to this treatment that he so insistently and unequivocally desires that any doubt in the matter be cast swiftly aside. Specifically, he is an empirical naturalist, or a naturalistic empiricist, in the sense that there is for him no discontinuity or break or dualism between nature and social man.[42] "To me," he says, "human affairs, associative and personal, are projections, continuations, complications, of the nature which exists in the physical and pre-human world. There is no gulf, no two spheres of existence, no 'bifurcations.' "[43] Hence there is no such thing as a separation between nature and man, no "insertion of unaccountable and unnatural conditions and factors" since there is a "thoroughgoing continuity" in existence in space and time, a fact which is demonstrated solely by the progress of natural science, not philosophy. The traits, events, affairs which human experience demonstrates find their prototypes contained in nature.[44]

What is Dr. Dewey's philosophy of religion? Does he believe in God, the Creator and Redeemer of the world? What does he say about the supernatural and Revelation? His answers to these questions will in-

---

[40] John Dewey, "Half-Hearted Naturalism" in *The Journal of Philosophy*, XXIV, No. 3 (February 3, 1927), 57-64.
[41] *Ibid.*, p. 61.
[42] *Ibid.*, pp. 57-58.
[43] *Ibid.*, p. 58.
[44] *Ibid.*

dicate definitely where he stands on the question of naturalism. As a matter of fact, Dewey does not believe in God,[45] nor in any religion, much less in Christianity,[46] consequently he rejects Revelation[47] and the supernatural.[48] He tells his readers that the word "God" does not mean a particular Being in any sense. "God," actually, "denotes the unity of all ideal ends arousing us to desire and actions." [49] "God" means solely ideal ends which in specific situations influence our volition and emotion "in contrast with the doctrine of religions that 'God' designates of some kind of Being having prior and therefore non-ideal existence." [50] God, therefore, the Creator and Redeemer of the world and of man, does not exist. He simply is not and never was. Hence Dewey does not believe *in any religion;* in fact, he is opposed to all religions which have relation to the super-empirical. This is very evident in his later works and particularly clear in the first chapter of *A Common Faith,* entitled, "Religion versus the Religious," [51] where he main-

---

[45] Cf. *A Common Faith* (New Haven: Yale University Press, 1934), pp. 41-54, 24, 32. *The Quest for Certainty,* pp. 303-305; 310-311. Reviewing this book in the *Journal of Philosophy,* XXVII, No. 1, (Jan. 2, 1930), 14, C. I. Lewis of Harvard says: "This is a completer and better rounded statement of the author's point of view than any which has preceded it, and on some points it is a clearer one." Cf. *Living Philosophies,* p. 22.

[46] Cf. *A Common Faith,* pp. 1-2, 30-43. *Living Philosophies,* pp. 23, 34-35. *The Quest for Certainty,* pp. 10, 292-293, 304.

[47] Cf. *A Common Faith,* pp. 26-27, 29, 33, 38-39, 85-87; *Living Philosophies,* pp. 21, 34; *The Quest for Certainty,* p. 306.

[48] *A Common Faith,* pp. 1-2, 29, 34, 73, 76, 80-81, 83-84; *Living Philosophies,* pp. 28-29, 43; *Experience and Nature,* Chap. VII, pp. 54 ff, 81 ff.; *Philosophy and Civilization,* pp. 7, 85

[49] *A Common Faith,* p. 42.

[50] *Ibid.* His idea is that the word "God" represents " a unification of ideal values that is essentially imaginative in origin when the imagination supervenes in conduct. . . ." *Ibid.,* p. 43.

[51] *Ibid.,* pp. 1-28.

tains that the progress of culture and science has completely discredited the supernatural and all religions
that were allied with it, though he is unwilling to
admit that "everything of a religious" nature is
thereby to be dismissed.[52]   The supernatural and religious were begotten in superstition, the products of
fear due to human inability to control the universe.[53]
The unseen power in control of human destiny is
not the Creator, God, but an ideal which influences
us in so far as we are motivated by the spirit of our
various callings.   The religious attitude actually and
truly means the quality that is connected through
imagination with a comprehensive general attitude
like that manifested in art, science, and good citizenship.[54]   Science has challenged successfully the very
idea of the supernatural.   Theologians miss the point
that science is a method by which beliefs are changed
as well as tested and that its subject matter, developed
under improved technique, must not be identified
with any fixed beliefs and ideas, a characteristic
which "is itself a hold-over of ancient and still current dogmatic habits of thought which are opposed
to science in its actuality and which science is undermining." [55]   He denies the possibility of any Revela-

---

[52] *Ibid.*, pp. 1-2.
[53] *The Quest for Certainty*, p. 10, cf. p. 292.
[54] *A Common Faith*, p. 23. "Faith in the divine author and authority in which Western civilization confided, inherited ideas of the
soul and its destiny, of fixed revelation, of completely stable institutions . . . have been made impossible for the cultivated mind of
the Western world." *Living Philosophies*, p. 34. "The extra-em-
pirical" in religion must be eliminated, i.e., there must be "a surrender of that supernaturalism and fixed dogma and rigid institu-
tionalism with which Christianity has been historically associated."
Ibid., p. 28. Cf. *The Quest for Certainty*, p. 255 and *A Common
Faith*, p. 76.
[55] *A Common Faith*, p. 39. Cf. *Character and Events*, II, 456-457.

tion or any "special and isolated channel of access to the truths" of religion.[56] Faith is not unwavering, unhesitant belief in God's Revelation. Instead it is "the power of intelligence to imagine a future which is the projection of the desirable in the present, and to invent the instrumentalities of its realization, [which] is our salvation."[57] Hence it follows implicitly that Dewey thinks that the Ten Commandments and the natural law are obsolete. They did not arise in experience, they are prior to it, they pretend to stability and seek to preserve their integrity no matter what changes culture and civilization produce. Therefore they are useless, false, and relics of a superstitious age. The fact is that Dewey believes Christianity has failed, that in any case it was bound to do so, since it started off on the false dualistic basis of natural and supernatural. We may conclude legitimately that Dewey is an atheist. There can be no doubt of it. He is not an agnostic since he holds that "generalized agnosticism is only a half-way elimination of the supernatural. Its meaning departs when the intellectual outlook is directed wholly to the natural."[58] This makes it certain that, even if metaphysically or ontologically he may be classed as an agnostic, as when he asserts that philosophy should abandon the search for ultimate reality,[59] he is an atheistic naturalist, whose sole faith lies in the method of intelligence, who doubts only to find the solution in the here and now of things in experience and "not because some inaccessible super-

[56] *A Common Faith,* p. 29. Cf. *Living Philosophies,* p. 21.
[57] Dewey, *Creative Intelligence,* p. 69.
[58] *A Common Faith,* p. 86.
[59] *The Quest for Certainty,* p. 311., cf. Demiashkevich, *op. cit.,* 113.

natural lurks behind whatever *we* can know." [60]   He is a naturalistic positivist, substantially in agreement with Comte, only that he has arrived at a more complete positivism.[61]   Consonant with his philosophical experimentalism and its denial of the abiding, fixed, and absolute, of God, supernaturalism, Revelation, and Christianity, Dewey rejects the concept of the moral law as a doctrine of externally fixed and unchanging principles implanted in human nature by the natural law and supplemented by Revelation. Since there is no eternal Lawgiver, the idea of a universal moral law prescribing definitely fixed and abiding principles is repugnant to the minds of men trained in the scientific attitude.   Such superstitious notions have disappeared from natural science. Ethical theory, hitherto "singularly hypnotized by the notion that its business is to discover some final end or good or some ultimate and supreme law," [62] must free itself from such hypnotism and "advance to a belief in a plurality of changing, moving, individualized goods and ends, and to a belief that principles, criteria, laws, are intellectual instruments for analyzing individual or unique situations." [63]   There is no *Summum Bonum,* no one supreme and final good and end, but as many goods as there are specific situations requiring improvement.   Therefore, a law presupposing uniformity in morals is not only undesirable but impossible.[64]   "Morals *are* social.   The question of ought, should be, is a question of better and

[60] *A Common Faith*, p. 86.

[61] Demiashkevich, *An Introduction to the Philosophy of Education*, p. 113.

[62] *Reconstruction in Philosophy*, p. 161.

[63] *Ibid.*, pp. 162-163.

[64] *Ibid.* p. 166.

worse *in* social affairs." [65] Since knowledge is the result of the interaction between the human organism
and the environment, so too, conduct is based on experiences which are acquired through the same reaction.[66] To be moral, then, means to be social, "to be
fully and adequately what one is capable of becoming
through association with others in all the offices of
life." [67] The naturalistic human aim in conduct is
an abundant life shared by all, achieved by "growth
itself . . . the only moral end." [68] "success and failure

---

[65] John Dewey, *Human Nature and Conduct* (New York: The
Modern Library, 1930), p. 319. He holds that "every moral situation is a unique situation having its own irreplaceable good," not
to be adjudicated by a fixed principle. The pragmatic rule of discovering the ethical meaning of an idea by seeking its consequences
is the only way to arrive at a moral judgment. Methods of inquiry,
observation, analysis, hypothesis, the inquiry which is intelligent
are the only ones which can determine moral values. *Reconstruction in Philosophy*, pp. 163-164. Curti tells us that: "Having
long felt troubled by the dualism in traditional conceptions of science
and morals, Dewey developed 'instrumentalism' as a critical method
for inquiry into morals, which, in the spirit of Hegel, are thought
of as social rather than as individual. The philosophy of instrumentalism is an attempt to adapt the scientist's technique of hypotheses, checked through experiment and experience, to the problems of society. Existing morals and institutions, as well as new
proposals, are to be tested by their effectiveness in promoting the
fullest development of all individuals in free association and cooperation." *The Social Ideas of American Educators*, p. 507. Cf.
Human Nature and Conduct, pp. 326-327.

[66] There is no innate moral faculty or conscience. Dewey says:
"if it is recognized that knowing is carried on through the medium
of natural factors, the assumption of special agencies for moral
knowing becomes outlawed and incredible." *Human Nature and
Conduct*, p. 185. Cf. pp. 58, 314-315, *Ibid.*

[67] *Democracy and Education*, p. 415. There is no *ought*, no universal moral duties with eternal sanctions, no moral law written
in the heart of man, impervious to change. Extrinsic motivation,
induced by eternal consequences, duty accomplished because of the
Commandments, because of God's Will and Love is detrimental to
the individual and society since it rests on the false dualism of the
natural and supernatural. Cf. *Ibid.*, 402 ff. and *Human Nature
and Conduct*, Part IV, Section IV.

[68] *Reconstruction in Philosophy*, p. 177.

are the primary 'categories' of life." [69]   The *a priori*, non-experimental sanctions are non-existent. Values justify themselves by experimental scientific technique and ethical principles of conduct are to be judged solely by their success as social consequences. The doctrine of evolution shows us that moral judgments are hypotheses to be used in a scientific experimental technique, thus banishing forever the idea of fixed and immutable principles of conduct. [70] And the moral and social are but two phases of the identical experience; they cannot be separated, since "The moral and the social quality of conduct are, in the last analysis, identical with each other." [71]   It is therefore legitimate to conclude that Dewey's theory of morals is naturalistic, monistic, relativistic, and pragmatic, not only because it excludes an eternal Lawgiver and an eternal code but also because it finds its reason for existence solely in changing experience. There are therefore no absolute moral standards of any kind.   And furthermore the mental and moral outlook is socialized, finding its full realization in shared interests.   Thus judgments of value are the result of social environment and change with it. Fundamental moral judgments are not stable and

[69] *Creative Intelligence*, p. 13.
[70] *Influence of Darwin on Philosophy*, pp. 68-69. Evolutionary method proves "there is no separate body of moral rules; no separate subject matter of moral knowledge, and hence no such thing as an isolated ethical science. If the business of morals is not to speculate upon man's final end and upon an ultimate standard of right, it is to utilize physiology, anthropology, and psychology to discover all that can be discovered of man, his organic powers and propensities," *Ibid.*, p. 69; Cf. *Reconstruction in Philosophy*, pp. 163-165.
[71] *Democracy and Education*, p. 415.

abiding; they are not built on eternal and natural law.

Just as morals change with the vicissitudes of social life, so too with truth and good in the Deweyan philosophy. It is not concerned with antecedent, everlasting, *a priori* truths, demonstration, nor certitude. Truths at all times have a hypothetic quality. "They are true *if:* if certain other things eventually present themselves; and when these latter things occur they in turn suggest further possibilities; the operation of doubt—inquiry—finding recurs." [72] The meaning of truth in instrumentalism is that a thing is true if it works. Dewey tells us clearly that "the effective working of an idea and its truth are one and the same thing." [73] This theory of truth is founded on the doctrine of evolution. It means simply that what is useful and gives satisfaction is true; when it fails in this test it is no longer so. Truths are never abiding, stable, secure, but change in experience; even the true can and does become false.

Likewise the good, to which incidentally the true is subject, is not absolute and unchanging but varying, subject itself to the changing criterion of utility and satisfaction. Here experimentalism has the final say, not the intellect, deciding what actions are in accord with right reason and revealed law. "Good,"

---

[72] *Experience and Nature,* pp. 154-155. He tells us that "knowledge is an affair of *making* sure, not of grasping antecedently given sureties. What is already known, what is accepted as truth . . . is held subject to use, and is at the mercy of the discoveries which it makes possible. It has to be adjusted to the latter and not the latter to it. When things are defined as instruments, their value and validity reside in what proceeds from them; consequences not antecedents supply meaning and verity." *Ibid.,* p. 154.

[73] *The Influence of Darwin on Philosophy,* p. 143; Cf. *Reconstruction in Philosophy,* pp. 156-157.

says Dewey, "consists in the meaning that is experienced to belong to an activity when conflict and entanglement of various incompatible impulses and habits terminate in a unified orderly release of action." [74] Thus we may safely conclude that Dewey's biological instrumentalistic theories concerning morals, truth, and good are a logical consequence flowing from his outlook on life and his attitude towards it. Since he holds that this life contains the solution of all experiential problems, since morals are limited simply to social habits which are subject themselves to continual change, since truth and good find their criteria solely in the workability and resultant satisfaction of successful hypotheses, there is nothing eternal, changeless, and absolute in morals, truth, or good. There is no eternal Being from whom they flow, in whom they have the reason of their existence.

This brings us to the examination of Dewey's educational theory. And in studying its content it is important to bear in mind that his philosophy of life and his philosophy of education are basically one. "The educational point of view enables one," he says, "to envisage the philosophic problems where they arise and thrive, where they are at home, and where acceptance or rejection makes a difference in practice." [75] Hence he conceives of philosophy as being a generalized theory of education. Since the former

---

[74] *Human Nature and Conduct,* p. 210.
[75] *Democracy and Education,* p. 383. "'Philosophy of Education' is not an external application of ready-made ideas to a system of practice having a radically different origin and purpose: it is only an explicit formulation of the problems of the formation of right mental and moral habitudes in respect to the difficulties of contemporary social life." *Ibid.,* p. 386.

is completely and exclusively naturalistic, so too must the latter be. From the moment that he posits evolutionism as the explanation of all life, including man, and substitutes a naturalistic cosmic setting for a supernatural one, it is only logical that his education should ignore God, the supernatural, religion, the Ten Commandments, the eternal moral law, the soul, immortality, everything in fact which is above and beyond the purely empirical realm of existence. Education is not a preparation for life here and hereafter but a necessity of social life, in the social environment of the present. And since "the educative process is a continuous process of growth," [76] this very preparation for life is itself an unconscious result not consciously motivated; that is, the child is educated into a complete, full childhood, not for manhood which, because of growth, will itself be a result which can take care of itself when the time comes. Education is for the present, for growth which abandons all foresight of probable consequences even in this world. It has no infinite goal any more than human life has. [77] On the principle that everything is in continuous change, education is conceived as continuous growing and unfolding, excluding the very idea of the "unfolding of latent powers toward a definite

---

[76] *Ibid.*, p. 63.

[77] *Ibid.*, pp. 65-70. "The future just as future lacks urgency and body. To get ready for something, one knows not what nor why, is to throw away the leverage that exists, and to seek for motive power in a vague chance. . . . The future prepared for is a long way off; plenty of time will intervene before it becomes a present. Why be in a hurry about getting ready for it?" *Ibid.*, pp. 63-64. And even this future is bounded by earthly confines within which man finds his origin and end. There is no need for the motivation of eternity since there is no immortal soul or destiny.

goal." [78]   There is no terminus of perfection or completion. [79]   Motivated by experimental evolutionism and its laws of *growth* and *change* in the natural environment, Dewey's economy of education is confined within the precarious range of human experience, in "continuity through renewal." [80]   "Education, in its broadest sense, is the means of this social continuity of life." [81]   The sole and final reason for teaching and learning is the attainment by transmission and communication of shared social interests.   Education has one sole function, the social one.   Hence any system which aims at individual *transformation* and *conversion* by the development of intelligence and character, moulded and modeled after a Divine prototype in accord with an eternal moral law, fails to serve the human naturalistic destiny of growth in the social organism.   The very principle of authority implicit in such an out-moded theory represses individuality and correct freedom[82] because there are no such enti-

---

[78] *Ibid.*, p. 65.

[79] "The conception that growth and progress are just approximations to a final unchanging goal is the last infirmity of the mind in its transition from a static to a dynamic understanding of life." *Ibid.*, p. 66.

[80] *Ibid.*, p. 2.

[81] *Ibid.*, p. 3.

[82] Note that Dewey ignores the question of moral freedom as well as that of the self-determining person, because in his theory there is no personal conscious self. "Regarding freedom," he says, "the important thing to bear in mind is that it designates a mental attitude rather than external unconstraint of movements, but that this quality of mind cannot develop without a fair leeway of movements in exploration, experimentation, application, etc." *Democracy and Education*, p. 357. In other words, human thinking is determined by its physical and social conditions of existence alone. Here we have naturalistic determinism with its educational implications, with its emphasis on social control in learning to the exclusion of "purely individual consciousness," essential in supernatural education. *Ibid.*, p. 356.

ties as a supreme eternal authority or a private personal conscious agent. The individual, first and last, is simply an agent in social reorganization.[83]

Therefore, the function of the school is really to transform pupil experience not pupil personality. Natural conditions are to be scientifically improved, not the individual nature. Ethical instruction is actually given in an incidental, practical manner by the indirect control exercised by social schooling in which sociality and interest are *the* motives, not *duty* or *obligation* inspired by reasons flowing from an eternal and abiding law. The urgency of the present situation supplies naturalistic motivation rather than that connected with immortality.[84] Dewey's doctrine of personality is naturalistic, resting as it does on the theory that the ultimate substrate of human mental life lies in the interaction between the human organism and its environment, not in a spiritual psyche or soul.[85] Personality, therefore, is not the subsistence of an individual, intelligent, nature, living and acting autonomously, the subject to which are referred the attitudes, ideals, principles, and conduct of a rational creature motivated by an eternal moral law. Rather

---

[83] *Ibid.*, pp. 340 ff. "Since in reality," he assures us, "there is nothing to which education is subordinate save more education." "Education is all one with growing; it has no end beyond itself. The criterion of the value of school education is the extent in which it creates a desire for continued growth and supplies means for making the desire effective in fact." *Ibid.*, pp. 60, 62.

[84] *Ibid.*, pp. 351 ff. Cf. Horne *The Democratic Philosophy of Education*, pp. 426-427. "Assured and integrated individuality is the product of definite social relationships and publicly acknowledged functions." John Dewey, *Individualism Old and New*, p. 53. "True individualism is a product of the relaxation of the grip of the authority of customs and traditions as standards of belief." *Democracy and Education*, p. 356.

[85] Cf. *Experience and Nature*, Chap VII, "Nature, Life and Body-Mind."

it is individual growth coincident with and produced
by social efficiency. Personal culture and social efficiency are synonymous. Everything that makes for
social service develops personality. There is no dualism between the individual and society, since "the
single person, as the 'real person,' is no longer either
a physical body or a rational substance," but an
aspect of the social organism.[86] "What one is as a person is what one is as associated with others, in a free
give and take of intercourse."[87] Therefore there is
to be no perfecting of an "inner" personality,[88] which
is the very core of Christian education. The ego is to
be considered as essentially a shareable experience
achieving itself in the social milieu, never superior
to, nor subsisting independently of it, since its reason for existence and nourishment is to be found
therein. Personal consciousness in this theory can
never contact the superphysical or the superhuman.
Thus in limiting the culture of personality to social
efficiency, Dewey continues on his naturalistic course.[89]
In identifying the personal and the social in nature,
Dewey absorbs individual personality in sociality instead of placing it on the superior level. Hence personal rights, freedom, and divine assistance are eliminated. Viewed from this angle, any education which
would pretend to the formation of Christian saints,
which would have as its primary aim soul culture,

---

[86] *Philosophy and Civilization*, p. 159.

[87] *Democracy and Education*, p. 143. Dewey believes that: "What
is termed spiritual culture has usually been futile, with something
rotten about it, just because it has been conceived as a thing which
a man might have internally—and therefore exclusively." *Ibid.*

[88] *Ibid.*

[89] Cf. Horne, *op. cit.*, pp. 159-161; Childs, *Education and the
Philosophy of Experimentalism*, pp. 87-91, 127-128, 232-233.

which would inspire the child to find himself by losing himself for others because of God's love and
man's consequent brotherhood, in order to achieve
the supernatural at the expense of the natural, would
be futile. Character formation after the Deweyan
manner is developed in the way knowledge is gained
since such knowledge influences conduct. First-hand
knowledge gained in activities provides the power to
guide conduct, and such intellectual attitudes as are
involved in learning from these activities are moral
traits, v.g., open-mindedness, single-mindedness, sincerity, breadth of outlook, thoroughness, and "assumption of responsibility for developing the consequences of ideas which are accepted." [90] In a word,
intelligence and character are two aspects of one practical activity. Conscience, basic to Christian character formation, does not exist. There is no moral
sense in the person, no restrictions, no criteria set up
outside nature to guide personal conduct. The only
convictions which can exist are those acquired
through testing in experience. Truthfulness, chastity,
honesty, etc., are moral traits solely because they are
derived from social relationships, and they adapt
themselves to the latter at all times. "The moral and
the social quality of conduct are, in the last analysis,
identical with each other." [91] Since moral knowledge
is not something vastly superior to ordinary knowledge, to separate them, to distinguish between conscience and consciousness, is detrimental to the last

---

[90] *Democracy and Education*, p. 414.
[91] *Ibid.*, p. 415. "To possess virtue does not signify to have cultivated a few nameable and exclusive traits; it means to be fully
and adequately what one is capable of becoming through association with others in all the offices of life." *Ibid.*

degree in education. "Moral education," he says, "in school is practically hopeless when we set up the development of character as a supreme end." [92] Knowledge in fact is virtue because it is the conviction gained by testing things in experience. "In truth, the problem of moral education in the schools is one with the problem of securing knowledge—the knowledge connected with the system of impulses and habits." [93] Desirable knowledge is that which is gained from social activities which develop social growth. Thus "the measure of the worth of the administration, curriculum, and methods of instruction of the school is the extent to which they are animated by a social spirit." [94] So all aims and values in education are moral, that is to say, social. "Discipline, natural development, culture, social efficiency, are moral traits—marks of a person who is a worthy member of that society which it is the business of education to further." [95] "Education is such a life," not a means to it. "To maintain capacity for such education is the essence of morals." [96] This naturalistic doctrine ignores completely the principle that character formation is inseparable from religious education; that life, thought, word and action should be

---

[92] *Ibid.*, p. 411. He is steadfastly against catechetical instruction or lessons dealing with moral truths because of the "servile regard" and the dependence both beget. "To attempt to get . . . results from lessons about morals in a democratic society is to rely on sentimental magic." *Ibid.*

[93] *Ibid.*, p. 413.

[94] *Ibid.*, p. 415.

[95] *Ibid.*, p. 417. It is not enough to be good. The person must be good in the sense of having "capacity to live as a social member . . . Discipline, culture, social efficiency, personal refinement, improvement of character are but phases of the growth of capacity nobly to share in such balanced experience." *Ibid.*

[96] *Ibid.*

dominated ultimately not by social impulse and circumstances, but by masterful and consistent purpose
in the pupil dominated by principles related to a
supernatural, immortal destiny. The Christian ideal,
therefore, to inculcate a definite group of supernatural principles into the heart and mind of the
pupil is foreign to Dewey's ideal, since he is fundamentally non-theistic, non-Christian, and purely
social in his outlook. What training his pupils get
flows from a scientific social experimental outlook in
which growth is its own end, in which the individual
in continuous relation with the social organism ful-
fills his earthbound destiny, in which the individual
in this sense is the final value, in which "Maximum
meaningful living in the present is the best preparation for the future." [97]   Ethics and culture divorced
from Revelation become relative, utilitarian, subject
to change in the changing scene. The conflicting
tendencies and needs of man are fused in sociality,
not in a supernatural synthesis. The natural dis-
solves itself in the social; personal freedom, personal
rights and duties, and obedience to supernatural
authority are rejected for social determinism. Self-
denial and self-realization give way to the interests of
societal progress. Since moral education is the relationship between knowledge and conduct, not between eternal moral law and conduct, Dewey insists
that social learning be the unifying end of education.
To this end there must be an internal organic unity
between method, subject matter, and growth. Hence

---

[97] Childs, *Education and the Philosophy of Experimentalism,* p.
89. In fine, "the social process provides its own regulative principles
within itself and does not have to be controlled by external standards or outside authorities." *Ibid.,* p. 90.

learning must be "the accompaniment of continuous activities or occupations which have a social aim and utilize the materials of typical social situations. For under such conditions, the school becomes itself a form of social life, a miniature community and one in close interaction with other modes of associated experience beyond school walls." [98] All values that are not social are rejected. Restraint, humility, obedience, trust and faith in the teacher, which "begets the listening attitude," are rejected. The home is no longer the fundamental primary source of character and intellectual education. [99] The vital function of the teacher's personality in education is ignored, the emphasis being placed on social tools and environment. The example and authority of the teacher are minimized, his authority is indirect. Intelligence becomes naturalized and limited under the domination of the scientific method. Values in the school are man-centered, not reality-centered, finding their worth in desirable connections and consequences, in direct experience. There is no "end outside of the educative process to which education is subordinate." [100] According to this educational theory, "we live in a practical, changing, naturalistic world," [101] and therefore the criteria of good educational aims are those of good social democracy. Pupils must develop the flexible attitude which seeks

[98] *Democracy and Education*, p. 418.
[99] In the Index to *Democracy and Education*, which comprises fifteen pages, no reference is made to the home, the cradle of Christian education.
[100] *Ibid.*, p. 117.
[101] Horne, *The Democratic Philosophy of Education*, p. 134; cf. *Democracy and Education*, pp. 117-122.

to outgrow existing social conditions. Intelligence is not to be coerced by a ready-made *ought* imposed by Christian authority. Here is the core of Dewey's thought. As Horne says: "Not even the aim of democracy in education and in society is permitted to lay an obligation or claim on human life. For the ought is substituted the intelligent direction of an activity." [102] There are no final values or ends, no final good outside of nature. The individual is merely an agent of change; truth, morality, honesty, etc., are relative to socialization and shared interests the end all of life. Social efficiency is "the socialization of *mind* which is actively concerned in making experiences more communicable." [103] Finally this social efficiency is industrial efficiency coupled with good citizenship with "faith in the social utility of encouraging every individual to make his own choice intelligent." This is the business of education. [104]

It would take us too far afield to treat Dewey's idea of interest and discipline which ignores conscience and naturalizes duty and obligation. [105] Suffice it to say that there is no place for prayer or meditation on the truths of eternal life. Whatever interest the pupil acquires is derived from material which produces constant activity and absorbs his whole attention here and now. The essence of discipline is the ability to plan and carry out plans of action despite confusion and difficulty. [106] Dewey's naturalism is

---

[102] Horne, *op. cit.*, p. 137.
[103] *Democracy and Education*, p. 141.
[104] *Ibid.*, p. 141.
[105] *Ibid.*, p. 147.
[106] *Ibid.*, pp. 150-151. "Discipline is positive. To cow the spirit, to subdue inclinations, to compel obedience, to mortify the flesh, to make a subordinate perform an incongenial task—these things are

clear when he confesses that: "In last analysis, *all* the educator can do is modify stimuli so that response will as surely as is possible result in the formation of desirable intellectual and emotional dispositions." [107] The basic interests in education are scientific, social, economic, and naturalistic. These consume his whole interest to the absolute neglect of the personal, the humanistic, the supernaturalistic life. Education is the tool to transform mankind into "a society in which every person shall be occupied in something which makes the lives of others better worth living." [108] in which each individual's interest is un-coerced but congenial to his aptitudes. The schools must project the type of society which is desirable by forming the student mind in a miniature society to the end that in due time the larger one outside may be gradually modified. Hence vocational educa-tion consists in exercising intelligence not apart from but within "activity which puts nature to human use." [109] Truth lies in solving problems. Living and making a living are one. The method of scientific experimentation supplants reason guided by abiding principles. The school is an occupational one wherein the questioning attitude, the proving for oneself takes the place of faith, trust, and authority. A new class of students is to be sent forth to build a

[107] *Ibid.,* p. 212.
[108] *Ibid.,* p. 369.   Cf. pp. 364 ff.
[109] *Ibid.,* 374.

or are not disciplinary according as they do or do not tend to the development of power to recognize what one is about and to per-sistence in accomplishment." *Ibid.,* pp. 151-152.

man-centered, not God or Christ-centered, society.
New loyalties for old, changing values and morals for
unchanging and eternal ones, are to satisfy human
nature. Socialism is to permeate the classroom and
the curriculum, so that we may get "a community
of workers at once highly individualized through following one's aptitude and highly socialized through
rendering useful service." [110]   Man must be devoted
to the service of society instead of God, to the natural
instead of the supernatural. Here is "stark naturalism untouched by emotion . . . man lifting himself
into sociality by the might of his own intelligent control of nature . . . Comte's positivism without his love
and worship of man . . . the supremacy of the scientific
method in the educational process as the means of
transforming a competitive industrialism into a co-
öperative community . . . Philosophy becomes sociology, and religion becomes a science . . . man has
lost his self and his God, but he still has his own
adaptive behavior and that of his fellow organisms." [111]   We conclude that Dewey, America's outstanding educator, is definitely and completely naturalistic in philosophy, religion, and education. And
since few writers have expressed so pointedly or so
often that truth that all education must have its underlying philosophy of life we must perforce class
his education as naturalistic. We go further and
state it is socialistic naturalism without God, without
Christ, without religion, without soul, without immortality. Every single strain in it from the in-

---

[110] Horne, *op. cit.*, p. 453.
[111] *Ibid.*, p. 454.

fluence of Hegel to the inspiration of Darwin finds its place within his system.[112]

---

[112] We have quoted extensively from *Democracy and Education* for two reasons. The first is because it is one of the most widely used texts in the field of educational philosophy. Cf. Horne, *The Democratic Philosophy of Education*, p. IX. Secondly, because Dewey himself notes that few philosophers as distinct from teachers ever examined it despite the fact that it contained for many years the fullest exposition of his philosophy. While he has written copiously on education and philosophy since it was published, his basic views on the subject which we are considering are to be found in this volume. Cf. "From Absolutism to Experimentalism," p. 23.

CHAPTER V

Kilpatrick and Rugg as Exponents of Naturalism in Education

Professor William Heard Kilpatrick has greatly helped by his writing and teaching to extend the influence of Dewey's experimental naturalism in American education. Stressing in a particular manner the latter's naturalistic attitude of mind, as well as the principles of change which it involves, he has perfected, in the sense of making clearer, the implications inherent in an educational outlook which has broken away completely from supernaturalism, the super-empirical, the fixed and abiding in life. Thus Dewey's thought has permeated the thinking of very many American teachers, and progressive naturalistic education in particular has advanced its dynamic position.[1] Dewey's influence on Kilpatrick has been tremendous. Kandel sums it up very well when he tells us that the latter has been the principal popularizer of the practical implications of the philosophy and education theory of the former.[2] Doughton says that: "The foremost of the disciples and expositors

[1] Isaac Doughton, *Modern Public Education*, pp. 611-612. Cf. William Heard Kilpatrick, *Education for a Changing Civilization* (New York: The Macmillan Co., 1928), pp. 85, 106, 112, wherein will be seen how fully the author has taken over Dewey's basic philosophy.

[2] Isaac L. Kandel, "The Philosophy Underlying the System of Education in the United States," in the *Educational Yearbook*, 1929, of the International Institute of Teachers College, Columbia University, p. 537.

of Dewey is William H. Kilpatrick." [3]   Curti names
him as the first of those through whose instrumentality Dewey's liberal social philosophy made itself
felt among the teachers of the United States.[4]   Woelfel, Thomas, and Demiashkevich are all of the same
opinion.[5]   It is important to note this recognition on
the part of writers on American educational theory.
Kilpatrick himself has no hesitation in acknowledg-
ing his admiration for and deep indebtedness to his
master whom he considers the "greatest American
thinker." [6]   From all this we are left no choice but to

[3] *op. cit.,* p. 611.

[4] Merle Curti, *The Social Ideas of American Educators,* p. 561.
Rugg says of him: "Interested in fundamental forces, underlying
principles, and significant trends, he integrated into a systematic
philosophy of educational method the essential ideas of biological
evolution and dynamic psychology as developed by James, Thorndike, Woodworth, and others." H. Rugg and A. Schumaker, *The
Child-Centered School* (New York: World Book Co., Copyright,
1928), p. 47. "Professor Kilpatrick, strategically located in the first
and most influential of the new teachers' colleges, has succeeded not
only in making the philosophy of the child-centered school intelligible to thousands of teachers in service, but also in inciting widespread experimentation with the new point of view." *Ibid.,* p. 46.

[5] Norman Woelfel, *Molders of the American Mind,* pp. 119, 132;
Godfrey H. Thomson, *A Modern Philosophy of Education,* pp. 46,
63; Michael Demiashkevich, *An Introduction to the Philosophy of
Education,* pp. 135-138.

[6] William Heard Kilpatrick, *Our Educational Task* (Chapel Hill:
The University of North Carolina Press, 1930), p. 74. "We are indeed," he tells us, "indebted to him. He has helped us to see more
broadly and deeper down, and, we believe, more truly than without
him had been our lot to see. For these things we are deeply
grateful. Not only has Professor Dewey helped us who feel it so,
but we believe that he has helped a much larger number than
know it. Every school child in our country is probably witness of
the fact. And still further, some of us believe—feel compelled to
believe in spite of the danger of mistake when any age would eval-
uate itself—that the world has in and through John Dewey taken
great steps forward in its thinking, steps which it will never with-
draw and for which his name will stand clearer as time shall run.
. . . Possibly Professor Dewey has most helped us by showing
how in scientific method may be found a way of philosophizing

class Kilpatrick with the naturalistic school of which Dewey is the leader.

His own influence on American education has been and continues to be quite important. Due to the fact that he has been on the faculty of Teachers College, Columbia University, since 1909 and Professor of the Philosophy of Education since 1918, he has helped to mould the minds of very many present day teachers in American schools. We agree with Doughton who states that:

> Unquestionably, Kilpatrick, from his strategic position, has done more to stimulate discussion and experimentation in the field of education than any other single individual, even more than Dewey himself. Thousands of students, graduate and undergrad-

---

which puts common sense, science, and philosophy, all three in continuous relation. . . . Beginning with man's life in and of itself, however and wherever it may be found, he gets from it the ways and means of making life better to live here and now and still better henceforth. Thus from life itself he gets his stuff to begin with, and the ways of working it up into something ever better. Thus comes his logic, a revolution in itself; in like manner his psychology so knit and fashioned in and with his logic that none can disentangle the two. So has his method worked. Beginning in this way with life it was easy for him—*and easy for us now that he has shown us*—to get from biology a bent or turn that runs through all and makes all quick with life itself, so that each part lends itself, as does no other point of view to every effort to make life better." W. H. Kilpatrick, Introduction, *John Dewey, the Man and His Philosophy* (Cambridge: Harvard University Press, 1930), pp. 3-4. Italics mine. When the Epstein bust of Dewey was unveiled, Kilpatrick said: "As we look to the ancient days for comparison I see in Professor Dewey the modest sincerity of Socrates, the radical constructive thinking of Plato, the balanced outlook of Aristotle. . . . These [contributions] and more are so conceived as to constitute the most thorough-going grasp yet achieved of how civilization is to be placed on a functional and dynamic basis." "Remarks at the Unveiling of Dr. Dewey's Bust," in *School and Society*, XXVIII (Dec. 22, 1928), 779.

142 *Naturalism in American Education*

uate, teachers, administrators, and theorists, have sat under his instruction at Teachers College, and countless other thousands of educators and lay citizens have read his writings or heard him lecture on conduct forum discussions outside the College.[7]

His influence in the field of educational philosophy may be gauged from the fact that his *Source Book in the Philosophy of Education* is one of the two texts, Dewey's *Democracy and Education* being the other, most widely used.[8]

Kilpatrick's attitude toward life is based definitely on a philosophy of change. He feels that the time has come, in fact has long since arrived, when "we must have a philosophy that not only takes positive recognition of the fact of change but one that includes within it change as an essential element."[9]

---

[7] Doughton, *op. cit.*, pp. 611-612. Kandel tells us that the "philosophy enunciated by Dewey and interpreted by Kilpatrick has been stimulating and in a sense has dominated educational thinking in the last two decades. To some extent it has been incorporated in the practice of some progressive schools, and in some directions has had an invigorating influence on that of the public schools." Kandel, "The Philosophy Underlying the System of Education in the United States," *loc. cit.*, p. 538. Thus we note how extensive this naturalistic education philosophy is in American education.

[8] Henry W. Mack, "Comparative Content of Educational Philosophy Text Books" in *Education*, XLIX (Dec. 1928), 236-244. Kilpatrick's *Source Book* is published in revised edition by The Macmillan Co., 1934. This contains two new chapters, one on "Right and Wrong," the other "Regard for Others" (Chapter IX and X) not found in previous editions. As an indication of his development we note, too, that this edition omits Aristotle in the Index of Sources whereas the older ones, v. g., the 1928 edition, had two references to him as well as three in the Index of Subjects. On the other hand, John Dewey merits one hundred and fifty-four quotations from thirty-nine sources as compared with eighty-five quotations from twenty-four sources in the 1928 edition. While Dewey increases in importance, Aristotle is neglected or ignored.

[9] *Education for a Changing Civilization*, p. 41.

Favoring Heraclitus, he rejects absolutely the philosophies of Aristotle and the Scholastics, determined to combat the "subtle indoctrination" of their assumptions.[10] The old traditional solutions which held steadfastly to reality, potency, and act, change as bounded and predictable, growth towards a definite goal, the abiding in values and doctrines and institutions, all in fact which tried to reconcile change with changelessness have failed. Darwin's *Origin of Species* proved this to be so by showing that the species was not fixed, immutable, or "spiritual" in nature. Hence his assumption of change has loosened the bounds set upon it by Aristotle, and since new species have come into existence in the past there is no telling what the future may bring in this respect. "In James's startling words, the lid is thus taken off the universe. The future is yet to be determined. No prior formulation will certainly hold in any realm. All old certainties are questioned."[11] Henceforth all fixed formulations are discarded. "Darwinian change shakes the foundation of every vested interest of whatever kind."[12] And we find ourselves living in the midst of a new world dominated by evolution,[13] the development of science,

---

[10] *Ibid.*, p. 43.

[11] *Ibid.*, p. 44, cf. 41-43. Note Dewey's influence here since Kilpatrick refers us to *The Influence of Darwin in Philosophy*, and follows its interpretation of the opposition offered to *The Origin of Species*, believing that this "is probably better viewed as voicing a conflict in philosophies" rather than protesting against the theological implications of the theses. *Education for a Changing Civilization*, p. 43.

[12] *Ibid.*, p. 44.

[13] Darwinian evolution is still "remaking our hitherto dominant philosophic, moral and religious outlooks." W. H. Kilpatrick, *A Reconstructed Theory of the Educative Process* (New York: Bureau of Publications, Teachers College, Columbia University, 1935), p. 1.

scientific methods of attack and industrial production, all of which have coalesced and interacted to
bring about a new civilization and a new social life
in which traditional modes of thinking and living
find no longer any justification for their continuance.
Authoritarian thought and outlook in church and
state, based on the essential nature of things, has
given way to the successes of democracy, science, and
industrial development.[14]   The effects of scientific
thinking and invention have brought about a condition of social life "subject to continual change," [15]
which has reflected itself in the behavior of home and
community life as the result of greater comforts and
greater leisure.   Yet while evolution and science
have decisively oriented the general mental outlook,
a cultural lag in contrast to material advancement is
too apparent.   Thought and social life have not kept
pace with the discoveries of natural science and the
new ways of living.   Aristotle is still in vogue as evidenced by the attitude of Catholics, KuKluxers, and
Protestant Fundamentalists, all of whom accept him
as "their chiefest leader in denying to philosophy, religion and morals the right to shift from a static to a
dynamic basis." [16]   The danger of this social lag "is
very great and grows daily greater." [17]   There is pressing need for an integrated social outlook with new
and satisfactory objects of allegiance to take the place
of outworn ideas and institutions founded on an out-
moded authoritarianism.[18]   In other words, a philos-

[14] W. H. Kilpatrick, *The Educational Frontier* (New York: D.
Appleton-Century Company, 1933), pp. 122-123.
[15] *Ibid.*, p. 123. Cf. W. H. Kilpatrick, *Our Educational Task*, p. 23.
[16] *Our Educational Task*, p. 28.   Cf. pp. 25-27.
[17] *Ibid.*
[18] *The Educational Frontier*, p. 131.

ophy of life resting on universal first principles, primarily interested in the permanent and abiding, is unable to solve the problems of the present social crisis.

Since "experience is indeed the beginning and end of all things," therefore, "all our interest and endeavor is to appreciate, understand and control and so improve experience." [19] "Man's whole being and structure, mind and heart included, we may well assume, have come gradually into existence through meeting the demands of a universe essentially precarious. Effort to effect is of the very essence of man. Mind, soul, and body are all built to it." [20] This is the doctrine of evolution in terms of struggle and survival. "Men live and die" while the world will continue to go on. [21]

Hence Kilpatrick does not believe in a Creator, in personal immortality, in a supernatural destiny, or a hereafter. Man finds the reason of his existence, its explanation and justification in a process of evolution. The aim of mankind, therefore, must be to improve experience, to invent a better social order by an intelligent social and economic understanding of it, to the end that all may enjoy rich and happy living, using all the means at their disposal, including art, music, and religion, to make life better instead

---

[19] *Our Educational Task*, p. 89. Concerning this he tells us that: "Those who may wish to read further in the line here suggested are directed principally to Professor Dewey's writings, *Experience and Nature* . . . *Human Nature and Conduct* . . . and *Reconstruction in Philosophy* . . ." *Ibid.*, p. 90, footnote. Here we may recall the fact that these books are exclusively naturalistic, evolutionistic, and experimentalistic.

[20] *Our Educational Task*, pp. 54-55. Cf. *Education for a Changing Civilization*, p. 79.

[21] *Our Educational Task*, p. 75.

of manipulating them largely as an "escape" from life to forgetfulness in a mythical hereafter.[22] In a word, mankind needs "a democratic social order, which means criticism and social judgment" and "citizens who will work for the common good." [23] This can be accomplished only by means of the one "essential factor which makes and explains the modern world and gives to it its differentiating characteristic . . . the presence of tested thought and its applications to the affairs of men. This changes not only our ways of living but changes if possible even more our mental outlook." [24] "Life is in fact lived experimentally. Always we face uncertainty in a world ever on the go. Our efforts to deal with such a world are but trials. In this world ends as well as means must be held subject to review as events continually develop." [25]

In his glorification of experimentalism and tested thought and the application of both to all human living, Kilpatrick is essentially naturalistic. In his attitude towards the type of mental outlook engendered by both, he is likewise anti-supernaturalistic. His writings furnish ample proof of this.[26] He feels

---

[22] W. H. Kilpatrick, *Education and the Social Crisis* (New York: Liveright & Co. 1932), pp. 50-51.

[23] *Ibid.* pp. 48-49.

[24] *Education for a Changing Civilization,* p. 49.

[25] Kilpatrick in Foreword to *Education and the Philosophy of Experimentalism* by John L. Childs, p. xiv. Here as elsewhere Kilpatrick follows the thesis of Dewey's naturalistic *Quest for Certainty.* His attitude is confirmed by the approval which he accords to the naturalistic philosophy of experimentalism as expounded by Childs.

[26] For example, in his *Education and the Social Crisis,* we find "the essence of a social and educational philosophy based not upon absolutistic concepts of the individual and society, but upon pragmatic experience, that is, upon the reality that challenges and tests individual and group intelligence here and now." Editor's note, p. ii.

that men must have a new faith founded solely on *methods of attack*. Since old solutions are inadequate there must be "positive faith in man's power to think and by testing to prove his thought correct to within the limits of the testing. In scientific method there is a new kind and sense of security. . . . The method has vindicated itself by testing more accurately. And man did it. Man is therein vindicated." [27]

Like Dewey, Kilpatrick holds that the goal of life lies entirely within the process of growth, since the very end of life is growth. [28] The basic fundamental ethical value of mankind is capacity and freedom to grow. Hence behavior cannot be subject to external authority, fixed ideas, eternal morals. Growth, social growth by means of experimentation, is the only true means whereby human existence is justified and made secure. The core of all living is to be found in this present existence, in the here and now. There is no hereafter and consequently no need to prepare for it. The final and all-important problem is to improve this life by better social and economic arrangements. Only a philosophy of change, of experimentalism, and the questioning mind, continually examining, planning, searching, progressing in the planning process are equal to this task. All other solutions have failed.

Kilpatrick's position in regard to the supernatural is of course evident. Since, according to him, "experience is indeed the beginning and end of all things," he clearly does not believe in God. This

---

[27] *Education for a Changing Civilization*, p. 17. Cf. *Educational Task*, pp. 54, 79-80, 85-86, 90-91.

[28] *Education for a Changing Civilization*, p. 134. Both consider this growth process as unending, as "that continuous reconstruction of experience which adds new meanings to life and yields further power to control subsequent experience." Childs, *op. cit.*, p. 217.

atheistic attitude is confirmed by his remarks on religion in all his writings.   He feels that "The last
stronghold of tradition under the guise of authoritarian morals and religion was at length all but destroyed by the World War." [29]   Like Dewey, he does
not believe in any revealed religion, much less in
Christianity. "Possibly most moderns will agree," he
says, "that as much as in us lies we have done with
final statements, that orthodoxy has been and remains a hateful thing, that things do change and we
propose to hold to the consequent necessary right of
question and revision, that the word faith has been
used in repellent senses." [30]   When he calls orthodoxy,
i.e., Christianity, "a hateful thing," he states in no
uncertain language his position.   And by implication
he indicts all that Christianity has done to mould
Western civilization, especially in regard to education.   This we consider to be the touchstone of his
naturalistic theory.   He tells us that evolution, applied science, and higher criticism are completing the
well deserved destruction of the authority of revelation and theology.[31]   The breakdown of Christianity
has been under way steadily since the thirteenth century, through the Renaissance, the Reformation, and
the Enlightenment.[32]   The result is that mankind refuses more and more to subordinate itself to this obsolete traditional authoritarianism.   The new attitude
of mind with its testing of thought "has got in its
work," by breaking down the authority of the Bible
while simultaneously generating and spreading "the

---

[29] *The Educational Frontier,* p. 123.
[30] *Our Educational Task,* pp. 82-83.
[31] *Ibid.,* p. 25.
[32] *Ibid.,* pp. 24-25.

general habit of questioning *why.*"[33]   Traditional religion no longer fills the need of a *cause.*   Therefore, religious energy and enthusiasm must be brought to the service of the real cause of a new civilization.   This alone is worthy of our greatest zeal and effort.[34]   And so man must learn to have faith in himself, i.e., he must have an attitude of mind begetting a firm hope and confidence in himself so that through his best scientific effort he may control by means of experimental knowledge as much as he can within the unpredictable stream of life, experience for the improvement of society.[35]   This is naturalistic faith in man himself and "in the methods of attack" whereby he controls unexpected obstacles on his way through this life.   It is entirely opposed to that supernatural faith of Christianity which enables the mind under the influence of the will and of grace to give unwavering assent to revealed truths resting on God's authority.   It is faith in man, in effort, in scientific method, not in God, in revelation, and religion.

From all this we may expect by implication a

---

[33] *Education for a Changing Civilization,* pp. 35-36. Cf. 32-34.

[34] *Our Educational Task* p. 21. This too is Dewey's solution. His *Common Faith* denies the validity of all religions, including Christianity, and insists on transferring religious interest to the field of social life and interest. In a chapel talk given before the students of Teachers College, Columbia University, which was later published in *The New Era,* Vol. II, No. 46 (October, 1930), 119, under the title "How Shall we Think about Religion?", Kilpatrick said: "It seems to be true that an increasing number of serious and intelligently religious people do not use the 'God concept', do not 'pray' and do not even know what 'worship' means, are indifferent to immortality, and count the bible (of whatever kind) to have no more authority than its teachings inherently carry. These may be prophets of a new day." This gives us a good indication of his religious position.

[35] W. H. Kilpatrick, Unpublished Ms. quoted in *Source Book in the Philosophy of Education,* Revised edition, p. 187.

naturalistic code of morals. And in fact he asserts that "the old moorings of morals, religion and philosophy" no longer hold us fast.[36] Continued change due to scientific thinking and invention has brought to the fore new and urgent moral problems. "Our youth no longer accepts authoritarian morals." [37] It will have nothing to do with any code of morality based on a rejected tradition. It wants to know *why* wrong is wrong and right is right apart altogether from the traditional say so. It is solving its moral problems in its own way, not by custom, convention, or the command of its elders.[38] Speaking of this new attitude in morals on the part of our young people, he tells us that:

> More and more do they insist on why's that shall be to them convincing . . . the results of this need not, in spite of common fears, be wholly bad. May it not lead to actual progress in morals? If creative thought can accomplish so much in natural science, why not also here? Is it the taboos with which our forebears so effectually beclouded moral action that prevent us now from expecting progress in the ways of living together? . . . A new situation in morals confronts. The old plan has broken down. It does not fit the fact of ever rapid change. A new procedure must be found . . . we must help our youth to find the only real au-

---

[36] *Our Educational Task*, p. 3.

[37] *Education for a Changing Civilization*, p. 50.

[38] On this point we quote what he says in *Education and the Social Crisis*, p. 64, "Parents, for example, do not have the right—though probably most still claim it—to fix the future thinking of their children." Nor does he concede this right to teachers.

thority . . . of 'how it works when tried. . . .'
Authoritarianism in morals dies. A better
morality must survive.[39]

Here we note that morals *are* social, not fixed or
eternal, but pragmatic, experimental, and relative.
The working out of them in social life, the adjustment to it which they present in the test of change,
is the *only way,* the only basis on which they may be
justified.[40] There is no difficulty in judging such a
code, if it may be called a code and not a theory, of
morals as naturalistic in the extreme. Based on a
philosophy of change which ignores God, it judges
experimentally what is right and wrong. What is
right today may be wrong tomorrow. There is no
eternal or natural law, no conscience, no commandments. For instance, Kilpatrick holds that the mo-
nogamous family, like all human institutions, is man-
made. He feels it should, therefore, be put on a dynamic basis, moulded to meet human needs and
wishes.[41] Changed ways of living necessitate changed
ways of behavior. Growing life built on a study of
consequences is the only criterion which will enable
morals to keep abreast of the social changes in life,
society, and the family.[42] We must have "inherent
morals" instead of "authoritarian morality," [43] that is,
conduct must be justified by why's which find their
reason and justification "by their consequences for

---

[39] *Education for a Changing Civilization,* pp. 81-82.
[40] *Ibid.,* p. 109. Cf. pp. 58-60.
[41] *Ibid.,* pp. 18 ff.; *Our Educational Task,* pp. 54, 74.
[42] *Our Educational Task,* pp. 92-93. "Indeed it is chiefly because
we live in this kind of world of change and decay that we have
been compelled to give up the old static logic of fixed entities and
final distinctions." *Ibid.,* p. 87.
[43] *Education for a Changing Civilization,* p. 36.

life." [44]   All moral problems must be "amenable to thought and experiment." [45]   In point of fact "the value of testing by consequences slowly but surely makes its way." [46]   Foolish prudery is disappearing, facts are being faced, and with wise leadership "the outlook for the future is for finer and better morals." [47]

Kilpatrick is perfectly frank in his plea for naturalistic and social morals. It would be hard to find a more clearly expressed dynamic naturalism. His thesis is that of Dewey, only it is more popularly expressed, more easy to understand. There is no doubt that while his philosophy is experimental naturalism, his religious attitude is atheistic, and consequently his morals and ethics are purely social. The only evils that exist are social ones. The only preparation requisite for life is that "for adequate management of social affairs." [48]

Our new civilization with its social cultural lag requires adjustment. The present generation must be adapted to a dynamic situation and this problem is "essentially educative." [49]   An efficient educational system is therefore imperative. Religion has no place in it, since education is not preparation for a hereafter. There is no body-mind dualism, no universe fixed-in-advance in which change is negligible. Educational thought must recognize the actual and essential factor in life which is *change*. Hence many cur-

---

[44] *Ibid.*, p. 19.
[45] *Ibid.*, p. 20.
[46] *Ibid.*, p. 21.
[47] *Education for a Changing Civilization*, p. 38.
[48] *Our Educational Task*, p. 48. Cf. pp. 50-51.
[49] *Ibid.*, p. 48. Cf. *Education for a Changing Civilization*, p. 49.

rent phases of emphasis in learning must "undergo great transformation." [50] Hence there will be no definite religious instruction, no fixed-in-advance moral teaching, no place for God, in this new education. Education is to be concerned with the good social life and nothing else. As we would expect, Kilpatrick's philosophy of education is that of the group, "of which," he tells us, "Professor Dewey is the most distinguished member." [51]

We may remark in passing that character formation in the sense of transformation, the moulding of the life of the pupil after that of the Divine model, is not the first essential of this type of naturalistic education. Neither is the paramount importance of the personality of the teacher and his influence on the learners in many intangible ways stressed. Method is the thing now. And this is exactly in line with a philosophy based on experimentalism. The aim is to give the child an attitude and a method which will enable him to control his environment and solve the obstacles that may arise. The aim, attitude, and method are in their exclusiveness, of course, completely naturalistic. The school is to be life, not learning about life, the emphasis being on the learning child who is to be provided with a novel plan of activity to fit a newly unfolding situation for the reason that "A novelly developing world requires consciously devised procedures, devised in terms of the novel elements and as these present themselves. . . . Conscious action adapts the old to the novelly de-

---

[50] W. H. Kilpatrick, "Philosophy and Research," in *School and Society*, XXX, No. 759 (July 13, 1929), p. 43.

[51] W. H. Kilpatrick, "The Philosophy of American Education," *Teachers College Record*, XXX, No. 1 (Oct. 1928) p. 13.

veloping situation." [52] In this way education prepares
for the precarious world in which life becomes increasingly complex, full of the new uncertainties and
problems which science, invention, and social evolution bring in their train.   There is no room here for
static *a priori* schemes of training.   The "strangle-
hold of tradition" is thus broken.[53]

A new system adequate to the shifting character of
modern life, one which prepares children to adjust
themselves to change, which provides them with the
temper and technique of experimentalism, is essential.   Its chief responsibility is to inculcate a fundamentally new outlook which views civilization as in
process, which sees that change is the most important
factor in modern life and that intelligence must
grapple with it in order to make life better.[54]   It must
therefore receive its guidance from a philosophy of
change and, instead of specific preparation for a fixed
goal, must help to remake logic, ethics, and religion
so that they may through experimentation and trial
by consequences prove aids in bringing thought
abreast of scientific discovery.[55]   The majority of
traditional philosophies of education conceived the
goal of education as something external, which was
detrimental to the student.   When, for example, this
goal was life after death, education was "prostituted,"
becoming simply "a training to a preordained set of
habits and attitudes or an indoctrination in a prior
chosen system of thought, and the individual [was]

---

[52] *A Reconstructed Theory of the Educative Process,* p. 9.

[53] *Education for a Changing Civilization,* p. 135.

[54] *Education and the Social Crisis,* p. 53.

[55] *Education for a Changing Civilization,* p. 83.

denied his very personality. No such goal or procedure can be permanently satisfactory." [56]

Instead of aiming at this obsolete static goal, education must produce pupils temperamentally and intellectually able to think in terms of the common welfare in freedom from prejudice and from any simply
private good. "The goal for education is to continue
and enrich this life process by better thought and act,
and this in turn is education again. Education thus
is in life and for life. Its goal is internal in the
process. Such a goal is the only one that fits a growing world. Continued growing is its essence and
end." [57] Education, therefore, is concerned absolutely
and finally with this life, with continual growth in
this world, with the reconstruction of life experience.
It is "the very warp and woof of life itself." [58]

This is naturalistic education in its most complete
form. Supernaturalistic education is rejected completely and therefore God, Revelation, the Ten Commandments, the ultimate eternal goal of Heaven are
put out of court. They have no case. The educator
has no concern at all with them unless it be to ob-
literate whatever traces they have left. Henceforth
tested experience is the sole basis for judging, and
therefore it is the task of education to build dispositions which will cultivate search on this foundation,
openminded scientific search increasing in growth as
age increases. [59] In a word, the new attitude towards

---

[56] *Ibid.,* p. 132.
[57] *Ibid.,* p. 134. Kilpatrick refers us here to Dewey's *Democracy
and Education,* Chapter IV, entitled "Education as Growth," pp. 49-
62. We note therefore that he is in complete accord with Dewey's
conception.
[58] *A Reconstructed Theory of the Educative Process,* p. 16.
[59] *Our Educational Task,* p. 103

life which evolution, the new physics, and industrialism have introduced, necessitating the reorganization
of individual and social behavior, insists on this new
education.[60]   Hence school procedures, objectives,
methods, and curriculum must shelve the static ideal
in favor of the dynamic one; and "our young people
must build such dynamic outlook, insight, habits, and
attitudes as will enable them to hold their course
amid change," [61] so that as they grow in age they may
increasingly possess the acquired ability to decide
problems for themselves, persuaded that old solutions
are insufficient, that intelligent use of the best scientific methods of attack, "including the method of
criticizing methods," [62] will arm them with a critical
attitude toward the unknown future in which
nothing is stable or abiding.   Instead of accepting un-
questioningly the achievements which traditional
education presented on the basis of a psychology of
learning which viewed education as the acquisition of
textbook information, a more reliable psychology and
changes in social life demand that actual experiencing take place in the school.   Only in this way can
the child grow in a changing civilization.[63]   The essential aim of education is to make all "come to an
intelligent understanding of our social and economic
situation." [64]

It is abundantly clear that in this educational
philosophy there is no place for authority.   Anything
like an eternal law prescribing fixed rules or regula-

---

[60] *A Reconstructed Theory of the Educative Process,* p. 1.
[61] *Education for a Changing Civilization,* p. 85.
[62] *Ibid.,* p. 86.
[63] *Ibid.,* pp. 95-96.
[64] *Education and the Social Crisis,* p. 50.

tions is proscribed in favor of criticism and the pursuit of "worthwhile social activities." [65]   All that is envisaged is the ideal mundane future of social life and "what we can do to bring that ideal into being." [66] There is no mention of eternal welfare. "The school exists to make life better." [67]   It must be "a school of life, of actual experiencing" [68] and it must be social in the sense that the pupils must share experience in shared enterprises, common aims, and opposed purposes, so that they may learn to adjust themselves to the larger group of the Great Society. In these pupil enterprises learning conditions are best found and essential social characteristics are built up; attitudes and ideals come from these situations which children recognize as their own, for which they alone are responsible.[69] Thus in this school which remains like life, experimental, "strong-charactered, social-minded, self-governing persons" [70] will be formed. The urgent need is that education will build in the school the kind of social attitudes needed for an ever improving type of life. It must produce the type of thinking which leads to responsible consequences, testing its results by shared known outcomes in the economic, ethical, and esthetic aspects, all in the setting of the social process.[71] Pupils must be taught to expect social changes and that "becoming" is a law of life, that they must wish and seek the common good, and with this in view criticize existing and hy-

[65] *Ibid.*, p. 58.
[66] *Ibid.*
[67] *A Reconstructed Theory of the Educative Process*, p. 25.
[68] *Education for a Changing Civilization*, p. 112.
[69] *Ibid.*, pp. 115-119.
[70] *Ibid.*, p. 130.
[71] *Education and the Social Crisis*, p. 57.

pothetical institutions.[72] This is socialistic naturalism
in education. The best attainable basis is only a
naturalistic one. And the conscious aim is "that the
pupils shall learn to criticize our institutional life." [73]
Institutional life includes the Church, religion, and
morals. Everything is to be subjected to criticism.
The school is to inaugurate changes in society, and
is therefore not to be confined to the passing on of
accepted values as understood in a static civilization.
Open-mindedness, scientific methods, experimentalism: these are the values, the methods which the new
school is to transmit; no indoctrination is to be permitted, nothing rigid, unquestionable, and authoritative like that upon which Christianity insisted. The
school room is to be "remade to a more social point
of view." [74] Instead of stated subject matter settled-
in-advance, content must henceforth be "the study of
problems vital within the lives of the young people
and . . . the undertaking of enterprises significant
within the community." [75]

In this way a new social emphasis, social responsibility, social intelligence, and social attitudes will be
found.[76] Instead of subject matter with conventional
solutions of problems and a curriculum based on
docility in the student and authority in the teacher,
all founded on a false educational philosophy, we
shall have one in accord with the significant factors
of change, using experimental method, testing
thought by its results, controlling within limits, all

[72] *Ibid.*, p. 60.
[73] *Ibid.*, p. 61.
[74] *Ibid.*, p. 80.
[75] *Ibid.*
[76] *Ibid.*, pp. 84-85.

oriented socially. The contents of the new curriculum will consist primarily, therefore, of ways of behaving, not in useless preparation for adult living. "The mind is not best used as a granary or a place for cold storage. It is best used when it is put to work now conducting enterprises and meeting problems that call out present efforts." [77]

Thus growth is facilitated and continuous growth is carried on in our changing social world. And the curriculum is such "a succession of school experiences as will best bring and constitute the continuous reconstruction of experience." [78] This is Dewey's thesis expressed, we may say, in Dewey's very words. In its exclusiveness it is evidently anti-Christian, anti-spiritual. It is entirely natural. There is no place here for the virtues of sacrifice, humility, self-restraint, docility, and obedience as these are understood in Christian education. Whatever motives exist rest on a purely natural social basis. This is the denial of immortal living. Dewey's conception of growth is repeated. The essence of the new curriculum "is the child actively at work needing for his present experiences better ways of behaving." [79] Thus the pupils are trained so that they may be able to think for themselves in religion, in morals, in philosophy, with no dependence on man or God.[80]

There is no doubt Kilpatrick is anti-Christian in philosophy, in religion, in education. His conception of life is evolutionistic and naturalistic in its very essence. Man's place in the universe and in his

---

[77] *Education for a Changing Civilization,* p. 122.
[78] *Ibid.,* p. 123.
[79] *Ibid.,* p.125.
[80] *Ibid.,* p. 109.

societal relations is likewise naturalistic. There is only one domain of knowledge—the physical and social sciences—and only one method of arriving at truth—the experimental method. Knowledge is power, social life is the end of mankind. Religion has been supplanted by science. Revelation, the supernatural, faith, morality in the Christian sense have been rejected. Applied intelligence is the sole authority. Morals are social, scientific, and relative. There is nothing unconditional, absolute, or change-less about them. Moral life and moral concepts depend purely upon economic, social, and political conditions. Education is, therefore, based on a naturalistic, socialistic, and experimentalistic philosophy of life. Children are to be scientifically trained to accept changing principles adapted to scientific progress. Since life in all its aspects is confined to earthly existence, education has for its sole aim this life of reality. There is nothing beyond it, above it. To live the good life in the social organism is man's greatest and highest calling. Hence the natural and social sciences are the source of life. The classics, literature, all traditional humanistic culture is relegated to the past. The core of Kilpatrick's education is the *attitude* towards life which it inculcates. This is a critical experimental and social outlook. In this is to be found the means which will regenerate the earth. After this life there is nothing more. No immortality, no God, no judgment. Man is for life and life is for man.

RUGG

Harold Rugg is an important figure in American education. In his comprehensive study of seventeen educators whom he terms "Molders of the American Mind," Woelfel lists Rugg among those who stress the implications of modern experimental naturalism, finding only instrumental value in tradition and science.[81] His position as professor of education at Teachers College, Columbia University, since 1920, from which strategic vantage point he has necessarily influenced many students and teachers of education, together with his treatises entitled *The Child-Centered School,*[82] *Culture and Education in America,*[83] *The Great Technology*[84] and *The Rugg Social Science Course,*[85] all representing important contributions to contemporary educational effort, have established him as an outstanding influence in education in this country.[86]

---

[81] Norman Woelfel, *Molders of the American Mind,* (New York: Columbia University Press), pp. 118-119, 139.

[82] Harold Rugg and Ann Schumaker, *op. cit.* This is an appraisal of the new education.

[83] New York: Harcourt, Brace and Company, 1931. This is his "preface to a theory of life and education and a tentative program to meet the staggering problems of social reconstruction," *op. cit.,* p. viii.

[84] New York: The John Day Company, 1933.

[85] This course consists of six volumes including Workbooks and Teacher's Guides for each volume, all published by Ginn & Co., New York.

Vol. I. *An Introduction to American Civilization,* 1929.
Vol. II. *Changing Civilizations in the Modern World,* 1930.
Vol. II[I]. *A History of American Civilization: Economic and Social,* 1930.
Vol. IV. *A History of American Government and Culture,* 1931.
Vol. V. *An Introduction to Problems of American Culture,* 1931.
Vol. VI. *Changing Governments and Changing Cultures,* 1932.

[86] Woelfel, speaking of *The Rugg Social Science Course,* says: "Rugg has single-handedly taken the responsibility of putting together in educationally usable form a prodigious amount of compounded history, geography, sociology, and economics relevant to the American scene . . . he has cleared a way which will be a lasting example to hesitant workers in these fields." Woelfel, *op. cit.,* p. 215. By permission of the publishers.

Rugg's philosophical outlook is confined to this earth and this life. It is entirely naturalistic in conception, aims, and ideals. Nowhere do we discover any vision of a hereafter, an immortality, or a God. He feels that a new epoch in civilization is at hand. He calls it the Great Technology within which lies the potential with which to produce a culture of beauty, enlightened tolerance, and abundance for all. Man having at last dominated nature is free to enjoy and to use both body and mind for creative purposes.[87] This great epoch is to be launched and marked "by the effort of reason and the adventure of beauty." [88] Hence a social structure which will actualize and realize the potential economy of abundance, and at the same time allow ways of complete personal living within it, must be designed.

In his search for a philosophy of life, individual and social, he has examined the characteristic intellectual forces and concepts which according to him have up to now contributed to the development of American culture. The result is the formation of a synthesis consisting of the scientific attitude of mind with its method of experimental inquiry and the concepts of the creative artist with his attitude of appreciative awareness. This new synthesis of knowledge, exclusively naturalistic in conception and extent, enables him to propose a new social philosophy

---

[87] *The Great Technology*, pp. 18-19. The Great Technology "is 'great' because man no longer need be the cringing slave of nature. Great . . . because work of any prolongation can become a happy and creative experience. Great because at last the scientific method will be applied to *all* of man's social problems—to government and to the Man-Man relationships as well as to Man-Thing relationships—great because Man at last can live creatively both as Artist and as Technologist." *Ibid.*, p. 19.

[88] *Ibid.*

which he feels should motivate social reconstruction through educational reconstruction.[89]

"Our dichotomy," he tells us, "consists of the pragmatic-social attitude and the attitude of self-cultivation—the heart of the 'new individualism.' "[90] To have an expressive program of living, these two attitudes, basically different in orientation, in emotional and intellectual content, in norms and instruments, must be combined. Scientific method and experimentation are essential in the Great Technology. The scientific attitude of mind continually questioning authority, postulating change, criticizing established ways of living, experimentally trying out new ways, is basic to the progressive betterment of life. Its ruthless scientific analysis has proven the inadequacy of the old loyalties and at the same time indicated the experimental way to everlasting salvation.[91]

---

[89] In his *Culture and Education in America,* Rugg discusses the intellectual forces which have contributed to the development of American culture. While there are ninety-five references to Dewey and sixty to Emerson, the number which refer to Peirce, James, Whitman, and Louis Sullivan number about fifty in a total of 1189 references to 412 authors. Cf. H. C. Minnich, Review, *Journal of Education Research,* XXIV (Dec. 1931), 385-386. One seeks in vain for Christian concepts in this impressive array. They are simply excluded. The dedication of his book is self-explanatory. We are informed that: "This book is dedicated to a company of creative students of American culture: *John Dewey* for phrasing clearly the experimental method of knowing, *Charles Beard* for his documentation of the interrelationships of economic, political and social life, *Louis Sullivan,* integrator of American culture, *Alfred Stieglitz,* the voice of the creative American . . . *Randolph Bourne, Waldo Frank,* and *Van Wyck Brooks* for launching a creative analysis of American culture, *Frederick Howe* for his school of opinion—a pioneer attempt to build a true cultural group." *Culture and Education,* p. v.

[90] *Ibid.,* p. 215; cf. *The Great Technology,* p. 260.

[91] *Culture and Education,* p. 141. Cf. p. 268. He believes that the pragmatic concepts have "brought enlightenment and ousted superstition." *Ibid.,* p. 222.

Nevertheless instrumentalism alone, with its insistence on thinking as problem-solving, experience as making and doing, learning as an active process and happiness as succeeding and getting forward, does not satisfy the *whole man*. The exactitude which it introduced "came at the expense of total vision. . . . The devotion to consumption of analysis, problem-solving, experimental knowing, led to a thoroughgoing emphasis on life as 'becoming,' not as 'being.' It enthroned science and ignored art. . . . It emphasized education at the expense of culture, and tended to minimize the rôle of 'continuity in one's interior life.' " [92] Furthermore, pragmatism enslaved the individual by magnifying the importance of the group. The domination of the concepts of adaptation and adjustment to society worked to the neglect of the individual and to the formation of personal culture.[93] Hence, while the experimental method has its definite place in the maintenance of a progressive society, the individual, the unit of society, must also make use of other modes of response, other intellectual sources and controls of conduct, other methods of knowledge than the scientific. "There is," Rugg tells us, "the artist and his characteristic 'way of knowing.' There is contemplation, appreciative awareness, as well as problem solving. There is *feeling-import* as well as idea . . . and so, to make an adequate critique of the pragmatic theory of life, we turn to the concepts of the artist." [94] Man living creatively is the goal of this expressive philosophy of life. Man enjoying the ecstasy of happiness through con-

---

[92] *Ibid.,* p. 111.
[93] *Ibid.,* pp. 219, 134, 222.
[94] *Ibid.,* p.142.

templation and meditation on the worth of life, believing in "the integrity of the natural thing," con-
fidently believing in self, "the whole self and the
whole society . . . society conceived as a multitude of
proud affirming selves," [95] not man building, making
money, gaining power, this the aim. To Dewey's
indispensable social experimental thinking for security, the "bold awareness of the integrity of one's
self" [96] must be added. Here we have Rugg's ideal
of the individual and of society. Emotional satisfaction in self-cultivation and self-expression, the completeness of the natural thing, is the goal of life.
There is no place for God or the supernatural. They
are not even considered. The natural is the final
goal. The "gathering-together-of-the-self . . . (which
means) a mental and emotional snythesis . . . a uni-
tary thing, a fusion of total physiology, emotion,
meaning," [97] alone can give the necessary dynamic
power to a complete theory of living. When the cultured person meets a situation demanding reflective
thought, he shall approach it experimentally, reviewing the facts, testing hypotheses, and so on. But not
all his life situations are of this nature. There are
those which demand only "appreciative awareness
with the embracing, gathering-together attitude of
contemplation. In such situations he will not be a
problem solver, measuring, analyzing, comparing de-
tails, reducing error. He will be a receptive, detached, accepting person, thrilling, appreciating, enjoying." [98] "The self-cultivated man," says Rugg,

---

[95] *Ibid.*, p. 229.
[96] *Ibid.*, p. 241, footnote.
[97] *Ibid.*, p. 230.
[98] *Ibid.*, pp. 250-251.

"embraces life. He exults in the glorious existing moment. He contemplates the essential goodness of things . . . he seeks to become aware, to believe, to embrace. He is content with the living moment and will not destroy its preciousness with a fear for the morrow. He glories in the discovery of another integral self rather than in a victory over another human being." [99] In other words the Good Life is something more than problem solving. It includes the enterprises of creative effort as well as moments of sheer appreciation of living. "These appreciational experiences are moments of awareness of life in which the Person embraces life, revels in the beauty of nature and of men and their products." [100] Life is social and asocial. Man is a tester of hypotheses, it is true; but he is also a person of appreciation and awareness, "receptive, detached . . . thrilling, appreciating, enjoying." [101] The cultured person "is both pragmatist and artist, at once a maker and doer and a creative appreciator of life." [102] This is really the

---

[99] *Ibid.,* p. 230. There are many sensory experiences which demand a "consummatory" and not a "preparatory" behavior, Rugg believes. These experiences "are situations to be lived, seized, enjoyed, thrilled over. There is the dynamic love of nature, the primary base of which is sensuous." *Ibid.,* p. 225.

[100] *The Great Technology,* p. 222.

[101] *Culture and Education,* p. 251.

[102] *Ibid.,* p. 361. Powys sums up his attitude when he says: "A cultured person . . . regards Nature with what might be called a Goethean, rather than a too Newtonian, eye. He trains himself to see and to feel rather than to analyze and to explain. His attitude to Nature is indeed what Milton said all poetry should be, 'simple, sensuous, and passionate.' The ecstasy he derives from Nature will vary with each individual temperament; but it will have this in common, that it draws its life *from life* rather than from the dissection of the cadaver of life." John Cowper Powys. *The Meaning of Culture* (New York: W. W. Norton and Co., Inc., 1929), pp. 164-165, quoted by Rugg with marked approval in *Culture and Education,* p. 233.

sum and substance of his philosophy of life and education.

From all this it is evident that Rugg is naturalistic. A sensualistic atmosphere runs through his synthesis which is Rousseauean in expression and conception. This is all the more significant in one whose temper has been considerably influenced by science.[103] Rugg's naturalism is less restrained than that of Dewey and Kilpatrick and therefore of a type which would prove more attractive to the average mind loosed from its moorings to Christianity. In its exclusive consummatory enjoyment of daily pleasures which it regards as ultimate it is hedonistic. Much of life is considered as "being," not "becoming" in the sense of consummation, not preparation,[104] and its directive norm and control is the "inner truth" which each person possesses through assimilated experience constantly changing and improving. There is no concern at any time with an inner *frein vital*, natural law, or conscience in the Christian meaning of these terms. It is purely a naturalistic humanism exulting, glorying, thrilling, and enjoying personal pleasures. When Rugg speaks of "the complete expression of individuality of self in rhythmic movement in the dance . . . (of) the sensitive integrated adjustments of the body in physical games . . . of the esthetic enjoyment of ideas, the self-absorbed thrill of meditative reverie, the play of human relationships," [105] all as consum-

---

[103] He was a professional engineer for six years previous to his entry into the field of education. *The Great Technology*, publisher's note, p. vi.

[104] "Being," according to Rugg means simply "conscious awareness," self-cultivation, the enjoyment of the "ultimate experiences of daily life." *Culture and Education*, p. 226.

[105] *Ibid.*, p. 225.

matory, final in themselves, not ordered to any other
end but the exultation of "the glorious existing movement," he leaves no doubt in our minds that he is
hedonistic.

The center of life towards which all efforts must
be directed henceforth lies in happy and creative experience. Hence the concept of creative labor, so
fundamentally important in the production of personality, must be the basic foundation on which the
society of the Great Technology is to be erected.[106]
His ideal is an economy which enables every man to
exercise his creative abilities without inhibition.
His new social order will be one "in which *all people
engage in creative expressive activities.* All, or nearly
all, will become craftsmen *in addition to being contributors of quantity goods and socially useful goods
and services.*"[107] He does not mention the feeble,
the old, or the sick, or the parts they may play in this
existence of creative activity which is constructed on
a dynamic and progressive outlook on life. In this
regime the highest point of culture will be found in
artistic self-cultivation.

While Rugg is persuaded that the liberal pragmatic Left represented by James, Dewey, and the
"evolutionists, accepting the scientific method and
the pragmatic sanctions for life," stands for "a more
soundly intelligent and independent-minded group"
than that represented by the conservative Right, including Irving Babbitt, Paul Elmer More, and the

---

[106] *The Great Technology,* p. 213. Rugg believes that the center
of life for all men is to be found either in leisure, art, or labor.
Ibid., p. 210. He visualizes no other, since his naturalism believes
in no hereafter.
[107] *Ibid.,* p. 217.

"brothers in the rank and file of American pulpits," [108] he feels that it is the creative artists, novelists, poets, etc., who have gotten their critical and artistic concepts from the inspiration of Emerson and Whitman who are laying the foundation of a national American culture.[109] Emerson's influence on him is marked. "In Emerson . . .," he feels, "we have achieved our goal. We have found a great steersman of the American mind, a seer and advocate of the wholeness of life." [110] His was the first "Olympian" mind that *laid the basis for a new philosophy of American culture.*" [111] It was he who "produced the first American *Weltanschauung,* founded in feeling as well as in intellect, in art as well as in science, in reverence as well as in knowledge." [112]

---

[108] *Culture and Education,* pp. 194-195.

[109] *Ibid.,* p. 210. Emerson and Whitman, according to Rugg are the heralds of the creative mind in America. They are the first overview men, "trumpeters of Self and Society." *Ibid.,* p. 146.

[110] *Ibid.,* p. 150.

[111] *Ibid.,* p. 156.

[112] *Ibid.,* pp. 156-157. Ralph Waldo Emerson (1803-1882), the philosopher of New England Transcendentalism, was a pantheistic naturalist. Breaking with tradition, he arrived at the point where he could state that Christianity no longer interested him. A monist, he held that the world was one with God, that nature was the incarnation of the divine, and that man was one with nature. As a part of nature, man is capable of an intuitive knowledge of its essence. This knowledge transcends the knowledge of sense. Emerson favored intuition, insight, and receptivity over metaphysical, logical and rational knowledge. His emphasis lay on the sanctity of the inner self while the external world was more a cause of joy than investigation. Optimism in regard to nature and man is the keynote of this thought. Hence his naturalistic delight in living, in the beautiful, the good, and the true. The source of all values lay in the creative activity of the individual. Self-culture and individualism received more emphasis than society and social duties. Harvey Gates Townsend, *Philosophical Ideas in the United States,* pp. 85-95; Woodbridge Riley, *American Thought,* pp. 140-154; Arthur Kenyon Rogers, *English and American Philosophy Since 1800,* p. 213. While Emerson represents a reaction against two centuries of Calvinism and its doctrine of the depravity of man and materialistic

However, Emerson needed the aid of Walt Whitman, according to Rugg, in order to produce the integration of the American character, in order to shake the Puritan out of his mold. Since Emerson, despite his poetic speech, was definitely inclined to the intellectual approach of life, he required the supplemental singing of Whitman to arouse the emotional and poetic spirit dormant in the American mind. Thus Emerson and Whitman, Man Thinking and Man Feeling, "launched the vital study of the economic, political, and social forces of America, and cast the outlines for the social and literary criticism of our own day." [113]

---

[113] *Culture and Education,* p. 163. Cf. p. 157. The two basic ideas in Whitman's philosophy were the self and democracy. In making the self the highest thing in nature, Rugg feels that Whitman rebuked the inferiority of Puritanism. "Poet that he was, he foresaw the rôle of the intuitive in scientific discovery." *Ibid.,* p. 163. Whitman was a crass naturalist. Long tells us that "there are objections to Whitman . . . some of his effusions indicate a lack of the fine moral sense that distinguishes nearly all American poets, and a few others are unpardonable. . . . Good taste need not and will not read what only bad taste could have written or published." William Joseph Long, *American Literature* (New York: Ginn and Company, 1923), p. 371. Long continues: "Of democracy, as related to law, government, society, he (Whitman) had no conception; his verse is largely a glorification of men's bodies rather than of their minds or institutions. As Lanier said, Whitman's democracy was, in effect, 'the worst kind of aristocracy, being an aristocracy of nature's favorites in the matter of muscle.'" *Ibid.,* p. 378. And again, "Some of his lines are vulgar or in bad taste. ...He is a fatalist; he allies himself with both good and evil...." *Ibid.,* p. 380.

---

deism, Rugg represents in a minor key a reaction against materialistic pragmatism and its emphasis on things and society. There is no doubt that Rugg has drunk deeply at the Emersonian fount stript of its pantheism and belief in God. His is an evolutionary naturalism couched very often in the language of the Sage of Concord. Like Emerson, he has no place for Christianity of an ultimate moral law. More than Emerson, he has no place for a deity.

It appears, therefore, that Emerson and Whitman appeal greatly to Rugg. One cannot fail to get this impression after reading his interpretation and approval of them. [114] Their naturalism as well as their cult of individualism is evident. And yet it is from them Rugg would have us devise an organic view of American life with their naturalistic concepts as the basis of a new national philosophy of life. Here indeed do we find the main naturalistic motives in Rugg. Christian principles are completely lacking.

Rugg is not a Christian. He does not believe in Christianity because it is a system of bondage. Because of it, medieval culture, "anesthetized by myth and superstition," failed.[115] His summary of Christian civilization for the first ten centuries shows his evident bias toward revealed religion.[116] He does not agree with philosophies, the Christian included, which demand acquiescence to accepted standards.[117] The Church is one of the face-to-face groups set up by the new industrialism whose object is propaganda and censorship. He puts it on the same level as the press, radio, and all agencies of propaganda and cen-

---

[114] Cf. *Culture and Education,* pp. 145-164.

[115] *Ibid.,* p. 21. During the later Middle Ages he tells us, "the Occidental mind became liberated from its bondage to the future and was refocused on material things. Food, shelter, and clothing began to usurp the place of Heaven in men's minds." *Ibid.,* p. 19.

[116] "For a thousand years," he says, "Christian Europe had lived isolated and relatively primitive. Life was essentially a spiritual parole, preparation for a world to come. For fifty generations and more the propaedeutic criterion for conduct was passed on from fathers to sons. Measurement languished. Science remained unborn. The standard of living was niggardly." *Ibid.* Today the church and religious groups are essentially self-aggrandizing conflict groups, defending and enhancing their positions. *The Great Technology,* p. 194.

[117] *The Great Technology,* p. 193.

sorship, which he believes are the chief obstacles to the creation of a new "climate" of opinion in America.

Rugg's naturalism is clearly evident in his principles of conduct. Since he holds that the old loyalties which bound men are rapidly disappearing, new objects of allegiance centered solely in the Self and Society must come forward to take their legitimate place. Three of these refer to the individual, four to the social group. With regard to the former, allegiance to the integrity of one's self, i.e., confident superiority and belief in the rightness of oneself, is the criterion and essence of a true personal philosophy of life.[118] Added to this is the belief and trust "in the validity and value of every thought-out personal philosophy . . . the 'authentic inner truth' that emanates from another personality," [119] and "the obdurate determination to be happy," in the maintenance of the sacred continuity of one's inner life.[120] Equally essential are the four loyalties to society. These are belief in frequent association in true cultural groups, glad compromise in the maintenance of happy relations with others, the scientific attitude of mind in order to preserve and improve social relations, and one's contribution and assistance in the function and growth of local and national life.[121] "Life is regarded as an onward-moving succession of complex interrelated experiences, each unique, each oriented and made meaningful by the adoption of ap-

[118] *Culture and Education*, pp. 249,232.
[119] *Ibid.*, p. 249, cf. *The Great Technology*, p. 228.
[120] *Culture and Education*, p. 249.
[121] *The Great Technology*, p. 229. *Culture and Education*, pp. 249-250.

propriate attitudes." [122]   In this scheme of life we find
no place for God, for immortality, for revelation, for
the supernatural, for eternal law.   The Self and Society determine duties and obligations.   When these
are satisfied, nothing else remains.   Courage and integrity are the main motives for the realization of
the new culture of the Great Technology, which demands two fundamental attitudes in its objects of
allegiance, that of experimental inquiry and that of
appreciative awareness. [123]   Rugg speaks as an out-and-
out naturalist when he tells us that

> the measure of integrity of the acts of the
> Man-as-Artist is found in the organic physi-
> ology of the human body.   In the memory
> of one's nerve centers the continuum of ex-
> perience stores up millions of impressions
> of human faces, of the radiations of happy
> or harassed personalities, of beautiful land-
> scapes, of animal and plant life, of wind and
> weather.   The integrative nature of the hu-
> man organism constantly gathers these im-
> pressions together in a fine fusion of emo-
> tional and intellectional meaning.   The
> welding of these meanings and attitudes
> precipitates cue concepts which serve as per-
> sonal norms of reference. Fused inextricably
> together, they constitute one's personal phi-
> losophy of life.   They are what one is. [124]

In this comprehensive quotation we get an adequate
insight into his personal philosophy and physiological

---

[122] *Culture and Education*, p. 250.
[123] *The Great Technology*, p. 251.
[124] *Culture and Education*, p. 231.

psychology. Norms of conduct are purely personal, the result of meanings and attitudes received from nature through the nerve centers which are supposed to retain them. Thus through the integrated action of the nervous, glandular, and visceral system are begotten propulsive attitudes and mental patterns.[125] Not only does he not believe in any external divine law or rule of life, but he denies the existence of a soul or a subsisting mind created by God. He is against all dualisms in man and in philosophy.[126] His theory of conduct is that the objects of allegiance which govern man "are found in the assimilated internal experience of the man." [127] Hence he excludes all others emanating from an externally revealed source. He finds no place for the Ten Commandments or the moral law.

Rugg believes that the fundamental task which confronts America is the building of a new philosophy of life and education. "As we look upon life," he says correctly, "so we teach. What we believe, the loyalties to which we hold subtly determine the content and the method of our teaching." [128] This is explicitly true of his own theory of education. We find no provision in it, of course, for God, for religion, for the supernatural. The main problem which he envisages, and this is true of all his aims, is the task

---

[125] *Ibid.*, p. 228.

[126] "May we not now assume," he asks, "that philosophic dualisms are to be permanently counted out?" *Ibid.*, p. 128. "Properly," he continues, "the experimental knowers destroyed the archaic conception that intellect, feeling and will were three separated aspects of the mind," substituting instead "the concept of the integrative nature of the nervous system and of the human response...."*Ibid.*, p. 227.

[127] *Ibid.*, p. 231.

[128] *The Great Technology*, p. 258.

of changing men's minds psychologically through the instrumentality of education for the better social order of the Great Technology. A new social mind composed of tens of millions of new public minds is the need of the hour.[129] Education must provide a new synthesis of knowledge, as well as new attitudes in regard to the self and society. It is the instrument whereby alone the Great Technology with its abundance, tolerance, and beauty can be ushered in.[130] Its theory must be constructed out of human experience, embracing the asocial as well as the social. It "must take its data from the two sources (the social and the completely individual) and recognize the two parallel ways of responding—first, the experimental mode— the true mode of response to a social situation; second, the mode of appreciative awareness—essentially the mode of reaction to the highly individualistic experiences."[131] Thus it must be more comprehensive than the educational theory of pragmatic instrumentalism.[132]

---

[129] "New climates of opinion must be formed in the neighborhoods of America. Old stereotypes which lack foundation in scientifically established facts and in driving humane attitudes must be uprooted. New ones well founded in those respects must be erected in their places. But this is the task of education." *Ibid.,* pp. 287-288.

[130] *Ibid.,* pp. 288-289.

[131] *Culture and Education,* p. 254. The philosophy of education must embrace two attitudes, two outlooks on life. "The first is the experimental attitude, the scientific outlook that has enabled men increasingly to master nature. Education in this attitude will enable men to devise economic government and to master social relations. The second attitude is that of appreciative awareness. It is the all-embracing attitude of receptivity. . . . an educational system built upon either one or the other alone will be incomplete." *The Great Technology,* pp. 260-261.

[132] "It may indeed be suggested," he says, "that pragmatic instrumentalism can be interpreted broadly enough to include all the objects of allegiance which I have set down. If the interpretation

Rugg's educational aim is to produce a civilization of comprehending and creative men. The schools, therefore, must be places of living instead of literacy. Book education is rejected. Education which "utilizes all the traits of human beings—the body, brain, senses, sensibilities, emotions . . . (and) every phase of social life—household work, agriculture, handicrafts, business, government, neighborhood and social organizations, press, movies and radio," is the desirable type.[133] In other words, it must not be limited to the schools. It must "go on through all the natural activities of the community." [134] It must be such as will best prepare for the new social order, inculcating the application of the scientific method in the physical order as well as the social, teaching at the same time appreciation of life in the present as well as preparation for the problems of tomorrow, producing "a race of artists and craftsmen as well as an army of efficient technicians." [135] It must send forth critical students of the new industrial civilization, not pupils interested in writing "themes," learning the classics, etc. Education has finished with all

---

[133] *The Great Technology,* p. 254.
[134] *Ibid.*
[135] *Ibid.,* p. 257.

---

proves really to do so, I shall be happy to find that there is no issue between us." *Culture and Education,* p. 251. This is important because, since the sole difference between Dewey's theory of life and education and Rugg's lies in the emphasis which the latter puts on artistry and feeling in man, an emphasis, incidentally, purely naturalistic, then by implication, Rugg subscribes to all the Dewey concepts, differing from him only in his stress on individual culture in preference to social culture. His educational system, therefore, like Dewey's would lack Christian principles, Christian character formation, preparation for eternal life, and virtues like humility, self-restraint and mortification of the flesh—the very core of supernaturalistic education.

that. In other words, Rugg's ideal is that which is realized in *the best progressive schools.*[136] The intellectual core of his school program is "social science," not narrow intellectual subjects, as well as physical science, and direct first hand study of community and national affairs. This is to introduce students to changing civilization and culture. It is to provide an introduction to creative and appreciative arts including a work period in both. Rugg considers that *body education,* by which he means "an integration of informal physical play activities with the dance, music, pageantry and the like, . . . should constitute in a real way the very base of the whole scheme."[137] The content of the curriculum and its program of work is to be built "directly out of the problems, issues and characteristics of our changing society."[138] Among the basic concepts of the new program must be that of rapid change. The coming generations "must be practiced in the attitude of expectancy of change—change in industry and farming, change in transportation, communication and trade; and, therefore, change in standards and norms of life, in standards of morality, in family life."[139] This statement alone would be sufficient to brand Rugg as a naturalistic educator. In this respect he is in complete agreement with Dewey and Kilpatrick. His theory of conduct, like theirs, is *Relativity in Morals.* More than theirs, it is hedonistic since it desires to "pro-

[136] *Ibid.,* p. 263.
[137] *Ibid.,* p. 267. Cf. Rugg-Schumaker, *The Child-Centered School,* (Copyright, 1928, by World Book Co.), Chapter XIII "Rhythm and Bodily Education," pp. 165-183. "Personality," he tells us here, "is an orchestration of rhythms." This is his "slogan." This is the basis of individuality (p. 165).
[138] *The Great Technology,* p. 268.   [139] *Ibid.,* p. 269.

duce persons who are consciously aware of the glorious moments of life themselves—individuals not haunted, not hesitant, not wary in the non-technological, non-problem solving experiences of life." [140]   Thus he complements insufficient instrumentalism by a more sensual, earthly life which enjoys to the full the non-problem solving acts of life instead of viewing them as preparatory.   He believes that formal education gives no sense of values and does not practice students at all "in the art of critical evaluation of the standards of their times."   On the contrary, it merely teaches them to acquiesce in these standards. [141] Rugg, discussing learning, insists on "the unified nature of experience." [142]   The organism responds as a unit in the sense that each response is "an integration of physiology, intellect and emotion." [143]   He admits no dualistic separation of the faculties.   Creative experience "is a fusion of physiological processes, meaning, kinesthetic and emotional reaction." [144]   He desires an eclectic psychology built upon the concepts and generalizations of modern physiologists, endocrinologists, Gestalt behaviorists, psychoanalysts, and other psychologists.   A practicable synthesis of these is the urgent need of educational reconstruction. [145]   Like Dewey, he considers that: "As the essence of living is growth, so the very basis of maximum growth is 'education.' " [146]   This growth, however, is to be planned, not left to the varying interests of the students.   "A

---

[140] *Culture and Education*, p. 227.
[141] *The Great Technology*, p. 250.
[142] *Culture and Education*, p. 367.
[143] *Ibid.*
[144] *Ibid.*, p. 373.
[145] *The Great Technology*, p. 275.
[146] *Culture and Education*, p. 288.

planned education by a 'school,'" he says, "is the desideratum. The school is a definite social agency with a recognized function and is superior in educative importance to the home. . . ." [147] The goal of education is the creative craftsman "whose criterion of 'success' is in his own inner conception of integrity, a believer in the integrity of other persons, a socially adaptable person, frankly compromising for the sake of happy social communion, a pragmatic person contributing to society tolerantly, critical of its institutions, yet open-minded to experimental modes of living. The cultured person is our goal." [148] Therefore education means the provision of such an environment and experience as will develop in the pupils these traits, guaranteeing "maximum all-round growth, first as a person, and second as a contributing member of society." [149] This is the substance of his educational theory which is the result of his naturalistic philosophy. Life, growth, creative artistry, body cultivation, social adaptability—these are his basic concepts, exclusive and limited to earthly life. There is no such thing as preparation for Heaven, no concept of Original Sin, no idea of the Christian economy. Self and Society—these are his goals. Technology and Hedonism—these are his concerns. He is a complete naturalist in education as in philosophy, lacking in religious foundation. Everything is included, as far as he is concerned, when he concludes his *Culture and Education* by saying that: "through education we shall launch our twofold program of

---

[147] *Ibid.,* p. 297.
[148] *Ibid.,* p. 297.
[149] *Ibid.*

social reconstruction—the Effort of Reason and the Adventure of Beauty. 'Thus widens the Democratic Vista.' " [150]

---

[150] *Ibid.,* p. 401.

CHAPTER VI

THORNDIKE AS AN EXPONENT OF NATURALISM IN EDUCATION

Edward Lee Thorndike has acquired during the course of nearly half a century a position of tremendous influence in American education. His aim has been to construct a science of education. To this end, employing the experimental method and endeavoring to reach the precision of the physical and biological sciences, he has inaugurated the movement in favor of widespread application of quantitative measures to educational problems. As a scientist he has built up an experimental pedagogy based on careful observation and experimentation rather than on an *a priori* philosophy, with the result that in America educational technique and educational psychology have been revolutionized.[1] We may form an estimate of his influence from the words of Henry Suzzallo who tells us that:

> Thousands of graduate students have studied with him, and hundreds of thousands of classroom practitioners, school principals,

---

[1] H. Gordon Hullfish, *Aspects of Thorndike's Psychology in Their Relation to Educational Theory and Practice* (Columbus: Ohio State University Press), Contributions in Principles of Education, No. 1, 1926, p. 15; Merle Curti, *The Social Ideas of American Educators*, p. 460; Isaac Kandel, "The Philosophy Underlying the System of Education in the United States," *Educational Yearbook*, 1929, International Institute of Teachers College, p. 525-529.

supervisors, superintendents, staff specialists, college instructors, professors, and laymen who have never even heard his voice have modified their thought and practice in education under the influencing currents of his mind. Few scholars have had a more surpassing power for good in American education than Dr. Thorndike.[2]

In considering Thorndike's influence it is well to remember that he is convinced that, "it is the vice or the misfortune of thinkers about education to have chosen the methods of philosophy or of popular thought instead of those of science."[3] This statement quoted from his first important book indicates his strong objection to the idea that science is unfit or unequal to the task of determining educational objectives. There is no doubt in his mind that scientific methods may and should be employed in dealing

---

[2] Henry Suzzallo, "The Mind of a Scholar," *Teachers College Record*, XXVII, No. 6 (Feb., 1926), 581. Cattell is persuaded that it would be "impossible to write the history of education or of psychology without giving prominence to Thorndike's name. . . . In presenting Thorndike recently for an honorary degree at the University of Iowa, Dean Seashore truly said: 'No school is uninfluenced and no humanistic science is unaffected by his labor.'" J. McKeen Cattell, "Thorndike as Colleague and Friend," *Ibid.*, p. 463. Speaking of his work at Teachers College, Columbia University, Dean James E. Russell informs us that: "In developing the subject of educational psychology and in making it a fit study for students in all departments, Professor Thorndike has shaped the character of the College in its youth as no one else has done and as no one will ever again have the opportunity of doing." "Thorndike and Teachers College," *Ibid.*, p. 460. The issue of *Teachers College Record* from which these excerpts have been quoted was devoted entirely to articles in honor of E. L. Thorndike. It contains also an "Annotated Chronological Bibliography of Publications by E. L. Thorndike," pp. 466-515. Cf. Edwin G. Boring, *A History of Experimental Psychology*, p. 528.

[3] Edw. L. Thorndike, *Educational Psychology* (New York: Lemcke and Buechner, 1903), p. 164.

with the problems of ethics and ideals, that science should determine not only how to do things but also what should be done. In other words, the core of Thorndike's position lies basically in the belief that the ideals and objectives of living, like all facts, must be determined by scientific study. He places complete confidence in the validity of the experimental approach to the discovery of truth, to the exclusion of all others.[4]

In so far, therefore, as he adheres to the exclusive infallibility of the scientific method in determining the aims, objectives, and ideals of education, Thorndike is to be classed as a naturalist in education. Evidently he would exclude any philosophy of education which derives its unchanging principles from a supernatural source. Persuaded that the things we deal with in education are subject to measurement, he thinks that it is only after measurement we can form valid judgments regarding educational procedures. In other words, theory can only be con-

---

[4] Writing on this point, Gates says: "That his [Thorndike's] own ideas have profoundly influenced the attitudes towards educational objectives is evident in the works and acknowledgments of Professor Kilpatrick and other leaders in this field. Nor has his influence stopped here. Thorndike's works have—in the writer's opinion —exerted a great influence on the gradually changing methodology of ethics and the social sciences generally. A more profound influence than this can scarcely be imagined." Arthur I. Gates, "Contributions to the Psychology of the Elementary School Subjects," *Teachers College Record,* XXVII (Feb., 1926), 556. In a footnote Gates continues: "For example, in a series of essays on social psychology, sociology, economics, political science, jurisprudence, ethics and other social sciences comprising *The History and Prospects of the Social Sciences,* edited by H. E. Barnes (Knopf, 1925), not only is the influence of Professor Thorndike's work very evident in the treatment of the subject but many of the authors, all eminent in their field, express their acknowledgment of his contributions." *Ibid.,* footnote. Cf. Curti, *op. cit.* p. 461.

structed on the facts accumulated from scientific
methods and measurements.[5] Thorndike holds that:

> Whatever exists at all exists in some
> amount. To know it thoroughly involves
> knowing its quantity as well as its quality.
> Education is concerned with changes in
> human beings; a change is a difference be-
> tween two conditions; each of these condi-
> tions is known to us only by the products
> produced by it—things made, words spoken,
> acts performed, and the like. To measure
> any of these products means to define its
> amount in some way so that competent per-
> sons will know how large it is, better than
> they would without measurement. . . . We
> have faith that the objective products pro-
> duced, rather than the inner condition of
> the person whence they spring, are the
> proper point of attack for the measurer, at
> least in our day and generation.[6]

[5] "If those who object to quantitative thinking in education," he
says, "will set themselves at work to understand it; if those who
criticize its presuppositions and methods will do actual experimental work to improve its general logic and detailed procedure;
if those who are now at work in devising and using means of
measurement will continue their work, the next decade will bring
sure gains in both theory and practice." Edward Lee Thorndike,
"The Nature, Purposes, and General Methods of Measurements of
Educational Products," *Seventeenth Yearbook, National Society for
the Study of Education,* Part II, p. 24. Commenting on this statement, Hullfish says: "The premises are those which underlie the
behavioristic movement in psychology. Everything is but a con-
figuration of measurable, quantitative units." Hullfish, *Aspects
of Thorndike's Psychology in Their Relation to Educational
Theory and Practice,* p. 102.

[6] Thorndike, "The Nature, Purposes, and General Methods of
Measurements of Educational Products," p. 16. The purpose of
his *Introduction to The Theory of Mental and Social Measurements*
(New York: The Science Press, 1904), was to make clear to students
of education and social sciences the statistical methods most useful

Here we have his main attitude. Since the results of science have been generally accepted by mankind in the fields of physics, chemistry, and the physical sciences generally, and, to a lesser degree, in the biological, psychological, and social sciences, Thorndike thinks that on the whole scientific methods of attack are gaining ground. In recent times science and scholarship have separated truth from error thus adding greatly to the true which men can know if they will. "The methods of science," he says, "are impartial, paying no heed to the immediate satisfyingness of an idea to any individual. They require verification and test by prophecy. They produce thinkers whose minds are, with respect to the special problems involved, repositories of facts—systems of connections all tried and true—and so well fitted to have fruitful ideas." [7] Hence it is the duty of psychology

> to think of intellectual and moral traits along continuous scales, as physical science thinks of length, temperature, weight or density . . . this is just what it must do to get insight or control over the facts. And this it is now doing as a result of the general emphasis on quantitative methods in all the sciences and partly of the special em-

[7] Edward Lee Thorndike, *Human Learning* (New York: The Century Co., 1931), pp. 192-193.

in interpreting mental and social data. It was prepared as a guide to those who would use statistical methods in interpretations of human life and activity and "immediately became the professional Bible of students interested in the scientific aspects of the social sciences." B. R. Simpson et al. "Annotated Chronological Bibliography of Publications by E. L. Thorndike," *Teachers' College Record, loc. cit.*, p. 473.

phasis on variability and continuity in living things, due to the work of Darwin.[8]

In addition to this attitude toward scientific
method, a deeper current of naturalism is apparent
in Thorndike's thought. This comes from his belief
in evolution. He tells us very clearly that:

> Nowhere more truly than in his mental
> capacities is man a part of nature. His in-
> stincts, that is, his inborn tendencies to feel
> and act in certain ways, show throughout
> marks of kinship with the lower animals
> especially with our nearest relatives physi-
> cally, the primates. His sense powers show
> no new creation. His intellect we have seen
> to be a simple though extended variation
> from the general animal sort. This again is
> presaged by the similar variation in the case
> of the primates. Amongst the minds of
> animals that of man leads, not as a demigod
> from another planet, but as a king from the
> same race.[9]

---

[8] Edward Lee Thorndike, "Darwin's Contribution to Psychology," *The University of California Chronicle*, XII (Jan. 1910), 76.

[9] *Human Learning*, p. 182. "In the evolution of learning," according to Thorndike, "the primates link man to the general mammalian stock almost as surely as they do in physical form." *Ibid.*,
p. 179. His theory of the evolution of the human intellect "is that
the rich supply of ideas, the insights and reasonings which seem to
separate human learning so sharply from the great bulk of animal
learning, are themselves secondary results of the tremendous
increase in the number and fineness of the connections which the
human animal can form. A quantitative difference in associative
learning is by this theory the producer of the qualitative differences
which we call powers of ideation, analyses, abstract and general
notions, inference, and reasoning." *Ibid.*, p. 168. The "growth in
the number, speed of formation, delicacy, and complexity of associations possible for an animal reaches its acme in the case of man."
Ibid., p. 167.

This leaves no doubt in one's mind that Thorndike is a firm adherent to the Darwinian doctrine. This, in fact, was clear from the beginning of his scientific work. His doctoral dissertation, written when he was twenty-four, entitled *Animal Intelligence; An Experimental Study of the Associative Processes in Animals,*[10] with its scientific technique marked the real beginning of animal psychology as a science.[11] It showed his belief in evolution and his

---

[10] *The Psychological Review,* Monograph Supplements, II, No. 4 (Whole No. 8) (New York: The Macmillan Co., June, 1898), pp. 1-109.

[11] The main opposition to evolution in the last decade of the nineteenth century lay in its claim that man was the culmination of the animal series. Hence the evolutionists determined to demonstrate the continuity between the brute and man by concentrating on the problem of animal intelligence. The question at issue was how much mind existed in man and how much in the animal. Romanes, Darwin's friend, endeavored to develop a comparative psychology along the lines of comparative anatomy relying chiefly on the "anecdotal method" to achieve this purpose. His conclusions credited animals with the possession of mind. The attempt, however, fell into disrepute because of its manifestly unscientific procedure and its tendency to anthropomorphize the animal. C. Lloyd Morgan, desiring to prove the Darwinian hypothesis and at the same time hoping to offset the absurdity of Romanes' interpretation and the anecdotal method initiated his observations of animal behavior in controlled situations. His appeal to the law of parsimony, that it is not justifiable to conclude that any action is to be attributed to the performance of a higher psychical faculty if it can be credited to one lower in the psychological scale, forced him into a more conservative position. The position with regard to the law of parsimony was that if continuity could still be proved despite this limitation, evolution was vindicated whereas if it could not be so demonstrated then it was simply a failure of proof, not of theory. Loeb's work emphasized the conservative findings of Morgan and at the same time reacted against the anecdotal method. This reaction was especially felt in America where Thorndike's experimental laboratory technique and his classical animal experiments in 1898, the results of which were published in his doctoral dissertation, laid the foundations of a science of animal or comparative psychology. While his conclusions were still more conservative than Morgan's or Loeb's, the significance of his work, apart from that already noted, lay in his origination of the Law

188   *Naturalism in American Education*

desire to prove the continuity between the brute and man, for he tells us that "the main purpose of the study of the animal mind is to learn the development of mental life down through the phylum, to trace in particular the origin of human faculty."[12] This phylogenetic emphasis gives us proof of the evolutionary naturalism which oriented his first important contribution to science. As a psychologist believing in Darwin's doctrine, he was persuaded that because of the affinity between man and brute, experimentation on the latter would bring to light facts of value to human psychology. Despite his confidence in evolution, however, his experiments persuaded him that there were tremendous differences between human mentality and animal association.[13] Determined, nevertheless, to discover the origin and development of the human faculty by looking for the processes of

[12] *Animal Intelligence, Psychological Review,* p. 2.
[13] *Ibid.,* pp. 86-87.

of Effect, invented to explain how correct chance associations were retained through pleasure acting retroactively while unsuccessful responses were stamped out. Habit formation thus explained became the basis of his educational psychology; and the laws of exercise and effect were assumed to account for all learning. As Simpson says, his work's "greatest value doubtless lay in its contribution to a new viewpoint in general and in educational psychology. It clearly revealed the fallacy of the old structural viewpoint, and went far towards establishing upon the Stimulus-Response cornerstone the foundation for a dynamic psychology, emphasizing as it did, bonds and specific connections as the central factor in all learning. It bridged the gap between human and animal psychology, and by illuminating the genesis of human faculty greatly simplified our understanding of it." Benjamin R. Simpson, "Annotated Chronological Bibliography of Publications by E. L. Thorndike," *Teachers College Record,* XXVII, No. 6 (Feb., 1926), 467; Edwin G. Boring, *A History of Experimental Psychology,* pp. 233, 462-467, 552-556, 562; Robert Sessions Woodworth, "Contributions to Animal Psychology," *Teachers College Record, loc. cit.,* pp. 516-520.

association in animals,[14] he continued his experimentation and published his results in *The Mental Life of Monkeys*.[15] He concluded that there was an advance in the intelligence of monkeys over the mammals in general, i.e., "the change from a few, narrowly confined, practical associations to a multitude of all sorts." [16] This inclined him to the belief in the advance of man from the monkey, "an advance which in connection with a brain acting with increased delicacy and irritability, brings in its train the functions which mark off human mental faculty from that of all other animals." [17] Thorndike felt that the discovered advance in monkeys indicated beyond doubt the truth of evolution. The scientific method in the study of animals was demonstrating this to his satisfaction so that in November of the same year his article on "The Evolution of Human Intellect," based on the experimental study of animal intelli-

---

[14] *Ibid.*, p. 3.

[15] Edward Lee Thorndike, "The Mental Life of Monkeys: An Experimental Study," *The Psychological Review*, Monograph Supplements, III, No. 5 (Whole No. 15), May, 1901, pp. 1-57. He found that monkeys represented "progress in mental devolpment from the generalized mammalian type towards man:

1. In their sensory equipment, in the presence of focalized vision.
2. In their motor equipment, in the coordinate movements of the hand and eye.
3. In their instincts or inherited nervous connections, in their general physical and mental activity.
4. In their methods of learning or associative processes." *Ibid.*, p. 54.

[16] *Ibid.* p. 57.

[17] *Ibid.* This process noted in the monkeys was viewed by him as of vast importance since it seemed "highly probable that the so-called 'higher' intellectual processes of human beings are but secondary results of the general function of having free ideas and that this general function is the result of the formation after the fashion of the animals of a very great number of associations." *Ibid.*, pp. 56-57.

gence, appeared. The substance of his argument was that learning in animals from the lowest to the highest was due to the gradual selection of suitable responses to situations by means of association, this same type of learning being found in man in the acquisition of many skills. The higher type of learning, reasoning, which was found in man, he held to be really a secondary consequence of this very process of selecting and connecting. Thus the evolution of mind was seen going on from the simple connections made by fishes to the complex associations made by monkeys, this advance in complexity continuing from monkeys to man.

> The intellect of the infant six months to a year old is of the animal sort . . . the only obvious intellectual difference between him and a monkey is in the quantity and quality of the associations formed. In the evolution of the infant's mind to its adult condition we have the actual transition within an individual from the animal to the human type of intellect.[18]

---

[18] Edward Lee Thorndike, "The Evolution of the Human Intellect," *Popular Science Monthly*, 60 (1901), 61. A decade later he maintained the identical thesis and the same conclusions which he published in his *Animal Intelligence*. Here is his statement: "The intellectual evolution of the race consists in an increase in the number, delicacy, complexity, permanence and speed of formation of such associations. In man this increase reaches such a point that an apparently new type of mind results, which conceals the real continuity of the process. This mental evolution parallels the evolution of the cell structures of the brain from few and simple and gross to many and complex and delicate. Nowhere more truly than in his mental capacities is man a part of nature. . . . Amongst the minds of animals, that of man leads, not as a demigod from another planet, but as a king from the same race." Edward Lee Thorndike, *Animal Intelligence, Experimental Studies* (New York:

Thorndike's confidence, therefore, in evolutionary naturalism has been maintained unshaken during the three decades which have elapsed since he first attracted the attention of the scientific world. Beyond any doubt his belief in it and his alleged scientific evidence have both influenced thousands of American educators. It is the basis of his educational psychology and his outlook on educational theory. This is evident from several sources besides those already quoted. For instance, during the summer session of the University of California, 1909, he delivered an address entitled "Darwin's Contribution to Psychology" [19] in which he attempts an analysis of Darwin's contribution and influence on the methods and problems of psychology. [20]

He is in complete accord with the naturalism inherent in Darwin's doctrine. [21] He informs us approvingly that "Darwin gave psychology the evolutionary point of view," [22] by showing us the history and character of the evolutionary growth of the human mind which itself cannot be completely understood except in the light of its total past. [23] Despite all this, he says, psychologists have by no means fully

---

[19] This was published later in *The University of California Chronicle* (Berkley: The University Press), XII, No. 1 (Jan., 1910), pp. 65-80.

[20] *Ibid.*, pp. 67-69.

[21] *Ibid.*, p. 67.

[22] *Ibid.*, p. 70.

[23] "False psychology," says Thorndike, "had studied the human mind by itself alone and had taught that our minds were all made after one pattern mind, which worked as it did for no intelligible reason, but just because it did." *Ibid.*

The Macmillan Co., 1911), p. 294. This statement was repeated two decades later when he published his *Human Learning* in 1931. Cf. p. 182.

realized this lesson. "Human learning is still too often described with total neglect of animal learning." [24] This of course is not true in his own case. From the beginning he has built his educational psychology on this basis and this alone. With the scientific method as his sole instrument he has made careful observations and experiments on selected animals and from the data amassed he has given us his theories, all fully in accord with the Darwinian spirit.[25] Psychologists, he tells us, forgot that man's intellect is "no new creation, but a simple, though extended variation from the general animal type as found in our nearest physical relatives, the primates. Among the minds of animals that of man is chief, but also kinsman; ruler but also brother."[26] There are important implications in all this. Briefly, the human mind is in no sense the creation of a personal eternal God. Therefore, men's souls are not made after the image and likeness of God. One of the fundamental dogmas of Christianity and Revelation is rejected. Possibly the most important influence of Darwin, according to Thorndike, is "his influence in making psychology a natural science—in depriving

[24] *Ibid.* "But each decade since the *Origin of Species* appeared has shown a well marked increase in comparative and genetic psychology. Of our own countrymen, for instance, William James, Stanley Hall and John Dewey have consistently worked at psychology on a genetic basis." *Ibid.* He, himself, gave the principal impetus to the science of animal or comparative psychology. And the reason is clear. Because he was a naturalistic evolutionist.

[25] Here, according to Thorndike, is the history of man's mental development "not at the very beginning, but half way in its course, with the fishes . . . starting from this point our bodily descent is roughly as follows: fishes begat amphibia; amphibia begat reptiles; reptiles begat mammals; some early mamals begat the primates; some early primates begat man." *Ibid.,* p. 71.

[26] *Ibid.,* pp. 74-75.

teleological or supernatural causes from their last remnant of power in the minds of scientific men." [27] These are strong words. Only a definitely clear naturalist could make such a statement. And, significantly, it was made before a group of university students two decades ago.

There is no doubt in Thorndike's mind that "Darwin taught two great principles," for "all human thinking and conduct." [28]

> The first [he tells us] is the principle of evolution, of continuity, ... The second is the principle of naturalism,—that in life and in mind the same cause will always produce the same effect, that the bodies and minds of men are a part of nature, that their history is as natural as the history of the stars, their behavior as natural as the behavior of an atom of hydrogen. If there was time I could show how this same contribution has acted to transform our views of all human institutions, of the state, the church, education and every feature of civilization, and our treatment of every practical concern of life. [29]

It would be difficult to find a passage in the writings of any naturalist, the sense of which is so evident, so manifest. In the brief compass of this quotation, Thorndike, economical in the use of words after the exact scientific tradition, has explained all life, individual and social, all history and behavior, church,

---

[27] *Ibid.,* p. 76.
[28] *Ibid.,* p. 79.
[29] *Ibid.,* p. 7.

education, and civilization, and all beyond the per-
adventure of a doubt, according to his scientific credo,
eminently naturalistic. Supernaturalism has suc-
cumbed before the advance of science, which has gradually repudiated "the caprices of persons—of gods,
goddesses, fairies and elves—as explanations of one
physical event after another." [30]

In this significant article of Thorndike's on Darwin we note with especial interest his treatment of
primitive thinking and human superstition which,
according to his thesis, gradually gives way before
the progress of knowledge, common first and then
scientific, until Darwin's time when "men of science
had, of course, given up the cruder forms of belief in
the regulation of nature by personal caprices." [31] But
the enlightenment was still incomplete and superstition still continued, for these same scientists still

> kept a refined form of it in the case of liv-
> ing matter. . . . They had gradually become
> thorough naturalists in their astronomy,
> physics, chemistry, and, last of all, in their
> geology; but they did not see how to rely on
> nature alone in biology. They still rea-
> soned, like primitive men or babies, that
> animals and plants were as they were be-
> cause someone had chosen that they should
> be so. . . . So for species and adaptation

[30] *Ibid.,* p. 76. "The successions of day and night, for instance, are
easily seen to be regular, and to neither need nor heed the wishes
of men or gods. The sun does not stand still at anyone's caprice.
Only a fool will hope to delay its setting by sacrifices or to hasten
its rising by prayers." *Ibid.* The whole attitude here would deny
miracles, and supernatural facts recorded in the life of Christ.
Providence is absolutely rejected.

[31] *Ibid.,* p. 77; cf. pp. 76-77.

science still accepted a cause outside of
nature in the time-dishonored form of someone's personal wish. Darwin showed a
natural way. He found within nature
forces able to have produced species and
their adaptations. . . . And Darwin's work
did not suffer tl.e caprice of persons to be
considered a cause of mental events, of human psychology, of the history of men and
nations. These also are to be understood,
not by divining the intentions which they
might possibly serve, but by examining
them and the natural world of which they
are part. These, also, are to be controlled,
not by devices to change someone's intentions, but by straightforward work with
nature itself. Science and true religion now
teach man to be throughout, in psychology
as in physics, honest with nature and with
himself. No excuse is left for hoping and
fearing instead of thinking—for teasing and
bribing instead of working. Our intellects
and our characters are no more subjects for
magic, crude or refined, than the ebb and
flow of the tides or the sequence of day and
night.[32]

Curti tells us that when one examines the titles and
summaries of some thirty volumes and three hundred or more articles which Thorndike has written
one is struck by their technical and objective character.[33] And Cattell also informs us that Thorndike's
old professor, James, once said his pupil had, more
than anyone he knew, the power of seeing things

---

[32] *Ibid.*, pp. 77-78.
[33] Curti, *The Social Ideas of American Educators*, p. 459.

apart from acquired perspective and personal lik-
ing.[34] Be that as it may, the statement just quoted,
made before an important student gathering of a
leading American University, would seem to be an
exception.   It views everything human and divine
from the naturalistic evolutionary point of view.   It
interprets all life from this angle and this alone.   It
makes *straightforward work* with Christianity and
with God.   Christianity evidently is the "refined
form" of primitive superstitious thinking, to be cata-
logued with the reasoning "of primitive men or
babies."   In "personal caprices" Thorndike evidently
includes divine providence.   When he speaks of the
"caprice of persons" as the alleged cause of mind,
consciousness, man, and nations, evidently he means
the caprice of the Deity.   At least this idea is implicit
in his statement.

With all this as a background it is easy to understand Thorndike when he tells us that, "Philosophy,
ethics, and religion are concerned with the deeper
meanings of events in the natural world." [35] Furthermore, "intellectual and moral variations among men
show as a rule continuity, gradation, change little by
little." [36] Human character is an evolution after the
manner of the mental evolution of the human
species.[37] Man, not God, is the ruler of himself.   But
he is free only in so far as he can understand and
foresee events in the world.   He is captain of his own
soul only in so far as it acts in perfect law so that he

---

[34] Cattell, "Thorndike as Colleague and Friend," *loc. cit.,* p. 461.
[35] Edward L. Thorndike and Arthur J. Gates, *Elementary Principles of Education* (New York: The Macmillan Co., 1929), p. 53.
[36] "Darwin's Contribution to Psychology," *loc. cit.,* p. 75.
[37] *Ibid.,* p. 71.

can understand and foresee every response which he will make to every situation. This is the only way we can control our own selves. "It is only because our intellects and morals—the mind and spirit of man —are a part of nature, that we can be in any significant sense responsible for them, proud of their progress, or trustful of their future." [38] Morality, according to Thorndike is the creation of knowledge. Apart from good will and other humane characteristics, morals are the result of experimental knowledge.

> Morality itself, though often contrasted with or set apart from knowledge, is, except for the good will and certain other noble and humane qualities of character and temperament, a creation of knowledge. It is chiefly knowledge that saves the mother of today from throwing her baby to an idol, the consumptive from poisoning his neighbors, or the ruler from ruining his country. Many of the greatest disasters have been innocent in content.[39]

In other words, morality is good social behavior. It is the product of scientific knowledge which enables men to change their conduct for the better. There is no question of eternal sanctions here, no question of a natural law, no question of a revelation given to mankind to guide his conduct. "Morality in the broad sense is simply such thought and action as promotes the improvement and satisfaction of human wants. The 'right' thing to do in any case is

---

[38] *Ibid.*, p. 78.
[39] Edward Lee Thorndike, *Education: A First Book* (New York: The Macmillan Co., 1923 [first printed in 1912]), p. 39.

the thing which a man who could foresee all the consequences of all acts, and who considered fairly the welfare of all men, would in that case choose." [40] Actions are not good or bad in themselves. They become so when they do or do not satisfy human wants. Activities are right when they are beneficial, wrong when they are harmful.

> Things are not good or bad in and of themselves; a man's acts are neither right nor wrong apart from their effects; no condition is either satisfying or annoying in isolation. Things, conditions, and acts can be classified as good or bad, beneficial or harmful, satisfying or annoying, or as otherwise possessing value and significance only when viewed from some point of view. In the last analysis, decisions as to the value and significance of things with which education is concerned are based on desires, wants, cravings, or urges. [41]

Now since Thorndike considers happiness, appreciation of beauty, utility, service, property, leisure, and friendship as the absolute goods of life which alone give satisfaction to mankind, [42] and since, according to him, "right" and "wrong" are determined

---

[40] *Ibid.*, p. 28. "Usefulness or service is one great feature of morality. The substitution of the impersonal pleasures for the proprietary pleasures and for the still more selfish and gross forms of indulgence, is another. So far as it can properly do so the school should give time and energy to morality in the narrower sense of the cultivation of good will and of all the specific habits of performing right actions, such as honesty, courage, or cleanliness, and of avoiding wrong ones, such as cruelty, and injustice." "We should make use of nature and be useful to men." *Ibid.*

[41] Thorndike and Gates, *Elementary Principles of Education*, p. 16.

[42] *Education: A First Book*, p. 6. Curti, *Social Ideas of American Educators*, p. 464.

by the foreseen consequences of acts and the welfare of man,[43] we must conclude that his ethical altruism is naturalistic in origin, aim, and action. It is concentrated solely on this life. It leaves no place for consideration of another world and existence. Its ideals are coöperation and good will. Its main problem is to satisfy natural wants, not supernatural desires. No thing, event, act, or condition in life is desirable because it is valuable on account of its eternal significance. Anything is valuable precisely because it satisfies a want, craving, or impulse of someone. "Value or worth or goodness means power to satisfy wants. One thing or condition or act is more valuable or more worthy or better than another because it satisfies wants more fully, or satisfies more wants, or causes less deprivation of wants."[44] And these wants or interests are not determined by God; they have no reference to natural or positive Divine law. They are rather the kind which the structure and functioning of one's neurones dictate.[45] "There

---

[43] *Education: A First Book,* p. 29.

[44] *Elementary Principles of Education,* p. 17.

[45] Edward L. Thorndike and the staff of the Division of Psychology of the Institute of Educational Research, Teachers College, Columbia University, *The Psychology of Wants, Interests and Attitudes* (New York: D. Appleton-Century Co., Inc., 1935), p. 10. He tells us that: "A want or interest does not evoke the responses which either a benevolent deity of the species or the foresight of one of its more prudent members would choose in the premises. It evokes what the structure and functioning of the animal's neurones dictate." *Ibid.* Again he affirms that the force in all situations which calls forth responses "is natural and biological operating in and by the animal's connection system or neurones. There need be nothing logical or teleological about it; and never is anything mystical or capricious. An animal's wants and interests are features of his nature like his muscles, blood cells, or glands, and would illustrate the uniformity of nature as truly if we knew the truth about them." *Ibid.,* p. 9. Note that for Thorndike man is only an *animal.*

are no . . . royal roads to an easy inventory of an
animal's wants under a few logical, teleological, or
verbal principles. Actual observation of what happens is required." [46] Hence wants, cravings, desires,
and urges initiate and sustain all human activity. And
since they are natural, the product of the human
animal's neurones, their end is a natural one. There
is no room, therefore, in Thorndike's diagnosis of
wants, interests, etc., for spiritual, supernatural forces.
There is no place for ideals, aims, and purposes that
rise above the biological level. Since the origin of
desires is to be found in the "animal" and not ultimately in a Supreme Intelligence, we must conclude
that the explanation is basically naturalistic. Because
he maintains this belief, Thorndike can affirm that:

> Wants . . . are the final determinants of good
> and bad, useful and useless, right and
> wrong, beautiful and ugly. Things have
> value and importance only as they serve to
> satisfy the urges which lie back of some-
> body's strivings; they are called useless,
> bad, wrong, and the like only as they fail to
> contribute to, or positively thwart, some
> conscious being's efforts to satisfy his crav-
> ings. [47]

Thus it follows that since these wants and desires
must be improved and satisfied, man must possess
knowledge of natural laws and forces in human
nature. "In the work of making use of the forces
and laws of nature to satisfy human wants," says
Thorndike, "the main—almost the only—cause of suc-

[46] *Ibid.*, p. 10.
[47] *Elementary Principles of Education*, p. 17.

cess is knowledge of natural forces and laws. In the work of improving our own wants an important cause of success is knowledge of the forces and laws of human nature." [48]

The solution of human wants and desires, therefore, is to be found in a knowledge of nature, not in a knowledge of God, creation, and Redemption. There is only one issue here and it is definitely a natural one. Its reduction to a successful conclusion is to be found in natural, not supernatural satisfaction. All teleological principles are useless. Scientific observation of what happens is the essential. The supernatural is excluded. Wants, desires, attitudes are not, cannot be supernaturalistic. Hence the very heart of Christianity is denied.

Thorndike's naturalism comes to light in another very evident way, viz., in his belief in eugenics. [49] Thorndike believes the social inheritance and the race can be improved

> by teaching prospective parents to breed men, as they do plants and animals, by discovering the nature of the best stocks and by seeking to increase their fertility while decreasing the productivity of the poorest strains. To achieve this end, ideas and mores different from those now prevailing

---

[48] *Education: A First Book*, p. 35.

[49] Rusk thinks that: "The eugenic doctrine admittedly received its stimulus and derived its support from Darwin's evolutionary hypothesis; it is not, however, based on natural selection, which would lead in the case of human society only to a *laissez-faire* policy; rather is it based on the manifest improvement resulting from the application of human skill and control in the breeding of animals." Robert R. Rusk, *The Philosophical Bases of Education*, p. 51.

must be established since most persons still
feel a superstitious dread of tampering with
the question of who shall be born, though
no other question so deeply affects the welfare of man.[50]

This doctrine places him definitely in the ranks of
the naturalistic thinkers. His influence being what
it is, this is of tremendous importance. He has told
us recently that if mankind wants to improve the
nature of its descendants as much as it desires to improve the conditions of life for itself and for them,
it can do so even by "the simplest and crudest types
of selective breeding." [51]

Thorndike's main concern, then, is not the individual soul, but social welfare and a better civilization,
the sources of which lie ultimately in the genes. This
is clearly naturalistic. When he says that the only
or the best way, to improve mankind is by selective
breeding, he is going beyond limits permissible by
supernaturalism and the moral and natural law.
When he tells us that: "The general average tendency

---

[50] *Elementary Principles of Education*, p. 281.

[51] *Human Learning*, p. 199. It would even hope to produce within
a hundred generations a race whose average intellect would be
closer to that of Newton, Pasteur, Gladstone, and Edison than it
actually is to the modern average. "The danger that selection for
intellect will involve deterioration in health or mental balance or
morals or anything else is non-existent, or easily avoidable. As a
rule breeding better intellects will mean breeding men better in
other respects as well. The danger of deterioration in social conditions as a result of breeding for intellect or character is trivial.
The effect is much more likely to be a betterment. The more intelligent the race becomes, the better environment it will construct
for itself. The more its genes favor wisdom and justice, the better
the customs and laws it will create." *Ibid.* "There is no surer way
of improving civilization than by improving man's own nature."
Ibid., p. 200.

of the original intellectual and moral natures of children to be like the original natures of their ancestry is guaranteed beforehand by the accepted principles of biology," [52] he takes this stand with its full explicit and implicit naturalism, especially with reference to the individual moral nature. "In intellect and morals," he says, "as in bodily structure and features, men differ, differ by original nature, and differ by families. There are hereditary bonds by which one kind of intellect or character rather than another is produced. Selective breeding can alter a man's capacity to learn, to keep sane, to cherish justice or to be happy." [53]

There is a determinism in all this which discredits free-will. It is a mechanistic view of character and morals. There is a fatalistic tendency in such moral determinism, a logical result of the naturalistic philosophy of life which is Thorndike's. He believes in eugenics in the case of intellect and morals and thinks the doctrine should be "in every primer of psychology, sociology and education, and be accepted as a basis of practice by every wise family, church and state," [54] so that mankind may provide "for the original intellect and character of man in the future with a higher, purer source than the muddy streams of the past." [55] And why? Because "it is our duty to improve the face of the world and human customs and traditions so that men unborn may live in better con-

---

[52] Edward L. Thorndike, "Eugenics: With Special Reference to Intellect and Character," *The Popular Science Monthly*, LXXXIII (August, 1913), 129.

[53] *Ibid.*, p. 130.

[54] *Ibid.*, p. 131.

[55] *Ibid.*, p. 138.

ditions," and therefore, "it is doubly our duty to improve the original natures of these men themselves.
For there is no surer means of improving the conditions of life." [56]

There is no concern about immortality, in fact,
there is no belief in it. There is no thought of God
or the hereafter. It is a simple question of better
conditions in the present life. To this end human
customs and traditions must be improved. The old
Christian moral law will not serve. Revelation is
not in order. The scene, the aim, the means—all are
first and last natural. The method is the method of
science and the influence is Darwin's for

> in the long run, the only cure for national
> ills and the only foundation for progress is
> science, sure and verifiable knowledge, di-
> recting a good will toward men. And this
> good will itself can be aroused and increased
> only by use of the facts and laws of science.
> Even now . . . in the new view of the family,
> we may see the influence of Darwinism be-
> ginning to spread to statesmanship and
> social control. [57]

And this means that science, verifiable knowledge in
the experimental sense under the guidance of the
evolutionary theory, is the sole method of attaining
to truth. Nothing is abiding, unchangeable, beyond
the test of the scientific method, which is to be utilized in discovering controls of nature. Hence the
rôle of ethics and religion must be to "teach man to

---

[56] *Ibid.*
[57] "Darwin's Contribution to Psychology," *loc. cit.,* p. 80.

want the welfare of the future as well as the relief of the cripple before his eyes; and science must teach man to control his own future nature as well as the animals, plants, and the physical forces amongst which he will have to live." [58]

We shall now examine Thorndike's educational aims in the light of his naturalistic outlook on life. First of all, he tells us that:

> Education as a science, is concerned with the discovery of the most satisfactory adjustments of an individual to the people, things and conditions in the world. As an art, education is concerned with bringing about those changes in human nature, as distinguished from changes in the outside world, which result in the desired adjustment. . . . It is concerned with producing changes in human knowledge, skills, feelings, emotions, morals, in habits of every type. [59]

This definition of education as a science and an art is explicitly naturalistic because it limits itself to the discovery and manipulation of adjustments of in-

---

[58] *Human Learning*, p. 200. According to Thorndike: "It is a noble thing that human reason, bred of a myriad unreasoned happenings, and driven forth into life by whips made aeons ago with no thought of man's higher wants, can yet turn back to understand man's birth, survey his journey, chart and steer his future course, and free him from barriers without and defects within. Until the last removable impediment in man's own nature dies childless, human reason will not rest." *Ibid.* Thus Thorndike, in 1931, concludes his *Human Learning*. Down the years of scientific work his main evolutionary naturalism stands unmodified. The sources of man's future guidance lie within himself. The Creator has no function or place in the whole scheme of human evolution. The final destination is earthly welfare.

[59] *Elementary Principles of Education*, p. 6.

dividuals to the physical and social environment. It excludes preparation for eternal life, concentrating on the things of time. It claims the power of discovering these adjustments under the guidance of scientific and experimental method to the exclusion of standards dictated by a philosophy of education which draws its essential and basic principles from a supernatural source. The aims of such a system of education must of necessity be purely worldly. In fact, Thorndike makes this abundantly clear when he states that: "The chief aim of education . . . is to realize the fullest satisfaction of human wants." [60] As we have already seen, these human wants are natural in origin, aim, and purpose. There is no mention anywhere of the want of God, or immortality, or personal salvation. Hence the purpose of education is simply "to make men want the right things, and to make them better able so as to control all the forces of nature and themselves that they can satisfy these wants. We have to make use of nature, to cooperate with each other, and to improve ourselves." [61]

"Education is interested primarily in the general interrelation of man and his environment, in all the

---

[60] *Ibid.,* p. 20.

[61] *Education: A First Book,* p. 11. Thorndike lists three elements necessary to make human wants better. The first is increase of good will. With regard to this, he says, "To wish the welfare of all men is one of the best wants, for it is a want which every satisfier of all will satisfy." *Ibid.* The second is the cultivation of the impersonal pleasures. This consists in satisfaction similar to that gained by productive labor, health and study. The pleasures thus gained do not deter others from enjoying them. The third means of improving wants is the elimination of desires which produce dissatisfaction. "Such, for instance, are the wants represented by superstition," or things which do not exist, e.g., the power to com-

changes which make possible a better adjustment of
human nature to its surroundings." [62] In other words,

> The main immediate aims of education in
> our present democratic society are to enable
> each person to effect the types of adjustment
> to the physical world, to the economic,
> family, social, and civic situations and to
> attain the physical and mental health, the
> recreational, ethical religious, and intel-
> lectual resources which contribute the most
> to the welfare of the Great Society. [63]

Since Thorndike thinks that education must select
its aims from the variety of human wants, [64] and that
its purpose is to change individuals so that they may
have more humane and useful wants as well as the
power to satisfy them, [65] the question arises: How can
education realize this? What sanctions are there to
enable it to succeed in its naturalistic mission? The
answer lies in social pressure. Society must punish
the person who considers only his own wants. The
community has it in its power to exile parents who
consider only the wants of their children. "Social

---

[62] *Elementary Principles of Education*, p. 3. "Man," says Thorndike, "compared to other animals, is the foremost producer of
change. His life may be viewed as a continuous and determined
effort to change the world in which he lives." *Ibid.*, p. 1.

[63] *Ibid.*, p. 59. The religious resources which Thorndike refers to
in this quotation are of course naturalistic. Man "by educating
himself and others," according to him, ". . . aims to produce those
changes which result in improving his condition, in achieving a
better relation between himself and the rest of the world, in increasing his welfare, or in making his life better and richer." *Ibid.*, p. 15.

[64] *Education: A First Book*, p. 70.

[65] *Ibid.*, p. 52.

---

mand evil spirits. "Only those wants which the universe as it is
may somehow satisfy are worth keeping." *Ibid.*, p. 13.

pressure is required to prevent folly and injustice in
education as elsewhere. . . . The state can suppress
sectarian schools altogether if it thinks that an unfair
discrimination amongst wants is made by them." [66]
Society, therefore, is the ultimate judge of human
wants. It alone has the power to decide what is licit
and desirable for its welfare and the interests of its
members. There is no power beyond it, above it,
transcendent to it. With society as the final arbiter,
therefore, traditional educational aims as well as
ideas in happiness and culture must be criticized in
the light of reason alone. "Against such customary
aims, reason, seeing things as they are and weighing
the wants of all men impartially in terms of the common good, has fought and is winning." [67] In other
words, all human wants are to be measured from the
point of view of the common good, i.e., what society
or the state declares to be good. And education is to
produce as well as prevent certain changes in individuals so that the world of things and of men may
be better.[68] There is no mention of changing the individual, society and the universe with a view to ful-
filling God's will or promoting man's eternal salvation. Nor are there any attitudes, ideals and aims
of education, other than those of the biological categories of adaptation and adjustment.

What kind of education then, does Thorndike desire? He has come to the conclusion that education
as preparation for complete living, according to the
Spencerian formula, must be qualified. He thinks
that

[66] *Ibid.*, p. 13.
[67] *Ibid.*, p. 50.
[68] *Ibid.*, p. 1.

the doctrine—that education's business is to make the best possible specimen of humanity out of each man—is faulty. The aim of life is not to stock the world as a museum with perfected specimens for man or deity to contemplate. It is to make them all together an organized force for the welfare of the group. . . . Men have to live together and depend one upon another, not each trying to be the best possible creature in all ways, but each being taught to perform and take pleasure in, those services which it is for the common good that he would excel in. Nor is it desirable even from the point of view of individuals taken singly, that education should develop every man in all virtues. Each individual, by sex, race, hereditary equipment and the circumstances of time and place in which he is born, is made likely to meet certain situations rather than others during life, and it is to be competent and happy in those situations that he particularly needs to be taught."

This statement indicates the type of education which Thorndike proposes. The school does not exist to prepare human beings for God or eternity. This is clear. Nor does it exist to further complete individual development. Nature has predetermined each person's intellectual endowment. Therefore, it is the business of education as a science to discover by tests and measurements the abilities which pupils possess and to provide for the functioning of these so that the pupils may be fitted for the particular

---

[60] *Ibid.,* pp. 31-32.

services which, for the common good and their own welfare, they should perform. Hence the school curriculum must contain scientific, social, technical, and industrial subjects in order to provide special training for special ends.[70] In other words, vocational preparation is the goal of the new education and special information, skills, and habits are the means to attain this end.

Thus we have seen that Thorndike is distinctly naturalistic in his outlook on life and education. Naturalistic evolution forms the basis of his explanation of man, society, and the universe. It is the source of his educational psychology which in turn dictates his educational ideal. He has brought forward new ideas on original nature, individual differences, and laws of learning, on this foundation. Rejecting the doctrine of mind as a distinct entity created by God, denying completely the faculty theory of the scholastics,[71] he has endeavored to demonstrate that human mental life has grown up as a mediation between stimulus and reaction.[72] S—R bonds constitute the basis of all learning. This necessitates a specialized curriculum ordained to the preparation of individuals for special vocations in this life.

In Thorndike we note the constant tendency to speak of the intellectual process in physiological terms. In this way he reduces the immaterial to the material in order to arrive at what the naturalistic

---

[70] E. L. Thorndike, "The Opportunity of the High Schools," *Bookman*, XXIV (October, 1906), 180-184.

[71] Edward Lee Thorndike, *Educational Psychology*, Vol. 1: *The Original Nature of Man* (New York: Teachers College, Columbia University, 1913), 174.

[72] *Animal Intelligence, Psychological Review*, p. 108.

school of psychology considers a valid kind of experience. His physiological psychology gives us nothing but physiological explanations. The result is, as Wyatt justly observes, that he "has surprisingly little to tell us—even in his Educational Psychology, which would naturally consider matters obviously so important to an educationist—about volition or creative imagination or the various aspects of the emotions or sentiments, or even the development of character." [73]

In conclusion, therefore, we may say that there is little in Thorndike's science of education which agrees with the Christian ideal of preparation for this life and eternal destiny, while there is much that is characteristically opposed to it. His researches have aided the cause of all education, it is true, but we feel his interpretations have been on the whole exclusively one-sided and naturalistic. There can be no doubt of the fact that the naturalistic trend of present-day education in America has been given a strong impetus by his teachings and writings.

---

[73] H. G. Wyatt, *The Psychology of Intelligence and Will* (New York: Harcourt, Brace & Co., 1931), p. 74.

CHAPTER VII

NATURALISM IN TEACHER-TRAINING SCHOOLS AND INSTITUTIONS OF HIGHER LEARNING

In the last three chapters we adduced evidence to prove the naturalistic bent of four of the most distinguished contemporary leaders of education in the United States. In demonstrating their influence we showed to what a considerable extent their opinions and theories had permeated the educational thinking of the times. The problem which this chapter undertakes is to discover to what extent the teachers of America have been influenced by these naturalistic tendencies. What tangible evidence is there at hand to prove that naturalistic currents of thought are motivating the education of American youth? In a word, what evidence is there to demonstrate the fact that the philosophies of education professed by American teachers tend to naturalism?

For some time past it has been clear that considerable uncertainty in regard to aims, ideals, and goals exists in contemporary American education. "Changing conditions in industry, in economics, in political ideals, in social philosophy and in educational views and goals, have shaken the habits and loyalties of a generation ago." [1] Thoughtful educators are per-

---

[1] R. Bruce Raup, "What Teacher-Training Faculties Believe," *Educational Administration and Supervision*, XX, No. 5 (May, 1934), 341.

suaded "that there must be much that is very wrong in that intricate world of affairs which we call American education." [2] "As a matter of fact, theory has been profoundly influencing American School practice over a full generation, and generally in the direction of relaxed standards." [3] "In sharp contrast to education in most of the civilized countries, an outstanding characteristic of education in the United States is its virtually complete rejection of the disciplinary ideal in the fields both of mind and of morals." [4]

All of this points sharply to the fact that naturalism is at work in the school system. The question is: What headway has it made? Admittedly this is a difficult question. To probe the educational philosophies of the hundreds of thousands of American school teachers would be a vast undertaking. To date it has not been accomplished. In fact to do so, may well seem impossible, and hence the next best approach would be to examine the educational philosophies of the teachers colleges in the country. What are the philosophies of life and education in use in teacher-training institutions? "These instructors are key persons in America. Their influence flows steadily and quietly into every school room, to every school child of the land. What they believe, on crucial matters is of vital concern to the American nation." [5]

---

[2] David Snedden, *What's Wrong with American Education* (Philadelphia: J. B. Lippincott Co., 1927), p. iii.

[3] William C. Bagley, *Education, Crime, and Social Progress* (New York: The Macmillan Co., 1931), p. xii.

[4] *Ibid.*, p. vii.

[5] Raup, *loc. cit.*, p. 341.

This again is nearly an impossible task because of the great numbers concerned. Nevertheless there is one important survey which supplies tangible evidence in this regard. This is the investigation of the National Survey of the Education of Teachers which, under the direction of Dr. Raup, endeavored to discover the educational philosophies held by 2,000 faculty members in 70 American schools for the professional education of teachers.[6] This survey issued an instrument, or list, of seventy-nine agreement-disagreement statements grouped around seven basic categories or controversial issues which represented two opposed philosophies of life and education. One outlook favored traditional conservatism in educational thought and practice while the other espoused the philosophy of experimentalism as held by Dewey, Kilpatrick, and the naturalistic school of educational thought inspired by them.[7] The instructions issued

---

[6] "Educational Philosophies held by Faculty Members in Schools for the Professional Education of Teachers," III, Part VII, 459-507, Teacher Education Curricula, *National Survey of the Education of Teachers*, Bulletin 1933, No. 10 (Washington, D. C.: Office of Education, 1935). Dr. R. B. Raup is Associate Professor of Education, Teachers College, Columbia University.

[7] Raup used the instrument which he had prepared with the assistance of his graduate students F. E. Peterson and O. Williamson. Peterson had used it in investigating the educational philosophies of 551 teachers in teacher training institutions. Cf. Francis Edwin Peterson, *Philosophies of Education Current in the Preparation of Teachers in the United States, A Study of Four State Teachers Colleges, Twelve Normal Schools, and Nine Liberal Arts Colleges*, Teachers College, Columbia University. Contributions to Education, No. 528 (New York: Bureau of Publications, Teachers College, Columbia University, 1933). A brief explanation of these somewhat overlapping categories, around each of which ten or twelve statements are grouped, is essential to a clear understanding of the implications of the survey. The central theme of the Static-Dynamic category is the factor of change as conceived by Dewey, Kilpatrick, and their followers. The statements relating to the Static outlook are opposed to change as the essence of things while

with this list of agreement-disagreement statements
made it clear that the purpose of the investigation
was not to decide which outlook on life and education was inherently right or wrong but rather to dis-

those representing the Dynamic side favor the doctrine of change
with its implications for life and education. The tendency to favor
the Dynamic side in preference to the Static, according to the
viewpoint expressed in this dissertation, would indicate that the
voter was naturalistic. The point at issue in the Academic-Direct
Life is whether the school should be conceived as preparation for
life or as life, whereby the curriculum should be academic and
treated in its own right or consist of a series of life experiences as
the units of instruction. The controversy here is that which exists
between traditional and progressive naturalistic education. The
basic question in the Traditional Individualism-Socialization category is whether socialization after the ideal of Dewey, Kilpatrick,
etc., should or should not supplant the traditional ideal of the past
and, hence, whether or not the school should inculcate this socialistic spirit. The Passive-Active category centers on the question
whether formal discipline, instruction, indoctrination, and obedience as conceived by orthodox education should or should not surrender to the new education which lays emphasis on developing
the pupil's learning capacity by doing, experiencing, and experiment-
ing in actual life situations; whether the teacher with sanctions
of reward and punishment should inculcate knowledge and unchanging moral values in the minds of docile pupils, or whether
the emphasis should be placed on the child with his natural spontaneous interests, experience, and activities. The issue here is the
old one between traditional and progressive education. One category is devoted to the controversy between heredity and environment. The Separate Mind-Naturalistic View category bears more
directly on our problem. Does man possess an existential mind having its own distinct being or are man and nature one? The answer
to this question set forth in the statements centered around this
category would indicate an individual's position in regard to
naturalism and its educational implications. It is evident that
the material which comprises the categories and their statements
represents in a general way two definite philosophies of life and
education. The naturalistic side or outlook manifestly follows the
inspiration of Dewey, Kilpatrick, and the modern naturalistic
school, while the conservative leans definitely to the traditional
ideal. While traditional, conservative education is not devoid of
naturalistic tendencies, nevertheless it is certainly less extreme than
the doctrines which we have examined. In particular it differs at
various strategic points from those theories which we have found
to be typical of certain leaders in American education. Cf. Peterson, *op. cit.*, pp. 26-44; *National Survey of the Education of Teachers*, pp. 461-484.

cover which view these teachers preferred. This is an important point. Since we consider the naturalistic outlook inherently wrong, our interpretation of the results of the survey will go farther than mere consideration of preferences. Furthermore, while it is difficult to defend all experimental and statistical procedures, and while we maintain a wholesome scepticism in regard to conclusions obtained by such procedures, certain tangible facts are brought out in Raup's study which give concrete justification to the contention partially indicated in the preceding chapters that the naturalistic doctrines of Dewey, Kilpatrick, and other naturalistic educators are permeating the thinking of considerable numbers of the molders of American teachers. Bearing in mind the pertinent fact that the doctrines which represent the naturalistic outlook in the instrument are those proposed by Dewey, Kilpatrick, and modern experimental naturalists in education, we shall indicate in terms of percentages the reaction of these 2,000 teachers of teachers, to this philosophy of life and education, and their attitude toward some of the naturalistic issues.

TABLE I.[8] PERCENTAGES OF 2000 MEMBERS IN 70 TEACHER-TRAINING INSTITUTIONS TAKING THE CONSERVATIVE OR NATURALISTIC OUTLOOK

Conservative or Traditional Outlook		Liberal or Naturalistic Outlook	
Static	61%	Dynamic	39%
Academic	43%	Direct Life	57%
Science	47%	Philosophy	53%
Traditional Individualism.	36%	Socialization	64%
Heredity	56%	Environment	44%
Passive	53%	Active	47%
Separate Mind	50%	Naturalistic View	50%
Total	49.42%	Total	50.57%

[8] Cf. *National Survey of the Education of Teachers*, pp. 465, 468, 471, 474, 477, 480, 484.

This table shows us about 50% of these teachers favor, generally speaking, the naturalistic viewpoint. This means that about half of the instructors engaged in preparing future American teachers are familiar with and approve the naturalistic doctrines of Dewey, Kilpatrick, and their followers. They evidently prefer a system of education motivated by a philosophy of experimental naturalism which views life as a process of change and becoming. They reject all traditional philosophies and theories of education founded on unchanging and essential principles formulated by correct reason and guided by revelation, preferring instead the doctrine of change which should influence human life, conduct, and all institutions including the school. Viewing life through purely human and secular eyes, excluding by implication the existence of the Deity and of revealed religion, they regard education not as preparation for life here and hereafter, but as life to be lived here and now with the aid of nature and science alone. Hence they implicitly reject the Christian tradition in life and education. If 50% of this representative sampling of teachers definitely leans to naturalism, what percentage of professors in all teacher training institutions in the nation subscribe to the same view? There is no tangible evidence at hand on which to base a fair decision. All that we may say, so far as surveys on the question tell us, is that Peterson found practically the same percentage in favor of the naturalistic view when he studied the smaller sampling of 551 individuals in 25 institutions.[9] It is

---

[9] Cf. Peterson, *Philosophies of Education Current in the Preparation of Teachers in the United States,* Table II, p. 80. Peterson's

very significant that, when the 551 subjects of the Peterson study were included in the Raup survey, the percentage in favor of the naturalistic philosophy of life and education remained practically unchanged. It furnishes some grounds for believing that larger samplings still might show considerable numbers of teachers maintaining more or less the same attitude.

We shall now examine some of the more definitely naturalistic categories of the instrument. A vote in favor of the naturalistic view in the Separate Mind-Naturalistic View category would lead us to infer that this attitude would color all of the individual's judgments regarding the statements of the other categories. In other words, this is the touchstone category of naturalism in the whole instrument. We note, therefore, that, as indicated by Table I, 50% of these instructors believe in the statements of this category which hold that man is part of nature, not superior to it and hence not endowed with an immortal soul. This is significantly in accord with the percentage in favor of the naturalistic experimental outlook of the entire instrument. Furthermore, it is exactly in accord with Peterson's data on the same category in the smaller sampling.[10] Here again the results of the smaller sampling are confirmed when combined with those of the larger one. For instance, there can be no doubt of the naturalistic belief of anyone who agrees with the statement that:[11] "It is

---

[10] *Ibid.* Peterson found that 50% of 551 individuals in 25 institutions favored this naturalistic doctrine of mind.

[11] This is number 74. Cf. *National Survey of the Education of Teachers,* p. 480.

---

study showed that 51% of the teachers examined favored the naturalistic view.

more true to say that the self is the habits acquired by the individual in the course of his life than to say that the self must be there to acquire the habits." Raup tells us that among the ten statements of the instruments which commanded the most liberal, or as we should term it, naturalistic vote, this was one. In other words,[12] these teachers were more than usually pronounced in their approval of this particular naturalistic view. While Raup does not give the percentage which favored it, Peterson's 63% of 551 cases favoring it[13] gives us a fair idea of the possible percentage of the larger group approving it.

When the results for the category Traditional Individualism-Socialization are examined, one notes that 64% of these teachers favor the Dewey-Kilpatrick ideal which, while not espousing communism, at least looks to the improvement of society in the shape of an earthly utopia through socialization. The philosophy back of this socialism is of course naturalistic since it makes society man-centered and envisages only human measures for a new social order. Significantly enough, too, this is the largest percentage vote of the teachers on any of the single categories. Peterson found that 60% of his teachers favored socialization, which means that a definite increase is evident when these teachers are included in the larger group.[14] Raup tells us that the statement, "Without passing upon the merits of communism, we might find a valuable suggestion for us in Russia's current use of her public schools in carrying out a

---

[12] *Ibid.,* pp. 489-490.
[13] Peterson, *op. cit.,* p. 104
[14] *Ibid.,* p. 80.

deliberately planned social program in the nation," [15] was one of the ten which received the most liberal vote on the whole instrument. Here again Peterson gives us indication of the number favoring it when he tells us that 68% of his subjects voted for it.[16] These teachers agree with this statement inspired by Dewey-Kilpatrick naturalistic school of thought, thereby showing their preference for naturalistic social education.

In the Static-Dynamic category we find 39% of 2000 teachers favoring the naturalistic doctrine of change in life, institutions, and man. The naturalistic vote on this issue is not so pronounced as it is on the others, it is true, but we think the explanation of this inconsistency lies in the inability of these teachers to reduce to concrete application the full implications of the doctrine contained in the statements favoring change.[17]

From the evidence thus far adduced we conclude that about 50% of these molders of future teachers are clearly naturalistic. We need not be surprised then that experimental naturalism is making its way

---

[15] This is statement 46. Cf. *National Survey of the Education of Teachers,* pp. 489-490.

[16] Peterson, *op. cit.,* p. 104.

[17] Peterson found that 40% of his teachers favored the dynamic outlook. *Ibid.,* p. 80. Peterson makes this comment on his own conclusions: "That teachers are not generally aware of what lies behind the issues on which they voted is probably the most significant single conclusion from the study. . . . Through the opportunity afforded by the instrument for a cross-reference study of judgments, the scores show abundantly that many teachers are not sensitive to the inherent interrelatedness of issues." *Ibid.,* p. 125. This seems very true. Nevertheless, we note that it does confirm the impression of the naturalistic bent of these teachers as evidenced by the data adduced. This is all the more true since the categories evidently overlap and interpenetrate each other. The total percentage vote favoring the naturalistic outlook confirms this.

into the schools of America whose teachers are trained by instructors holding theories which have little in common with Christian ideals. Raup gives us some important evidence in regard to the differences in educational theory which exist between teachers of education, arts and languages, social science and history, physical science and mathematics, and administration.[18] He found that: "The most 'liberal' position is held by the teachers of education, showing in the aggregate a 59 - per cent liberal vote."[19] This means that among the various instructional groups in teacher training institutions, the teachers of education are more familiar with and approve more decidedly the naturalistic doctrines of Dewey and his disciples, and hence "are as a group without competition in liberality of view."[20] Must we not conclude, since the survey indicated that the other groups were by comparison more conservative,[21] that naturalism is permeating American education principally by way of educational philosophies after the fashion of Dewey, Kilpatrick, Rugg, Bode, Counts, and others who are endeavoring to break down the traditions of the past?

Before we close our examination of this survey, we desire to call attention to the fact that the most liberal group after the teachers of education is that composed of administrators. They stand midway between the former and the average of the other five

---

[18] He selected 50 teachers from each of these classes and compared their positions. *National Survey of the Education of Teachers,* p. 493.

[19] *Ibid.*

[20] *Ibid.,* p. 494.

[21] *Ibid.*

groups.[22] This is an important fact since administrators in the field of education perforce exercise considerable influence in determining educational policies. An interesting piece of evidence in regard to
the naturalistic leanings of educational administrators
may be derived from the fact that during the 1936
convention of the Department of Superintendence
of the National Education Association held in St.
Louis, 1500 sympathetic superintendents attended
the first meeting of the newly organized John Dewey
Society. The principals of this society are "Left-
wing professors, most of whose leaders are from
Teachers College, Columbia." [23] We feel that all this
indicates naturalistic tendencies in many of these important officials. In addition to the Raup group of
2000 instructors in teaching institutions which included Peterson's 551 members, we must call attention briefly to another group much more influential,
if decidedly smaller, which both Peterson and Raup
used in order to institute a comparison between the
scores of the former and the latter. This was a "jury"
of 30 educators, 27 of whom were professors (Ph.D.'s)
of education courses, the three others being graduate
students (M.A.'s) of Teachers College, Columbia
University.[24] This influential body voted 73% in
favor of the naturalistic philosophy and theory of
education propounded in one of the "outlooks" of

[22] *Ibid.*, p. 497.

[23] *Time*, XXVII, No. 10 (March 9, 1936), 49. "In proof that they
were feeling educationally progressive, . . . the delegates elected as
their president, Superintendent Archie Lloyd Threlkeld of Denver.
Dr. Threlkeld's was the first public school system in the United
States to adopt progressive methods of education on a city-wide
scale." *Ibid.*, p. 50.

[24] Peterson, *op. cit.*, p. 65. Cf. also pp. 53, 60, 64. Cf. *National
Survey of the Education of Teachers*, p 460.

the instrument. Seventy-nine per cent of these professors favored the view that man's mind, like his
body, is simply a part of nature.[25] It is clear that this
group is more decidedly naturalistic than the larger
one. The members of this body are, be it noted,
teachers of education, nineteen of whom teach at
Columbia University. It would seem that naturalistic theories of education are exerting their greatest
influence on and through teachers of education
courses, younger teachers, and those who have recently had courses in educational theory. Peterson
informs us that: "Younger teachers (those under
thirty-five years of age) scored considerably more on
the right side (i.e., the naturalistic outlook of the instrument) than did the older teachers (those between
the ages of forty-four and sixty-nine years, and holding no degrees of any kind)." [26]

In conclusion, we agree with Raup who, when sum-
marizing the final results of this survey of 2000 teachers, says that there is a marked correspondence between the total vote of this group in all the categories
of the instrument and of that of the Separate Mind-
Naturalistic View. As we have said, this is really, so
far as the instrument is concerned, the keynote to
naturalism in education. "Making allowance for
possible errors of judgment here," he says, "it still
may be said with strong evidence that this means that
in this group the beliefs which persons hold with regard to the relation of man and nature constitute the

---

[25] Peterson, *Philosophy of Education Current in the Preparation
of Teachers in the United States* . . ., Table II, p. 80.
[26] *Ibid.*, p. 124. "Teachers," he tells us, "who had recently taken
courses in general theory of education scored more on the right
side than teachers who have not pursued such courses." *Ibid.*, p. 125.

best index of how they will stand on all the other issues raised. The degree in which this is true should be cause for considerable thought with regard to our policies in the education of teachers." [27] We are in full accord with this statement. It justifies our contention that 50% of these teachers are naturalistic. This evidence forces us to agree with Peterson when he says that: "Within recent years teacher-training personnels have been changing in the direction of a more liberal point of view (i.e., a more naturalistic view), a movement which seems to be on the increase at the present time and likely to continue at a progressively rapid rate." [28] This evidence indicates that

[27] *National Survey of the Education of Teachers,* p. 503.

[28] Peterson, *op. cit.,* p. 125 . We believe that this instrument was both valid and reliable. It was valid because, subject to the limitations inherent in all such investigations, it did elicit the reactions of these teachers on two opposed philosophies of life and education. One entire year was devoted to the preparation and revision of the instrument. Educational experts aided in refining and clarifying the 79 statements through personal interviews and written comments solicited during several preliminary tryouts. The issues were fairly adequate. This is evident to anyone conversant with controversies current in modern American education. The seven categories based on the issues were judged by experts to be a strategic and adequate battery of tests. No reliance was placed on a teacher's reaction to a single statement, the index to his belief being based rather on the aggregate of ten or twelve related statements in each category. In order to test the validity of the scores in preliminary tryouts, Peterson checked the scores of many staff members of Teachers College, Columbia University, against the estimates which their close friends had already formed of their views on these issues. Prominent educators whose beliefs are well known marked the instrument in order that the results might be checked against their known doctrines. Significant agreement was found in every instance. This proves that there is a high degree of validity in the instrument. When the instrument was tested for reliability, Peterson found the correlation between scores made in successive markings to be close enough to suggest actual reliability. Besides this he made a statistical investigation of the internal or self-reliability of the instrument using the coefficient of correlation to make a three way check; this served to confirm his

considerable numbers of teachers of future teachers in America are imbued with the doctrines of John Dewey and his followers. It would seem to indicate also that the present generation of teachers is more inclined to experimental naturalism than were previous generations. Certainly the issues aroused by Dewey and Kilpatrick, not to mention lesser leaders, command more than passing interest.[29] Large numbers of teachers are reading these naturalistic treatises, some of which we have examined. Perusal of practically any widely used text in education will show that these books find a prominent place in required and preferred reading. It might seem that religious persuasion, traditions of the home, and habits of inherited thought would be sufficient to protect teachers from the philosophical implications of

---

[29] Cf. Ephraim Vern Sayers, *Educational Issues and Unity of Experience,* Teachers College, Columbia University Contributions to Education, No. 357, Bureau of Publications (New York: Teachers College, Columbia University, 1929). Note especially Chapter II, "Significant Contrasts in Educational Thought and Some Issues that Underlie Them," pp. 4-37. Sayers lists "twenty *prima facie* issues" selected after an examination of 100 books written by Dewey, Kilpatrick, and others. Peterson made these issues the basis of his instrument, adding others inspired by similar authors. Cf. Peterson, *op. cit.,* pp. 48, 139-142.

---

previous conclusions. Language difficulty was offset to a great extent by using the categories with their ten or twelve related statements. This procedure helped to lessen possible errors of comprehension, mistakes, etc. The secrecy and anonymity of the ballot called forth candid and free judgments. The fact that the instrument would be used later by the National Survey added to its prestige. The marking was accomplished with great care, changes, erasures, question marks, etc., clearly indicating interest and desire to be truthful. We conclude that the instrument was both reliable and valid. Cf. *Ibid.,* pp. 45-62, for his complete treatment of the validity and reliability of the instrument. To our mind, the remarkable agreement which is evident between Peterson's results and those of Raup in the National Survey serves to confirm both the validity and reliability.

these naturalistic educational theorists, while permitting them to accept gladly their worthwhile suggestions regarding methods of instruction, administration, and class room practices in general. However, this hope is not borne out to any great extent by the evidence adduced by the National Survey. And, after all, these molders of future teachers are expected to be more intelligent and better equipped to handle such problems. If many of these succumb, what may we expect from less favored teachers? Nor are the signs of the times propitious. Underneath the extraordinary interest in the new education in America lie signs of unceasing unrest and questioning. Behind this unstable equilibrium in education lies the uncertainty of philosophical and religious thought. We quote the following as an indication of how some feel though we deny the complete truth of the statements: "Everybody today is troubled about ideals, and there seems to be a profound disturbance of inner complacency in the American spirit. Something appears to have snapped among the forces which bound the people together into a nation of stable ideals and institutions. . . . Modern life no longer operates under any real guidance or supervision of the Christian church." [30] While "Experimental naturalism, just appearing over the horizon, seems actually to lay the foundations for a completely relevant synthesis of outlook," he continues, ". . . the Christian tradition as it has been known seems at present to be moving rather slowly but inevitably off the stage of modern America." [31] "If the Chris-

---

[30] Woelfel, *Molders of the American Mind.* (By permission of Columbia University Press), p. 6.   [31] *Ibid.*, p. 14.

tian tradition, as we have known it, passes, it probably will not be missed, because the infinitely numerous complex and penetrating influences of modern society will have imperceptibly replaced its functions."[32] These statements presented in a recent critical analysis of the philosophical and social views of seventeen leaders in American education synthesize the opinions of many important thinkers on the question. While we do not agree with Woelfel's interpretation, we feel that there is a grain of truth in the evidence which prompted them and which gives much ground for profound thought. Few doubt that certain pressing manifestations of a materialistic age are influencing the thinking of the oncoming generations. More than one piece of startling evidence has been brought forth in numerous essays and articles. *Recent Social Trends in the United States,*[33] to cite one source, indicates that: "The weakened grip of traditional Christianity upon educated opinion in the United States has been found reflected in general 'intellectual' periodicals, in scholarly journals, in the number of religious books published, in declining relative circulations of religious journals and in the attitudes reflected in mass circulation magazines. Evidence of the recent rebellion against authoritative monogamistic mores has been found not only in magazine articles, but in short stories, moving pictures and stage plays."[34] Hart's investigation shows

---

[32] *Ibid.,* p. 15. [33] Report of the President's Research Committee on Local Trends, one volume edition (New York: McGraw-Hill Book Co., Inc., 1933); by permission of the publishers.

[34] *Ibid.,* Chapter VIII, "Changing Social Attitudes and Interests," by Hornell Hart, p. 387. Cf. Christian Gauss, "The Decline of Religion," *Scribner's Magazine,* 95 (April, 1934), 241-246; Waldo Frank, *The Re-Discovery of America* (New York: Charles Scrib-

that until 1905 Christianity was still in high favor
but since then a decrease in power has taken place
until today it finds itself "being severely criticized
and opposed." [35] A brief examination of the Leuba
investigation concerning the belief in God and immortality of 1000 scientists (physical and biological)
and 406 historians, sociologists and psychologists gives
us some evidence which points to a considerable
amount of atheism and materialism among the intellectual leaders of the American nation. [36] "The ex-

---

[35] Hart, "Changing Social Attitudes and Interests," *op. cit.*, p. 403.
[36] James H. Leuba, *The Belief in God and Immortality, A Psychological, Anthropological and Statistical Study* (Boston: Sherman,
French and Co., 1916), Part II, *Statistical Study of the Belief in a
Personal God and in Personal Immortality in the United States*,
pp. 173-281. The groups chosen were students, scientists, historians,
sociologists, psychologists, and philosophers on the basis that their
beliefs "represent probably the public opinion of tomorrow." Leuba
chose two groups of scientists consisting of 500 persons each from
the 5500 names listed in *American Men of Science* (J. McKeen Cattell), to whom he gave two identical questionnaires. These two
groups were in turn subdivided into groups of 300 men of lesser
and 200 of greater eminence, the latter being chosen from the
starred names in the volume. Sixty per cent of one group of 500
were university and college professors. Cf. *Ibid.*, pp. 248-250. He
selected 202 (100 greater, 102 lesser) names of professors of history
(including church history) in universities and colleges from the 1911
membership list of the American Historical Association. *Ibid.*,
p. 258. From the 1913 list of the American Sociological Association
he selected two groups of sociologists, one consisting of 48 (23
greater, 25 lesser) professors of sociology and the other of 149 non-
teaching sociologists. *Ibid.*, pp. 262-263. After eliminating non-
teachers he selected 50 most distinguished and 57 lesser psychologists
from 288 names in the 1914 list of members of the American
Psychological Association. *Ibid.*, pp. 266-267. Leuba believes that
a relatively small number of individuals from each of these groups
would represent to a reliable degree the total of each group since
the selection was made by chance. He tells us that: "The probable
error resulting from such limitation is, moreover, mathematically
ascertainable. I have been assured by statisticians that results based
on the whole list of fifty-five hundred men of science and results

---

ner's Sons, 1929); Robert S. Lynd, *Middletown: A Study in Contemporary American Culture* (New York: Harcourt, Brace, 1929), p. 406.

pression, 'intellectual leader,' should not by any means be construed as a disclaimer of the importance of the moral influence exerted by these men. Most of them are teachers in schools of higher learning. In that capacity they should be, and doubtless are, in a very real sense, moral leaders. There is no class of men who, on the whole rival them for the influence exerted upon the educated public and upon the young men from whom are to come most of the leaders of the next generation."[37] The main conclusion of Leuba's investigation

> shows that in every class of persons investi-
> gated, the number of believers in God is
> less, and in most classes very much less than
> the number of non-believers, and that the
> number of believers in immortality is some-
> what larger than in a personal God; that
> among the more distinguished, unbelief is
> very much more frequent than among the
> less distinguished; and finally that not only
> the degree of ability, but also the kind of
> knowledge possessed, is significantly related
> to the rejection of those beliefs.[38]

[37] *Ibid.*, p. 227.
[38] *Ibid.*, pp. 277-279. Here are the percentages:

based on five hundred, would be to all intents and purposes the same. . . . In every one of the other groups my investigation included a larger proportion of the whole than in the case of the scientists." *Ibid.*, p. 221-222. Note, however, that his survey included two groups of 500 each selected from the total number of men of science listed in Cattell's volume, a procedure which insures more valid conclusions. We feel that this representative survey gives relatively sound evidence on the belief concerning God and immortality of the great majority of intellectual leaders in America. "The representative nature of our statistics," he says, "invests them with a very great significance, for if these groups do not include all the intellectual leaders of the United States, they certainly include the great majority of them." *Ibid.*, p. 277.

Believers in the God of the Christian Churches	Physicists	Biologists	Historians	Sociologists	Psychologists
Lesser Men	49.7%	39.1%	63.0%	29.2%	32.1%
Greater Men	34.8%	16.9%	32.9%	19.4%	13.2%
Believers in Immortality					
Lesser Men	57.1%	45.1%	67.6%	52.2%	26.9%
Greater Men	40.0%	25.4%	35.3%	27.1%	8.8%

Ibid., pp. 255, 261, 264, 268.

All this is a good indication of the atheistic and agnostic temper of the intellectual life of America. The fact that most of these people hold strategic posts in schools of higher learning enables us to conclude that naturalism in education is more firmly embedded in the country than was at first thought possible.[39] Another indication of the advance of naturalism is gleaned from the recent coalition of several independent movements of Humanism under the leadership of Charles Francis Potter.[40] The Associated Press on

---

[39] Elder tells us that: "In at least nine leading universities of the United States, the majority of the professors were unbelievers; among the most popular writers on science the greater number were infidels; the authors of public school texts, the syndicate writers for the newspapers, the contributors to standard magazines, were largely agnostics, materialists or out-and-out atheists. In fine, the most active and prolific sources of the nation's educative and cultural life were tainted, if not corrupted by infidelity. Unbelief in God was revealed as a definite cult." Benedict Elder, "The Worst Evil of Our Day," *The Fortnightly Review*, St. Louis, Mo., XXXIV, No. 21 (Nov. 1, 1927), 433. Cf. "The Worst Evil of Our Day," *ibid.*, No. 17 (Sept. 1, 1927), Part I, 347-349; Charles Bruehl, "Rampant Atheism and Immortalism," *The Homiletic and Pastoral Review*, XXVIII, No. 9 (June, 1928), 923-931.

[40] Potter founded *The First Humanist Society of New York* in 1929. *Humanizing Religion* (New York: Harper, 1933) contains on page 8 a copy of a manifesto signed by thirty-two so called Humanists. Here are some of the articles of this document: "Religious Humanists regard the universe as self-existing and not created." "Humanism believes that man is a part of nature and that he has

May 1, 1933, carried a summary of the credo of this body signed by "eleven eminent professors of philosophy, theology, economics, medicine and sociology, and twenty-three other leaders in editorial, literary, educational, and religious fields." [41] Leuba also gives us some idea of the situation among students in colleges regarding the Christian idea of God.[42] He found that in 97% of the answers from individuals between eighteen and twenty years of age in these nine colleges, 31% of the male and 11% of the female students conceived God as impersonal while the results showed 40.5% and 15.7% respectively if "doubtful" cases were added. He found also that "the proportion of disbelievers in immortality increases considerably from the freshman to the senior year in college. Considered all together, my data would indicate that from 40 to 50 per cent of the young men leaving college entertain an idea of God incompatible with the acceptance of the Christian religion, even as interpreted by the liberal clergy." [43] Amid

---

[41] Quoted by Mary Vincent Killeen, *Man in the New Humanism*, Ph.D. Dissertation (Washington, D. C.: The Catholic University of America, 1934), pp. 22-23.

[42] He received nearly one thousand answers to a questionnaire sent to members of various classes in non-technical departments of nine colleges of high rank as well as seventy-eight answers from two classes in one normal school. Leuba, *op. cit.*, p. 185.

[43] *Ibid.*, p. 203. Concluding his study of college students he thinks that: "The deepest impression left by these records is that, so far as religion is concerned our students are groveling in darkness. Christianity, as a system of belief, has utterly broken down, and nothing definite . . . has taken its place." *Ibid.*, p. 213. Commenting on Leuba's statements, Bruehl says: "These observations war-

---

emerged as the result of a continuous process." "Holding an organic view of life, humanists find that the traditional dualism of mind and body must be rejected." "We are convinced that the time has passed for theism, deism, modernism and the several varieties of 'new thought'! "

Naturalism in American Education

this prevalence of irreligion and the breakdown in moral standards to which naturalism in education has contributed not a little, we find the American Association for the Advancement of Atheism[44] establishing "chapters in twenty colleges and preparatory schools of the United States."[45] Charles Smith believes that *avowed* atheists in America number one hundred thousand.[46] Freeman Hopwood says: "The beauty of it is that we have so many atheists in the college faculties in America. But of course they can't

---

[44] This society generally known as the 4A's has for its subtitle: A Militant Foe of the Church and Clergy. Its charter of incorporation in the State of New York was granted in November, 1925. It is one of the first organized bodies, outside of Russia, dedicated to spread atheism. Cf. Homer Croy, "Atheism Beckons to Our Youth," *The World's Work*, LIV, No. 1 (May, 1927), 18-19.

[45] *Ibid.*, p. 19. The names of these institutions are: University of Rochester, Colgate University, Brown University, University of Colorado, University of Kansas, Cornell University, University of Tennessee, New York University, University of Chicago, Clark University, Phillips Exeter Academy, City College of Detroit, George Washington University, University of Denver, University of Texas, University of Kentucky, University of Wisconsin, University of California. These are listed in the records of the Association. Besides students, members of faculties belong to it. *Ibid.*

[46] *Ibid.*, p. 20 Smith was president of the Association when Croy wrote his article.

---

rant the Professor's conviction that belief in God and immortality is gradually disappearing. They are swept away as being incompatible with a scientific interpretation of the universe. Of course, a mechanistic evolutionary scheme, such as is usually taught in the modern college leaves no room for God and soul." Charles Bruehl, "Rampant Atheism and Immortalism," *loc. cit.*, p. 930 footnote. Cf. D. W Gilbert, "Is Materialism Our State Religion?" *The Catholic World*, CXL, No. 835 (Oct. 1934), 80-86; D. W. Gilbert, "Are Secular Universities Reactionary" *America*, 51 (June 9, 1934), 205-206; D. W. Gilbert with the collaboration of Students of Four State Universities, *Crucifying Christ in Our Colleges* (San Francisco: Alex Dulfer Printing Co., 1933). Bernard I. Bell, "Universities and Religious Indifference," *Atlantic Monthly*, 150 (Sept., 1932), 316-320. F. A. Cunningham, "In Their Generation," *America*, 51 (June 16, 1934), 229-230; Editorial Comment in *The Catholic World*, CXL, No. 837 (Dec. 1934), 257-263.

say much about it, as they would be thrown out, and
then where would their living come from? But they
encourage the students all they can. As the movement grows the professors will become more and
more open in their private beliefs." [47] The significant
thing about all this is that these apostles of atheism
are centering their attention on the young in the
colleges, preparatory schools, and high schools.[48] Another example of atheistic activity is that of The
American Anti-Bible Society which "has undertaken
a task which might well stagger a modern disbelieving
Hercules—to stamp out confidence in the Bible, and,
as part of its immediate program, to have the Gideon
Bibles taken out of all the hotels. For this purpose
the society, writes Esther A. Coster in the *Brooklyn
Daily Eagle,* plans to spend nearly $100,000 this
year." [49]

All of this indicates that intellectual leaders in
many instances as well as higher institutions of learning, strategic points in the nation's life, nourish an
atmosphere very often totally alien to, sometimes opposed to the Christian tradition. We have seen from
the various surveys studied briefly, that the naturalistic doctrines of education are in a comparatively

[47] Quoted by Croy, *ibid.,* p. 21. Hopwood is secretary of the 4A's.
He tells us that: "We sent out a questionnaire to the scientists of
America—cost us $400—and we found that 75 per cent are agnostics
and atheists." *Ibid.,* p. 22. The names of some of the chapters are:
"The Devil's Angels," "The Damned Souls," "The Circle of the God-
less," "The Legion of the Damned," "God's Black Sheep." Croy,
"Atheism Rampant in Our Schools," *The World's Work,* LIV, No.
2 (June, 1927), 141. Cf. John McGuire, "Atheism in the Public
Schools, *The Fortnightly Review,* XXXIV, No. 14 (July 15, 1937),
287-290.
[48] Croy, "Atheism Beckons to Our Youth," *loc cit.,* p. 22.
[49] "The Atheists' Intolerance," *The Literary Digest,* 96 (January
14, 1928), 29.

strong position in many of our teacher-training institutions. Not only is the climate of national opinion
naturalistic to a great degree, but the teachers who
live in it and assimilate it are more directly affected
in teacher-training institutions through philosophies
of life and education which base themselves on a doctrine of change and experimentalism. The problem
we undertook to diagnose may be said to be solved
in a general way, more than this being impossible
within the limits at our disposal and the purpose of
this work. Naturalism exists to a considerable
extent in American life and especially in American
education.[50]

[50] Cf. Manly H. Harper, *Social Beliefs and Attitudes of American
Educators,* Teachers College, Columbia University Contributions to
Education, No. 294, Bureau of Publications (New York: Teachers
College, Columbia University, 1927).

CHAPTER VIII

Naturalism vs. Christianity

The evidence adduced in the course of this study shows that naturalism has not only entered into, but has assumed a dominant rôle in, American education. We have confined ourselves, of necessity, in this treatment to main currents of naturalistic educational theory but we feel justified in stating that these influences have percolated into the educational system to a greater extent than is generally realized. The fact is all the more significant since American education has been for long related to the general life of the nation as an agency of social formation. In this connection we must bear in mind that, like the rest of Western civilization, our social structure is at present in a process of change which affects economic, political, moral, and religious issues. The school, because of its strategic position and its ever increasing scope, has a vital part to play in this transformation. In a sense it has taken the traditional place of the Church and the family as an agent of social adjustment in directing these changes and, of necessity, is guided in the process by the philosophy of those who teach the young. Today thousands of these teachers are deeply steeped in the philosophy of naturalism and either openly or covertly are inoculating the young people under their charge with new ideas concerning the nature of man and his place in society.

Naturalism as an attitude of mind has been spreading rapidly during the last four hundred years. As a result of this attitude, with its insistence on the all-sufficiency of scientific methods, man has constructed a new theory of life in which he finds himself continuous with nature and not superior to it. He is the product of evolution, not the creation of the Deity. Nature is the ultimate reason and justification of his existence, and earthly life, scientifically improved, is his goal. Morals are man made, relative as to time and place. Education is directed to this life alone and consequently should be a development along natural lines toward natural aims and purposes.

The seeds of this naturalistic outlook are to be found in the Renaissance, that period wherein man thought he had discovered himself by gradually turning from the eternal and the absolute to the temporal and the human. In contrast with the theocentric thought of the Middle Ages we find an anthropocentric philosophy which, gathering momentum from the Renaissance on to Deism, sets in motion naturalistic forces which give rise to the Enlightenment only to stem off into Materialism, Positivism, and evolutionism. The rejection of the Christian individual and social ideal was definitely facilitated by the liberal humanitarianism of the nineteenth century which, viewing religion and culture as entirely distinct and independent entities, banished religion from economic, social, and political life. Secularization was thus made possible. All this, as Dawson says,

> led to the discredit of a religion that had no power over social life and of a culture that

had no spiritual sanctions. It found at once its logical conclusion and its refutation in the yet more radical secularization of life which characterized the Marxian philosophy. While Liberalism had pushed religion to one side, Communism eliminated it altogether and thus prepared the way for the complete re-absorption of the individual in the social organism while at the same time it transformed the social organism into an economic mechanism. Thus Communism reduces the social process to the economic factor and treats the spiritual element in culture as something altogether secondary and derivative.[1]

Thus the twentieth century witnesses the full development of the completely naturalistic man, finally uprooted from Christianity "with his ideal of a perfectly uniform and standardized internationalism . . . preparing the destruction not only of Christianity but of human culture in general."[2] The communist doctrine represents the full-tide development of naturalism in Western civilization, while all forms of collectivism and totalitarianism are definite aspects of the same philosophy of life.[3] The tendency towards mass organization due to the mechanization of economic life is beginning to dominate the human personality by substituting a new relationship between society and the individual in place of the Chris-

[1] Christopher Dawson, *Enquiries into Religion and Culture* (New York: Sheed and Ward, 1936), Introduction, p. vi.

[2] Peter Wust, "Crisis in the West," translated by E. I. Watkin, in *Essays in Order* (New York: The Macmillan Co., 1931), p. 114. Cf. *Ibid.*, pp. 109, 112.

[3] Cf. Dawson, *Religion and the Modern State,* Introduction, p. xv.

tian ideal. This new relation in turn is being motivated by an anti-Christian ideal endowed with a spiritual force. The fact which really confronts us today,
as Dawson says, is "that the coming conflict is not
one between religion and secular civilization, but
rather between the God religious and the social religious,—in other words between the worship of God
and the cult of the state or of the race or of humanity." [4]   In other words, naturalism through its
offspring communism, national socialism, and liberal
humanitarianism, is giving rise to a new religion
which is man-centered as opposed to God-centered,
and whose social expression is the very antithesis of
the Christian ideal.[5]

> For the first time in the world's history the
> Kingdom of Antichrist has acquired politi-
> cal form and social substance and stands
> over against the Christian Church as a *coun-
> ter-church* with its own dogmas and its own
> moral standards, ruled by a centralized
> hierarchy and inspired by an intense will to
> world conquest.[6]

The heart of the conflict which shall decide the
future course of Western civilization lies therefore
between Christianity and naturalism in its various

---

[4] *Ibid.,* p. 57.

[5] Dawson says that "it is impossible to deny that Russian Communism does resemble a religion in many respects. Its attitude to
Marxian doctrines is not the attitude of an economist or a historian
towards a scientific theory, it is the attitude of a believer to the
gospel of salvation; Lenin is more than a political hero, he is the
canonized saint of Communism with a highly developed cultus of
his own; and the Communist ethic is religious in its absoluteness
and its unlimited claims to the spiritual allegiance of its followers."
Ibid., p. 58

[6] *Ibid.*

forms. The challenge to Christianity is definitely under way in extreme forms in certain European nations while the rest, themselves permeated to a great degree by naturalistic tenets, fear the outcome.

As we have seen in the course of this study, considerable opposition to the Christian religion and its philosophy of life exists in the minds of our most influential educational leaders, Dewey, Kilpatrick, Rugg, and Thorndike. But the opposition does not stop with these men because, as we have seen, thousands of teachers and leaders in the fields of the physical and social sciences are absolutely persuaded and will not be satisfied until America puts "aside resolutely such irreparably damaged entities as the Christian tradition." [7] That this naturalistic attitude is spreading cannot be doubted. Its very growth constitutes a direct challenge to Christianity. Proclaimed and expounded in the press, on the platform, and in the classroom, it is definitely influencing hundreds of thousands of teachers in the nation, and through them the body of our American youth, from the kindergarten to the University, and even beyond.

The period which has elapsed since the turn of the century has been characterized as "one of great religious uncertainty, a period in which old standards and attitudes have been very considerably modified." [8] During this time not only has traditional Christianity been losing prestige and interest,[9] but

---

[7] Norman Woelfel, *Molders of the American Mind,* p. 229.

[8] C. Luther Fry, with the assistance of Mary Frost Jessup, "Changes in Religious Organizations," *Recent Social Trends in the United States* (New York: McGraw-Hill Book Co.). vol. II, pp. 1018-1019. By permission of the publishers.

[9] Hornell Hart, "Changing Social Attitudes and Interest," *ibid.,* pp. 402, 404, 407, 412.

definite antagonism to its teachings has arisen in certain influential quarters.[10] We are persuaded that this "apparent shift from Biblical authority and religious sanctions to scientific and fractional authority and sanctions," [11] is a result of the growth of naturalism in America and constitutes a positive menace to the Christian tradition. It is imperative, therefore, that those of us who believe firmly in the teachings of Christianity should take stock of the situation in order to discover the reasons for this antagonism to Christian doctrine so that plans for a decisive counter-attack may be launched forthwith.

Christianity as a philosophy of life has been indicted because it is alleged that it has failed to relieve the lot of humanity. It has placed its center of gravity in the world beyond, concerning which man knows, and can know, nothing. The result has been that it has neglected the world of the present. It has even prevented and discouraged the progress of science by arbitrarily setting limits to the province of experimental investigation. It insists on the stratification of society to the consequent detriment of the democratic ideal. It has even approved of the capi-

[10] *Ibid.*, pp. 387, 408, 441. Hart says "that the greatest antagonism to Christianity is found in the magazines circulating in the most highly educated classes." *Ibid.*, p. 408.

[11] *Ibid.*, p. 390. Harry Emerson Fosdick thinks that "science today is religion's overwhelming successful competitor in showing men how to get what they want." "Will Science Displace God?" *Harper's Magazine,* 153 (August, 1926), p. 363. Changing religious attitudes and interests are reflected in books and magazines, the circulation data of which show losses by religious and gains by scientific periodicals. Hart, "Changing Social Attitudes and Interest," *op. cit.*, pp. 390, 397. Hart also thinks that Pragmatism "has become assimilated in public thought to such an extent that special articles no longer appear on this subject." *Ibid.*, p. 396. Meanwhile scientific and proletarian humanism based on Marxian doctrines begin to command definite interest. *Ibid.*

talistic order which has been responsible for the present economic crisis. Above all, it has proclaimed in no uncertain terms an outworn code of morality entirely unfitted for modern social life, while at the same time it has insisted on religious dogmas which fail to stand the test of experimental thought, thus holding the masses under the thraldom of authority. In short, Christianity has outlived its usefulness and must be discarded.

Various naturalistic substitutes for this "decadent" philosophy are being tried in contemporary civilization. The Russian communistic experiment, a logical development of naturalism, is endeavoring to found a new anti-Christian social order in which an improved economic and social organization is set up as the ultimate end of human life. European thinkers as a body seem to tend towards some sort of oriental mysticism or fatalism, while Nationalism and Statism dominate the populace. The American solution "is based on a combination of the political tradition of Liberalism and democracy with the material order of a standardized mass civilization." [12] This solution is causing much intellectual and moral unrest because of the contradiction which exists between its democratic ideals and its economic practice. There seems to be a growing demand from intellectual leaders on all sides for a new declaration of the meaning and purpose of life in terms of our changing democratic society. Educational leaders like Dewey, Kilpatrick, Rugg, Bode, Counts, and a host of others, openly professing the tenets of naturalism,

---

[12] Christopher Dawson, General Introduction, *Essays in Order*, p. xii.

as well as insisting that the solution of all our problems, economic, social, and political, be arrived at by means of the methods of experimental science, are in the vanguard of those clamoring for a change in our institutions. Socialistic tendencies are very much in evidence in their writings, and while they are not prepared to approve fully the communistic theory of life and education in making the well-being of society, even though it be a democratic one, the sole and exclusive aim of education, they are actually preparing the way for just such a development.

The naturalistic doctrines which they are teaching American youth have been indicated in this study. The results of such instruction are very evident and all the more important because of the commanding position which education enjoys.[13] American schools today are graduating a generation which has been taught, directly and indirectly, that all religion, including, of course, Christianity, is but the survival of a superstitious age. God is declared to be a myth; Jesus Christ a well-intentioned visionary. Man is merely the highest development of the evolutionary process; the moral law is a fable; the only object which can lay claim to our allegiance is society. This situation is not peculiar to our times. For several decades such indoctrination has been under way, increasing in momentum with the years. The highly important thing to be noted, however, is that whereas yesterday material prosperity and success were offered instead of the Christian philosophy of life, today

---

[13] Bode says: "Our faith in education has become a faith akin to the faith of religion." *The Educational Frontier,* William H. Kilpatrick, editor, p. 3.

nothing positive can be or is being offered in its stead, because the economic crisis has shown the shallowness of earth-bound hopes. The products of our schools today are simply urged to devote their efforts to the construction of a new social order from which the injustices and abuses inherent in the older one will be eliminated. The important point to be noted in this connection is that these abuses and injustices are always laid at the door of Christianity, never by any chance being attributed to naturalism and its offspring, nationalism, liberalism, and communism.

We have already called attention to the spirit of unrest, doubt, and uncertainty that harks over our civilization. "It would indeed seem," says Berdyaev, "that the old, the secular foundations of the West are trembling, things apparently stabilized by use and wont are shifting. Nowhere and in no single matter is solid earth felt underfoot: we are on volcanic ground, and any eruption is possible, natural or spiritual." [14] The history of this period in Western civilization will be the chronicle of one of its most critical epochs. The very departments of traditional life are menacingly beset while age-old principles stay their flight with dubious courage. They stand as timid sentinels of a vanished trust, guarding an assertively deceased order, the old order. Gone, too, is that wonted adherence to the truth of Christianity and that general acceptance of Christian moral principles which even in the nineteenth century still impressively dominated the minds of men. Yet no certain mode of living has been recognized in their

---

[14] Nicholas Berdyaev, *The End of Our Time* (New York: Sheed and Ward, 1933), p. 12.

stead. In America, discontent and uncertainty are
reflected in every phase of life. Bode thinks that

> A civilization that shows so many major
> maladjustments must have something seri-
> ously the matter with it. There probably
> never was a time during the past century
> when the American people were less sure
> of the essential finality of their institutions
> than they are at the present moment. But
> what is it that is wrong? On this point we
> seem to be pretty much at sea. For this sit-
> uation, education, owing to its inherent
> confusion, must accept a large measure of
> responsibility.[15]

We admit the truth of these statements but we
contend that the abuses which characterized the old
order and which led to its destruction were due, not
to the teaching of Christianity and its common sense
philosophy of life, but to the naturalistic philosophies
which have been gradually undermining our civilization and culture since the Protestant Reformation.
In America, for instance, due to the spread of naturalism and the consequent decline of Christianity, serious and far-reaching changes in belief and practice
concerning morals, sin, and family relations have
taken place. Hart tells us that: "The waning power
of religious sanctions is closely related with the rise
of antagonism against monogamistic sex mores." [16]
Thus the change of attitude in regard to religion has
brought in its train a serious change in the concept
of moral behavior. Moral agnosticism has followed

---

[15] *The Educational Frontier*, p. 6.
[16] Hart, "Changing Social Attitudes and Interests," *Recent Social
Trends in the United States*, (New York: McGraw-Hill Book Co.),
p. 423. By permission of the publishers.

logically on the heels of religious agnosticism to such
an extent that new attitudes towards divorce, sex, and
birth are threatening the very life of the family, the
unity of society.[17] Leighton informs us that there are
"in our social life many symptoms of moral confusion
and disintegration that present striking, and even
startling, analogies to the decadent paganism of the
Roman world under the Caesars. . . . The family life
is notoriously endangered among us, and in ever
increasing measure, by the rapidly growing frequency
of divorce, which in turn is but a symptom of deeper-
lying ethical laxity and confusion. The unblushing
effrontery and sensual suggestiveness of the lascivious
stage corrupt our youth. The appalling increase of
suicide among the young indicates a weakening sense
of personal responsibility . . . objective moral values
are no longer recognized."[18] He gives us the reason
for this when he states that, "There is plenty of
cheap and easy naturalism abroad."[19] In other words,
the fruits of naturalism are manifest in a definite de-

[17] "The United States has the highest divorce rate of the countries
for which statistics are available, with the possible exception of the
U. S. S. R. which had in 1926 the same divorce rate per 1000 inhabitants as did the United States." W. F. Ogburn, with the assistance
of Clark Tibbits, "The Family and Its Functions," *Recent Social
Trends*, vol I, p. 693. "*Sexual irregularities, easy divorce and sex
freedom in general have recently been approved to an extent entirely unprecedented in 1900-1905. . . .*" Hart, *loc. cit.*, p. 441.
"*Religious sanctions have been largely displaced by scientific sanctions* in discussions published in leading magazines. Applied science
has risen to a paramount position in the intellectual life reflected
in periodicals of opinion." *Ibid.*, p. 441. Cf. Frank S. Hopkins,
"After Religion, What?" *Harper's Magazine*, 168 (April, 1934), 526-
534; James Gillis, "The Decay of Domestic Virtue," *The Catholic
World*, 140 (Jan., 1935).
[18] Joseph Alexander Leighton, *Religion and the Mind of Today*
(New York: D. Appleton-Century Co., 1924), pp. 39-40; cf. Chapter
IV, *Ibid.*, "The Recrudescence of Paganism."
[19] *Ibid.*, p. 43.

cline in traditional religious belief and morals with a
consequent increase in Paganism.

At the same time, *"Crime has attained gigantic pro-
portions in the United States."* [20]   Overt lawlessness
costs fifteen thousand million dollars per year. "The
cost of running our National Government staggers
us when we contemplate a budget of over four bil-
lion dollars, but this . . . is no more than 25 per cent
of what it costs us to indulge our love of lawlessness." [21]   The fact which is of most concern is that
the Investigation of So-Called "Rackets" has revealed
that most criminal careers begin in childhood. [22]   Is
it not alarming to be told that the average age of our
prison population is about twenty-three years? [23]
Commenting on this, the editor of *The Elementary
School Journal* says: [24] "It is indeed an appalling fact
that, according to the most conservative estimates,
the cost of crime is at least three times as great as the

---

[20] *Crime and Crime Control, Investigation of So-Called "Rackets,"*
Digest of Hearings held before a Senate Subcommittee of the Com-
mittee on Commerce During the Year 1933 (Washington: United
States Government Printing office, 1934), p. 1.

[21] Harry Elmer Barnes, *ibid.*, p. 3.

[22] *Ibid.*, p. 5. "Today about 50 per cent of the arrests reported to
the federal government are for persons under 30 years of age, and
20 per cent are for those under 21 years." *Research Bulletin of the
National Education Association* XII, No. 5 (Nov., 1934), *Modern
Social and Educational Trends*, XIII, "Crime and Crime Punishment," p. 274. Published by the Research Division of the National
Educational Association, Washington, D. C.

[23] *Investigation of So-Called "Rackets,"* p. 6. Senator Royal S.
Copeland tells us that the nineteen-year-old group, numbering
12,418 individuals made up the largest age group in a total of
241,000 persons arrested in 1933. There were 1700 in the 15-year-
old-group, while 20 per cent were below 21 years of age. *Ibid.* Cf.
Courtney Ryley Cooper, "Criminal America," *The Saturday Evening
Post* (Sept. 28, 1935), 23, 72, 73, 74; S. A. Queen, W. B. Bodenhafer,
E. B. Harper, *Social Organization and Disorganization* (New York:
Thomas Crowell Co., 1935), pp. 30, 344, 425.

[24] XXXIV, No. 9 (May, 1934), 641.

cost of public elementary and secondary schools combined. Perhaps equally appalling is the youth of
criminal offenders." We agree with this statement
as we do when the author says that: "Even a cursory
examination of the evidence gathered by the Senate
Subcommittee makes it obvious that the problem of
the youthful criminal constitutes a definite challenge
to our educational and social policy." [25] This necessarily brief survey of religious, moral, social, and intellectual conditions in America indicates clearly a
canker of some sort at the heart of the nation.

Several factors are, of course, responsible for the
prevalence of crime, especially among the young.
The socio-economic conditions resulting from the industrial revolution and the consequent radical
changes in family life have contributed to it, no
doubt; but back of the crime wave and the other
social evils of divorce, relaxed moral standards, and
intellectual agnosticism is to be found the decline of
Christianity due to the growth of naturalism in
American life and education. [26]

---

[25] *Ibid.,* p. 645.

[26] Dr. Nicholas Murray Butler, noted educator and President of
Columbia University, warns us of the disappearance of religious
instruction from the curriculum of the tax-supported schools in the
following words: "A Christian minister, in addressing a nation-
wide public some little time since, made the statement that he had
asked a group of school children in the city of Chicago, 'Where is
Bethlehem? and Who was born there?' He added that not one of
the group had ever heard the word Bethlehem, had any notion of
its whereabouts, or knew Who was born there. Apparently the
word meant nothing whatever to them. This illustration, striking
in itself, might be multiplied many scores of times from the experience of any observer of the work of the present-day schools and of
the children enrolled in them. From the viewpoint of sound educational principle, this is a serious state of affairs . . ." Report of the
President of Columbia University for 1934, *Columbia University
Bulletin of Information* (New York: Morningside Heights, December 15, 1934), pp. 21-22.

The forces of change seem to have produced conditions which endanger American institutions and social life. Many seem to have lost confidence because they lack the sense of direction which the supernatural, religion, and reason combined to give man. They lack a unified philosophy of life which takes the whole man into consideration. This is the reason why the social philosophy current today is unable to furnish a solution to our social problems. Certain leaders in education admit fundamental failure in regard to the achievement of education during the last twenty years.[27] This has been a common indictment for some time. The root-cause of the failure, of course, is to be found in the false anti-Christian philosophers back of educational theory. Unless the evil is corrected, education will continue to lead to confusion and worse.

There can be no doubt "that what is wrong is the spirit of our civilization, and that so long as that spirit is unchanged no improvements in social or economic machinery will help us in the long run." [28] It is this naturalistic spirit which produced the false philosophies of Individualism, Socialism, Rational-

---

[27] Cf. *The Educational Frontier,* passim. Bode tells us that: ". . . there appears to be a growing sense that something is lacking. The average man is more sensitive than before to the need of some kind of chart or compass by which to shape his course." *Ibid.,* p. 10. Cf. Norman Foerster, "Education Leads the Way," *The American Review,* I, No. 4 (Sept., 1933), 385-408.

[28] Dawson, *Religion and the Modern State,* p. xii. It cannot be insisted upon too much or too often that individualism and capitalism, important factors in producing the trend towards collectivism or totalitarianism, two aspects of the same naturalistic tendency, were positively fostered by Protestantism. Cf. Amintore Fanfani, "Protestantism and Capitalism," Chapter VII in *Catholicism, Protestantism and Capitalism* (New York: Sheed and Ward, 1935), pp. 183-217.

ism, Liberalism, Materialism, and Positivism, the abuses of which have led to an insistent demand for the destruction of the old order. In every single nation in the world wherein these doctrines have been tried they have been found wanting. Each in turn had proclaimed in no uncertain terms that the millenium had arrived and with it the exodus and destruction of Christianity, but instead of solving the problems of humanity they have only added to the confusion of mankind. This is the world which naturalism created with its advocacy of scientific experimentation as the only approach to truth. This is the civilization which, breaking away from its supernatural moorings, first rejected the Church, then Christ, and finally God, and abandoning God, the Principle of Order, it has thrown the whole life of man into turmoil.[29] That is why Irving Babbitt warned us in 1924, in his *Democracy and Leadership,* that "the economic problem will be found to run into the political problem, the political problem in turn into the philosophical problem, and the philosophical problem itself to be almost indissolubly bound up at last with the religious problem."[30]

The wholesale breakdown of the economic system [says Mercier] and the threatened

[29] Sheen tells us: "The sixteenth century asked for a 'new Church,' the eighteenth for a 'new Christ,' the nineteenth for a 'new God,' and the twentieth for a 'new religion.' In response to these appeals and in the name of 'progress,' 'science,' and 'liberty,' the Church became a sect, Christ but a moral teacher, God the symbol for the ideal tendency in things, and religion an attitude of friendliness to the universe." Fulton J. Sheen, *Religion Without God* (New York: Longmans, Green and Co., 1928), p. 3.
[30] Quoted in *The Challenge of Humanism* by Louis J. A. Mercier, Foreword, iii.

collapse of the political systems of the nineteenth century which followed the unprecedented tragedy of the World War may
well lead us to inquire whether the quality
of our philosophical thought and its relation to religion, do not, indeed, need to be
re-examined.[31]

Thus one thing only is certain. The issue lies "between the Christian point of view and what used to
be called the pagan point of view, but is now more
commonly known as the modern point of view." [32]
In other words, "today we have to choose between the
complete expulsion of the spiritual element from human life or its recognition as the very foundation of
reality." [33] There can be no doubt that in proportion
as each school of philosophy based on naturalism has
endeavored to eliminate this spiritual element, the
ills of the individual and society have multiplied.
Individualism, Rationalism, Liberalism, and Positivism have run their courses only to end in frustration.
At the zero hour, Communism raised its standard of
revolt, offering its naturalistic panacea; and many,
not only in Russia but also in Europe and America,
are manifesting more than passing interest in its phi-

---

[31] *Ibid.* Mercier's *The Challenge of Humanism* "provides a con-
spectus of the current revival of ethical philosophy (or humanism)
in France and America, sketches the connection of the new humanism with that of former times, shows strikingly the challenge it
offers to the naturism of the past two hundred years, and carefully
discusses its relations to Christianity. The subject as a whole is
huge and intricate but Mercier handles it with Gallic clarity, selecting the leading ideas and weaving them into a true pattern." **G. R.**
Elliot, "Babbitt and Religion," *American Review,* II (February,
1934), 487.

[32] Dawson, *Religion and the Modern State,* p. xii.

[33] Dawson, *Essays in Order,* p. xx.

losophy. More numerous, however, in America are those who place their faith in the ultimate triumph of science. These constitute the group which is directing the training of American youth, a training which in ultimate analysis, is nothing more than a process of naturalization in which the realm of the contingent takes the commanding place to the exclusion of genuine thought based on spiritual principles which the mind of man craves. The result is that the youthful mind is being deprived of everything that it was formerly taught to value; it has lost faith in its own destiny and all its inner bonds seem broken.[34] The result is that we have our "lost generation" without ambition or enterprise adrift in a civilization which is not sure of its own direction because it has discarded its spiritual values.[35]

---

[34] In this connection we might ponder the following words of Babbitt: "All the nobler aspirations of man, all his notions of conduct, had clustered around the old-time conception of the soul and of the struggle between a higher and a lower self. The weakening of traditional belief has been followed by such an unsettling of all fixed standards, by such intellectual and moral chaos, that we are inclined to ask whether the modern man has not lost in force of will and character more than an equivalent of what he has gained in scientific knowledge of life. . . . The triumph of naturalism has been followed by a serious falling off, for the moment at least, in the more purely spiritual activities of man." I. Babbitt, *Masters of Modern French Criticism* (New York: Houghton, Mifflin, 1912), p. 239.

[35] Cf. Maxine Davis, *The Lost Generation* (New York: The Macmillan Co., 1936). Traveling 10,000 miles from coast to coast in four months, "She found tragedy in the fact that nowhere did youth count itself in a temporary jam. It no longer had even the conviction that it could or would emerge from its distress. She found native youth 'today accepts its fate with sheep-like apathy.' " "Today's Lost Generation," in *The Literary Digest*, 121 (April 4, 1936), 21. Sherwood Anderson's *Puzzled America* (New York: Charles Scribner's Sons, 1935), gives us a similar picture of the populace. He found it wanting belief, some ground to stand on, some meaning to life which would satisfy its cravings. Cf. R. L.

What shall be the fate of the youth adrift in the spiritual void which broods over our time? What shall happen to the civilization of which these young men and women form a part? Very many of our American educators predict the passing of Christianity and its traditions. "It may as well be frankly recognized by American educators," says the naturalistic Woelfel, "that the days of Christian cultural solidarity in America are over." [36] When the Christian tradition has passed, as many of these naturalistic educators seem to think it will, and carried away with it its authority and sanctions, then American youth in common with the youth of the world will build a new social order in which humanity will realize its dreams and ideals in the here and now instead of waiting in superstitious and vain hope for the Christian millennium. This is the way out of the world crisis proposed by the philosophy of scientific naturalism which American youth are being taught by many American educators. This solution is in agreement, so far as its anti-Christian character is concerned, with the other theories which naturalism has originated these many years in the world at large.

Christianity is opposed fundamentally to all these proposed solutions which it maintains are based on one-sided philosophies of life. It contends, furthermore, that the present crisis in civilization has its roots in the rejection of the Christian tradition. It believes that the only true and sane solution must be a religious one. "In other words," as Mercier says,

[36] Woelfel, *Molders of the American Mind*, pp. 229-230. By permission of Columbia University Press.

Duffus, review in the *New York Times Book Review* (April 7, 1935), p. 1.

"we have to look to our religion as well as to our philosophy *for the organization of this life* because, fundamentally, the organization of this life depends on our conception of the nature of man, and our conception of the nature of man depends upon our conception of God and of man's relation to Him." [37]

Christianity has God for its center, not man. It teaches that man not only is not simply continuous with nature, the highest product of the evolutionary process, but is the king of creation, a creature of God. It insists that he is composed of body and soul which form one substantial unit, a single substance, of which the animating principle is the soul. He is dependent on a First Cause, as well as on the world of which he forms an integral part. He is endowed with reason and will which distinguish him from the animals. This is why "he is self-determining and can even impose his will on the world. This is the reason that man has maintained a proud spirit throughout his history and gone from success to success in exploration and in the subjugation of nature, in the advance of science and development of social relations." [38]

On the other hand, the life of time and earth are not fully satisfying to him. He finds much in it, no matter how excellent, that only engenders a thirst in him for more. Wealth, success, health, society are not enough. He can only be fully satisfied in the possession of God, Who is his final end, the Supreme

---

[37] Louis J. A. Mercier, "The American Inheritance," an address before the Springfield City Club, Springfield, Massachusetts, January 13. 1936.

[38] M. C. D'Arcy. *Mirage and Truth* (New York: The Macmillan Co., 1935), pp. 153-154.

Good and Truth. This is his immortal destiny, the reason why he has been raised to a supernatural state by grace.[39] Herein lies the significance of the Christian religion and the philosophy of life which it inspires. It is diametrically opposed to the naturalistic theories which have claimed and are claiming supremacy over mankind. Today civilization must choose between Christianity and naturalism. There is no other way out of the modern dilemma.

The only real solution of the present crisis lies in the acceptance of the Christian philosophy of life and education. This is the only sane commonsense doctrine because it is based upon an organic conception of God, man, and life.

> This means that it takes into account the intimate relation that really exists between the natural and the spiritual, between God and man, between the soul and body. It sees also the relation between the individual and society, the Nation, the Church, and the State. It takes into consideration other relations, too, such as the relation of individuality to personality, of the intellect to the will, of reason to feeling. And last but not least, it sees the real relation between God and the world.[40]

---

[39] "Man's true excellence," says Dawson, "consists not in following the law of animal nature but in his resistance to it, and in his recognition of another law. The law of the animal world is the law of instinctive desire and brute force; there is no room in it for freedom or right or moral good. In man alone a new principle comes into play; for he recognizes that beyond the natural good of pleasure and self-fulfillment, there is a higher good which is independent of himself, a good that is unlimited, ideal, spiritual." Dawson, *Enquiries into Religion and Culture*, pp. 316-317.

[40] De Hovre-Jordan. *Catholicism in Education*, p. 39.

Motivated by such an outlook, it is able by the aid of reason enlightened by Revelation to answer the two basic questions of all education: Why does the child exist? What is his nature, what kind of a being is he? Holding that the child exists because God created him to know, love, and serve Him here so that he may be happy with Him hereafter, and at the same time realizing that he is a creature composed of body and soul made to the image and likeness of God, Christian education is essentially supernatural. Hence,

> since education consists essentially in pre- paring man for what he must do here be- low, in order to attain the sublime end for which he was created, it is clear that there can be no true education which is not wholly directed to man's last end, and that, in the present order of Providence, since God has revealed Himself to us in the Per- son of His Only Begotten Son, Who alone is 'the Way, the Truth, and the Life,' there can be no ideally perfect education which is not Christian education.[41]

This is the reason why revealed religion permeates the whole atmosphere of the Christian school, influ- encing constantly, aims, content, and method. In such an atmosphere the purpose of education is "the harmonious development of the faculties in this world with a view to a further and final felicity in the next." [42] This is why useful secular knowledge can

---

[41] Pius XI, "Christian Education of Youth," *Four Great Encyclicals* (New York: The Paulist Press, no date), p. 38.

[42] Gerald Vann, *On Being Human* (New York: Sheed and Ward, 1934), p. 22.

never be the first essential of education. Since it does not raise man to his highest perfection, it can never be the principle or the antecedent of ethical training or social unity or action. The first principle of true education must be based on a true analysis of human nature, on the recognition of what it is that makes man man and gives value to his life. Since man is a creature with an immortal destiny the core of all training must be such as enables the higher in man to dominate the lower, thus producing a development of character in which discipline and restraint play key parts in producing results which mere knowledge of facts never could produce. Thus when it comes to a question of selection between many facts and the commonsense which derives from the realization of the true nature of man and of the universe, the choice must always be with the latter. This is why

> Christianity, and nothing short of it, must be made the element and principle of education. Where it has been laid as the first stone, and acknowledged as the governing spirit, it will take up into itself, and assimilate, and give character to literature and science. Where Revealed Truth has given the aim and direction to Knowledge, Knowledge of all kinds will minister to Revealed Truth.[43]

Christian formation recognizing the true function of education to be a process of conversion or transformation does not insist too much on the etymological

---

[43] John Henry Newman, *Discussions and Arguments* (London: Longmans, 1899), p. 274.

meaning of the word, hoping to "draw education out of human nature itself and evolve it by its own un- aided powers." [44]   Rather does it view the child as he actually is with his capacities and defects.   This is why it devotes so much time to the training of the will and self-discipline by the inculcation of motives, ideals, and aims under the guidance and aid of religion so that the individual's mental and emo- tional life may be stabilized and developed, so that his intellect may attain truth and observe order.   This is all in marked contrast to naturalistic education which gives unlimited freedom to the will and op- poses the restraining of impulses.   Naturalistic educa- tion

> leaves the mind free to follow any principle
> or no principle, any destiny or no destiny,
> it takes its own origin for granted and cares
> not whither it tends.   It forgets that free-
> dom without law and law without author-
> ity, and authority without sanction are in
> the final analysis intellectual nothings.   Uni-
> versal education without opportunity for re-
> ligious and moral discipline as well as re-

[44] Pius XI, "Christian Education of Youth," pp. 37-38. The Pope tells us that: "Every form of pedagogic naturalism which in any way excludes or weakens supernatural Christian formation in the teaching of youth, is false. Every method of education founded, wholly or in part, on the denial or forgetfullness of original sin and of grace, and relying on the sole powers of human nature, is unsound. Such, generally speaking, are those modern systems, bearing various names which appeal to a pretended self-government and un- restrained freedom on the part of the child, and which diminish and even repress the teacher's authority, and action, attributing to the child an exclusive primacy of initiative, and an activity inde- pendent of any higher law, natural or divine, in the work of edu- cation." *Ibid.*, pp. 56-57.

ligious aid and moral supports, in the end
defeats its own purpose. . . . [45]

While the human environment, physical and
social, changes, instruction and training must be
adapted accordingly, while civic and industrial life
develops and education must prepare the child to
adjust himself to the new order, while scientific investigation enhances our knowledge of the child
mind and its operations and methods of instructions
are improved as a result, human nature and the ultimate principles which must determine the aims of
Christian education in general will never change.
This is why stress is continually laid upon the unchanging aspects of human life and education. Christian education "studies human life in all its aspects,
physical, psychological, social, civic, vocational, moral,
and religious. It sees man as a whole and seeing him
thus finds no difficulty in establishing a hierarchy of
values in the things that concern man." [46]   This is
why Christian education is concerned with the formation of the whole man.   While religious and
moral training are the heart of such formation, other
phases of education are not neglected.   Every reason-
able objective which progress has demanded has been
met.   Thus we find it imparting instruction in social
service, sound health, wholesome family life, economic efficiency, good citizenship, and profitable

---

[45] Albert F. Kaiser, "Naturalism and Education," *The Sign,* 13,
No. 8 (March, 1934), p. 492.

[46] Edward B. Jordan, "The Philosophy of Catholic Education,"
The National Catholic Educational Bulletin (Washington, D. C.:
National Catholic Education Association), XXVII, No. 4 (August,
1931), 17.

leisure, all inspired and motivated by the fact of man's ultimate destiny.[47]

It is well to bear this in mind now that we are in the midst of a crisis in culture. Naturalistic education has failed. Christian education continues to improve. The former was based on a false philosophy of life. The latter has the only sound viewpoint concerning man and life. Liberal humanitarianism or naturalism

> has proved incapable of providing an enduring basis for culture, and today its ideals are being swallowed up by the subversive forces it has itself liberated. . . . What we are suffering from is the morbid growth of a selfish civilization which has no end beyond itself—a monstrous cancer that destroys the face of nature and eats into the heart of humanity. As in the days of ancient Rome, but on a far larger scale, men have made themselves the masters of this world, and find themselves left with nothing but their own sterile lusts.[48]

This is the result of a naturalistic philosophy which has motivated all secular education including American. The results have been unhappy. Failure is manifest. The remedy is at hand. The Christian philosophy of life and education alone possesses it. In the not very distant future, American education will have to choose between a return to the philosophy of Christianity or a surrender to the philosophy of Communism.[49] Which shall it be?

---

[47] *Ibid.*

[48] Dawson, *Religion and the Modern State*, p. 143.

[49] Cf. Louis J. A. Mercier, "Naturalism or Humanism?" Chapter VIII in *The Challenge of Humanism*, pp. 256-271.

BIBLIOGRAPHY

Adams, Henry, *History of the United States of America,* Vol. I,
   New York: Charles Scribner's Sons, 1889.
Adams, James Truslow, "The Crisis in Character," *Harper's Maga-
   zine,* 167 (August, 1933), 257-267.
——, *The March of Democracy.* 2 vols. New York: Charles Scrib-
   ner's Sons, 1933.
Allers, Rudolph, *The Psychology of Character.* London: Sheed and
   Ward, 1931.
——, *The New Psychologies.* London: Sheed and Ward, 1933.
Anderson, Sherwood, *Puzzled America.* New York: Charles Scrib-
   ner's Sons, 1935.
Arnett, Claude E., *The Social Beliefs and Attitudes of American
   School Board Members.* Emporia, Kans.: Emporia Gazette
   Press, 1932.
"The Atheists' Intolerance," *The Literary Digest,* 96, No. 2 (Janu-
   ary 14, 1928), 29-30.
Attwater, Donald, Editor, *The Catholic Encyclopedia Dictionary.*
   New York: The Macmillan Co., 1931.
Babbitt, Irving, "President Eliot and American Education," *Forum.*
   LXXXI, No. 1 (January, 1929), 1-10.
——, *Rousseau and Romanticism.* Boston: Houghton Mifflin Co.,
   1929.
Bacon, Leonard Woolsey, *A History of American Christianity.*
   American Church History Series, XIII. New York: The Chris-
   tian Literature Co., 1897.
Bagley, William C., *Education, Crime, and Social Progress.* New
   York: The Macmillan Co., 1931.
——, *Determinism in Education.* Baltimore: Warwick and York,
   Inc., 1925.
Baldwin, James Mark, *Dictionary of Philosophy and Psychology.*
   Vol. II, New York: The Macmillan Co., 1902.
Balfour, Arthur J., *The Foundations of Belief.* New York: Long-
   mans Green and Co., 1895.
Bandas, Rudolph, *Contemporary Philosophy and Thomistic Prin-
   ciples.* New York: The Bruce Publishing Co., 1932.
Barnard, Henry, "Jean Jacques Rousseau," *Barnard's American
   Journal of Education.* V (1858), 459-486.
——, "Pestalozzianism in the United States," *Ibid.,* XXX (1880), 561-
   572.
——, *National Education in Europe.* 2nd ed. New York: Charles
   B. Norton, 1854.
Beard, Charles A. and Mary A., *The Rise of American Civilization.*
   2 vols. in 1. New York: The Macmillan Co., 1930.

Becker, Carl L., *The Declaration of Independence, A Study in the History of Political Idea.* New York: Harcourt, Brace and Co., 1922.

Bell, Bernard Iddings, "Economic Morality for the New Age," *Scribner's Magazine.* 95 (April, 1934), 269-274.

——, "Universities and Religious Indifference," *Atlantic Monthly.* 150 (September, 1932), 316-320.

Berdyaev, Nicholas, "The Bourgeois Spirit," *The Dublin Review.* 193 (October, 1933), 169-180.

——, *The End of Our Time.* New York: Sheed and Ward, 1934.

Bode, Boyd H., *Modern Educational Theories.* New York: The Macmillan Co., 1932.

——, *Conflicting Psychologies of Learning.* Boston: D. C. Heath and Co., 1929.

Boon, Richard G., *Education in the United States: Its History from the Earliest Settlements.* New York: D. Appleton and Co., 1902.

Boring, E. G., *A History of Experimental Psychology.* New York: The Century Co., 1929.

Bouscaren, T. L., "Horace Mann and the Public School," *America.* 30 (October 27, 1923), 46-47.

Boyd, William, *The History of Western Education.* 3rd edition. London: A. & C. Black, Ltd., 1932.

Brown, Samuel Windsor, *The Secularization of American Education.* Teachers College, Columbia University, Contributions to Education, No. 49. New York: Bureau of Publications, Teachers College, Columbia University, 1912.

Bruehl, Charles, "Rampant Atheism and Immortalism," *The Homiletic and Pastoral Review* XXVIII, No. 9 (June 1928), 923-931.

Burton, William H., *Introduction to Education.* New York: D. Appleton-Century Co., 1934.

Cattell J. McKeen, "Thorndike as Colleague and Friend," *Teachers College Record.* XXVII, No. 6 (February 1926), 461-465.

Ceulemans, J. B., "American Materialism," *Ecclesiastical Review.* XLV, No. 4 (October 1911), 406-427.

——, "Studies in American Philosophy," *Ecclesiastical Review.* XLV, No. 1 (July 1911), 27-45.

Ceybolt, Robert Francis, *The Public Schools of Colonial Boston, 1635-1775.* Cambridge: Harvard University Press, 1935.

Childs, John L., *Education and the Philosophy of Experimentalism.* New York: The Century Co., 1931.

Cohausz, Otto, *The Pope and Christian Education.* Translated by George D. Smith. New York: Benziger Bros., 1933.

Compayré, Gabriel, *Horace Mann and the Public School in the United States.* New York: Thomas Y. Crowell & Co., 1907.

Confrey, Burton, *Secularism in American Education, Its History.* Ph.D. Dissertation, The Catholic University of America, Washington, D. C., 1931.

Cooper, John M., "The Scientific Evidence Bearing upon Human Evolution," *Primitive Man.* Quarterly Bulletin of the Catholic Anthropological Conference. VIII, Nos. 1, 2 (January and April, 1935), 1-56.

Coram, Robert, *Political Inquiries: To Which is Added, a Plan for the General Establishment of Schools Throughout the United States.* Wilmington, Del.: Andrews and Brynberg, 1791.

Corcoran, T., "Child Labor Within School Years, From Dewey Back to Pestalozzi," *Thought.* VI, No. 1 (June 1931), 88-107.

Crime and Crime Control, Investigation of So-Called "Rackets," Digest of Hearings held before a (Senate) Subcommittee of the Committee on Commerce during the year 1933. Washington: Government Printing Office, 1934.

Counts, George S., "Dare Progressive Education Be Progressive," *Progressive Education.* 9 (April 1932), 257-263.

———, *The American Road to Culture.* New York: John Day Co., 1930.

———, *The Social Foundations of Education.* New York: Charles Scribner's Sons, 1934.

———, *Dare the School Build a New Social Order?* New York: John Day Co., 1932.

Cronin, Michael, *The Science of Ethics.* 2nd edition. Dublin: M. H. Gill and Son, Ltd., 1920.

Croy, Homer, "Atheism Rampant in Our Schools," *The World's Work.* LIV, No. 2 (June 1927), 140-147.

———, "Atheism Beckons to Our Youth," *ibid.,* No. 1 (May 1927), 18-26.

Cubberley, E. P., *The History of Education.* Boston: Houghton Mifflin Co., 1920.

———, *An Introduction to the Study of Education and Teaching.* Boston: Houghton Mifflin Co., 1925.

———, *Public Education in the United States.* Boston: Houghton Mifflin Co., 1919.

Cuff, Mary Louise, *The Limitations of the Education Theory of John Locke Specially for the Christian Teacher.* Ph.D. Dissertation. Washington, D. C.: Catholic University of America, 1920.

Culver, Raymond B., *Horace Mann and the Religion in the Massachusetts Public Schools.* New Haven: Yale University Press, 1929.

Cunningham F. A., "In Their Generation," *America.* 51 (June 1934) 229-230.

Curti, Merle, *The Social Ideas of American Educators.* New York.: Charles Scribner's Sons, 1935.

D'Arcy, M. C., *Mirage and Truth.* New York: The Macmillan Co., 1935.

Davidson, Thomas, *Rousseau and Education According to Nature.* New York: Charles Scribner's Sons, 1898.

———, *A History of Education.* New York: Charles Scribner's Sons, 1901.

Davis, Maxine, *The Lost Generation.* New York: The Macmillan Co., 1936.

264 *Naturalism in American Education*

Dawson, Christopher, *Progress and Religion: An Historical Enquiry.*
New York: Sheed and Ward, 1934.

——, *Religion and the Modern State.* New York: Sheed and Ward, 1935.

——, *Enquiries into Religion and Culture.* New York: Sheed and Ward, 1936.

De Hovre, Franz, *Philosophy and Education.* Translated by Edward B. Jordan. New York: Benziger Bros., 1931.

——, *Catholicism in Education.* Translated by Edward B. Jordan. New York: Benziger Bros., 1934.

Demiashkevich, Michael, *An Introduction to the Philosophy of Education.* New York: American Book Co., 1935.

Dewey, John, *A Common Faith.* New Haven: Yale University Press, 1934.

——, *Art as Experience.* New York: Minton, Balch and Co., 1934.

——, *Democracy and Education, An Introduction to the Philosophy of Education.* New York: The Macmillan Co., 1933.

——, *The Educational Frontier.* Edited by William H. Kilpatrick. New York: The Century Co., 1933.

——, *Philosophy and Civilization.* New York: Minton, Balch and Co., 1931.

——, *Human Nature and Conduct, An Introduction to Social Psychology,* with a new introduction by John Dewey. New York: The Modern Library, 1930.

——, *Individualism Old and New.* New York: Minton, Balch and Co., 1930.

——, *Construction and Criticism.* New York: Columbia University Press, 1930.

——, *Experience and Nature.* New York: W. W. Norton and Co., Inc., 1929.

——, *The Quest for Certainty: A Study of the Relations of Knowledge and Action.* New York: Minton, Balch and Co., 1929.

——, *Characters and Events, Popular Essays in Social and Political Philosophy.* Edited by Joseph Ratner. 2 vols. New York: Henry Holt and Co., 1929.

——, *The Public and Its Problems.* New York: Henry Holt, 1927; London: George Allen and Unwin Ltd.

——, *Reconstruction in Philosophy.* New York: Henry Holt and Co., 1920.

——, *Essays in Experimental Logic.* Chicago: University of Chicago Press, 1916.

——, *Influence of Darwin on Philosophy and Other Essays in Contemporary Thought.* New York: Henry Holt and Co., 1910.

——, *How We Think.* Boston: D. C. Heath and Co., 1910.

——, *The School and Society.* Chicago: University of Chicago Press, 1900.

——, "Half - Hearted Naturalism," *The Journal of Philosophy.* XXIV, No. 3 (February 3, 1927), 57-64.

——, "From Absolutism to Experimentalism," in *Contemporary American Philosophy, Personal Statements.* Edited by George

P. Adams and Wm. Pepperell Montague. Vol. II. New York: The Macmillan Co., 1930.

——, "A Credo" in *Living Philosophies. A Series of Intimate Credos.* New York: Simon and Schuster, 1931.

Dewey, John, *et al., Art and Education.* The Barnes Foundation Press, 1929.

Dewey, John, *et al., Creative Intelligence.* New York: Henry Holt and Co., 1917.

Dewey, John and Evelyn, *Schools of To-morrow.* New York: E. P. Dutton and Co., 1915.

Dewey, J. and Tufts, J. H., *Ethics.* Revised edition. New York: Henry Holt and Co., 1932.

De Wulf, M., *Scholasticism Old and New.* Translated by P. Coffey. Dublin: M. H. Gill and Son, Ltd., n.d.

Dexter, Edwin Grant, *A History of Education in the United States.* New York: The Macmillan Co., 1904.

Dingle, Reginald J., *The Faith and Modern Science.* London: Burns, Oates and Washbourne, Ltd., 1935.

Doughton, Isaac, *Modern Public Education, Its Philosophy and Background.* New York: D. Appleton-Century Co., 1935.

Drew, Samuel, *The Life of the Rev. Thomas Coke, LL.D.* New York: J. Soule and T. Mason, 1818.

Dudley, Owen Francis, *Will Men Be Like Gods?* New York: Longmans Green and Co., 1932.

Eby, Frederick and Arrowood, Charles Flinn, *The Development of Modern Education.* New York: Prentice-Hall, Inc., 1934.

"A Significant Invesitgation of Crime in the United Sates," *The Elementary School Journal,* XXXIV, No. 9, (May 1934), 641-645.

Elder, Benedict, "The Worst Evil of Our Day," *The Fortnightly Review.* XXXIV, No. 17 (September 1, 1927), 347-349.

——, "The Worst Evil of Our Day," *ibid.,* XXXIV, No. 21 (November 1, 1927), 433-435.

Eldridge, Seba, *The Organization of Life.* New York: Thomas Y. Crowell Co., 1925.

Eliot, Charles W., *Education for Efficiency and the New Definition of the Culivated Man.* Boston: Houghton Mifflin Co., 1909.

——, *The Religion of the Future.* Boston: John W. Luce and Co., 1909.

——, Introduction to *Spencer's Essays on Education.* Everyman's Library. London: J. M. Dent and Sons, 1911.

Everett, Samuel, Editor, *A Challenge to Secondary Education.* New York: D. Appleton-Century Co., 1935.

Fanfani, Amintore, *Catholicism, Protestantism and Capitalism.* New York: Sheed and Ward, 1935.

Feldman, William Taft, *The Philosophy Of John Dewey, a Critical Analysis.* Ph.D. Dissertation. Baltimore: The Johns Hopkins Press, 1934.

Fletcher, John Madison, *Psychology in Education.* New York: Doubleday, Doran and Co., Inc., 1934.

266   *Naturalism in American Education*

Flexner, Abraham, *Universities: American, English and German.* New York: Oxford University Press, 1930.

Foerster, F. W., *Marriage and the Sex-Problem.* Translated by Meyrick Booth. New York: Frederick A. Stokes Co., 1912.

Foerster, Norman, "The College, the Individual, and Society," *The American Review,* IV, No. 2 (December 1934), 129-146.

——, "Education Leads the Way," *ibid.* I (September 1933), 385-408.

Forman, Henry James, *Our Movie Made Children.* New York: The Macmillan Co., 1933.

Frank, Waldo, *The Re-Discovery of America.* New York: Charles Scribner's Sons, 1929.

Fry, C. Luther, with the assistance of Mary Frost Jessup, "Changes in Religious Organizations," *Recent Social Trends.* Edited by the President's Research Committee. New York: McGraw Hill 1933. Vol. II, 1009-1060

Gates, Arthur I., "Contributions to the Psychology of the Elementary School Subjects," *Teachers College Record,* XXVII (February 1926), 548-557.

Gauss, Christian, "The Decline of Religion," *Scribner's Magazine,* 95 (April 1934), 241-246.

Gilbert, D. W., "Are Secular Universities Reactionary?" *America,* 51 (June 1934), 204-206.

——, "Is Materialism Our State Religion?" *The Catholic World,* CXL, No. 835 (October 1934), 80-86.

Good, H. G., "The Sources of Spencer's Education," *Journal of Educational Research.* XIII, No. 5 (May 1926), 325-335.

Goodsell, Willystine, "The New Education as It Is: A Reply to Professor Kandel," *Teachers College Record.* XXXIV, No. 7 (April 1933), 539-551.

——, *Problems of the Family.* New York: The Century Co., 1928.

Graves, Frank Pierrepont, *A History of Education During the Middle Ages and the Transition to Modern Times.* New York: The Macmillan Co., 1910.

——, *Great Educators of Three Centuries, Their Work and Its Influence on Modern Education.* New York: The Macmillan Co., 1912.

——, *A History of Education in Modern Times.* New York: The Macmillan Co., 1917.

——, *A Student's History of Education.* New York: The Macmillan Co., 1921.

Griswold Rufus Wilmot, *The Republican Court, or American Society in the Days of Washington.* New York: D. Appleton and Co., 1864.

Hall, G. Stanley, *Life and Confessions of a Psychologist.* New York: D. Appleton and Co., 1923.

Halsey, Thomas Milton, and Wallace, Sneider Herbert, *A Bibliography of John Dewey.* New York: Columbia University Press, 1929.

Hansen, Allen Oscar, *Liberalism and American Education in the Eighteenth Century*, with An Introduction by Edward H. Reisner. New York: The Macmillan Co., 1926.

Harper, Manly H., *Social Beliefs and Attitudes of American Educators*. Teachers College, Columbia University Contributions to Education, No. 294, New York: Bureau of Publications, Teachers College, Columbia University, 1927.

Hart, Charles A., Editor, *Philosophy of Society*. Philadelphia: The Dolphin Press, 1934.

Hart, Hornell, "Changing Social Attitudes and Interests," Chapter VIII of *Recent Social Trends*, Edited by the President's Research Committee, New York: McGraw-Hill, 1933, Vol. 1.

Hayes, C. J. H., *A Political and Social History of Modern Europe*. New York: The Macmillan Co., 1917.

Hazlitt, Henry, "Progress without a God," *The Nation*. 131 (October 22, 1930), 446-447.

Hemelt, Theodore Mary, *Final Moral Values in Sociology*. Ph.D. Dissertation. Washington, D. C.: The Catholic University of America, 1929.

Hinsdale, B. A., "Notes on the History of Foreign Influences upon Education in the United States," *Report of the Commissioner of Education*, 1897-98. Washington, D. C.: The United States Bureau of Education, 1899. Vol. I.

——, *Horace Mann and the Common School Revival in the United States*. New York: Charles Scribner's Sons, 1898.

Hocking, William Ernest, *Types of Philosophy*. New York: Charles Scribner's Sons, 1929.

Holmes, Henry W., Editor, *John Dewey, the Man and His Philosophy*. Address Delivered in New York in Celebration of His Seventieth Birthday. Cambridge: Harvard University Press, 1930.

Honeywell, Roy J., *The Educational Work of Thomas Jefferson*. Cambridge. Harvard University Press, 1931.

Hook, Sidney, *The Meaning of Marx, A Symposium*. New York: Farrar and Rinehart, Inc., 1934.

Hopkins, Frank S., "After Religion, What?" *Harper's Magazine*, 168 (April 1934), 526-534.

Horne, Herman Harrell, *The Democratic Philosophy of Education*. New York: The Macmillan Co., 1933.

Hudson, William Henry, *Rousseau and Naturalism in Life and Thought*. New York: Charles Scribner's Sons, 1903.

Hull, Augustus L., *A Historical Sketch of the University of Georgia*. Atlanta: The Foote and Davies Co., 1894.

Hullfish, Gordon H., *Aspects of Thorndike's Psychology in Their Relation to Educational Theory and Practice*. Columbus: Ohio State University Press, 1926.

Humphrey, Edw. F., *Nationalism and Religion in America, 1774-1789*. Boston: Chipman Law Publishing Co., 1924.

Huxley, Thomas Henry, *Evidence as to Man's Place in Nature*. London: Williams and Norgate, 1863.

James, Henry, *Charles W. Eliot, President of Harvard, 1869-1909*. 2 vols. Boston: Houghton Mifflin Co., 1930.

James, William, *Pragmatism*. New York: Longmans Green and Co., 1926.

Janet, Paul and Seailles, Gabriel, *A History of the Problems of Philosophy*. Translated by Ada Monahan, edited by Henry Jones. 2 vols. London: Macmillan and Co., Ltd., 1902.

Johnson, George, *Catholic Education*. Washington, D. C.: National Council of Catholic Men, National Catholic Welfare Conference, 1934.

——, "Fundamentals of Education," *The Catholic Educational Association Bulletin*. XXII, No. 2 (February 1926), 9-16.

Jones, Howard Mumford, *American and French Culture, 1750-1848*. Chapel Hill: The University of North Carolina Press, 1927.

Jordan, Edward B., Review of "A Social Basis of Education," *The Catholic Educational Review*. XXXIII (April 1935), 246-248.

——, "The Philosophy of Catholic Education," *The National Catholic Educational Bulletin* XXVII, No. 4 (August 1931), 9-21.

Joyce, George Hayward, *Principles of Natural Theology*. 2nd ed. London: Longmans Green and Co., 1924.

Kaiser. Albert F., "Naturalism and Education," *The Sign*. XIII, No. 8 (March 1934), 490-492.

Kandel, Isaac L., "The Philosophy Underlying the System of Education in the United States," *Educational Yearbook of the International Institute of Teachers College, Columbia University, 1929*. New York: Bureau of Publications, Teachers College, Columbia University, 1930.

——, "Education and Social Disorder," *Teachers College Record*. XXXIV, No. 5 (February 1933), 359-367.

——, *Comparative Education*. Boston: Houghton Mifflin Co., 1933.

Kidd, Benjamin, *Social Evolution*. New York: The Macmillan Co., 1894.

Killeen, Mary Vincent, *Man in the New Humanism*. Ph.D. Dissertation. Washington, D. C.: The Catholic University of America, 1934.

Kilpatrick, William Heard, *A Reconstructed Theory of the Educative Process*. New York: Bureau of Publications, Teachers College, Columbia University, 1935.

——, *Source Book in the Philosophy of Education*. Revised edition. New York: The Macmillan Co., 1934.

——, Editor, *The Educational Frontier*. New York: D. Appleton-Century Co., 1933.

——, *Education and the Social Crisis*. New York: Liveright, Inc., 1932.

——, Foreword to *Education and the Philosophy of Experimentalism* by John L. Childs. New York: The Century Co., 1931.

——, Introduction to *John Dewey, the Man and His Philosophy*. Address Delivered in New York in Celebration of His Seventieth Birthday. Cambridge: Harvard University Press, 1930.

——, *Our Educational Task*. Chapel Hill: The University of North Carolina Press, 1930.

——, *Education for a Changing Civilization*. New York: The Macmillan Co., 1928.

——, "How Shall We Think about Religion?" *The New Era*. II, No. 46 (October 1930), 115-119.

——, "Philosophy and Research," *School and Society*. XXX, No. 759 (July 13, 1929), 39-48.

——, "The American Elementary School," *Teachers College Record*. XXX, No. 6 (March 1929), 513-527.

——, "The Philosophy of American Education," *Teachers College Record*. XXX, No. 1 (October 1928), 13.

——, "Remarks at the Unveiling of Dr. Dewey's Bust," *School and Society*, XXVIII (December 22, 1928), 778-780.

——, "The Philosophy of American Education," *Teachers College Record*. XXX, No. 1 (October 1928), 13-22.

Knight, Edgar W., *Education in the United States*. Boston: Ginn and Co., 1929.

Knox, Samuel, *An Essay on the Best System of Liberal Education Adapted to the Genius of the Government of the United States*. Baltimore: Warner and Hanna, 1799.

Koch, Adolf G., *Republican Religion: The American Revolution and the Cult of Reason*. New York: Henry Holt, 1933.

Kuehner, Quincy A., *A Philosophy of Education*. New York: Prentice-Hall, Inc., 1935.

Laguna, Theodore and Grace A., *Dogmatism and Evolution*. New York: The Macmillan Co., 1910.

Leighton, Joseph A., *Religion and the Mind of Today*. New York: D. Appleton and Co., 1924.

Leuba, James H., *The Belief in God and Immortality*. Boston: Sherman, French and Co., 1916.

Lewis, C. I., Review of Dewey's *The Quest for Certainty, Journal of Philosophy*, XXVII, No. 1 (January 2, 1930), 14-25.

Lindsay, E. E., and Holland, E. O., *College and University Administration*. New York: The Macmillan Co., 1930.

Lippman, Walter, *A Preface to Morals*. New York: The Macmillan Co., 1929.

Litt, Theodore, *Die Philosophie der Gegenwart und ihr Einfluss auf das Bildungsideale*. Leipzig: Teubner, 1925.

Locke, John, *Some Thoughts Concerning Education* with introduction and notes by Rev. R. H. Quick. New edition. Cambridge: University Press, 1892.

Loewenburg, Bert James, "The Reaction of American Scientists to Darwinism," *The American Historical Review*, XXXVIII, No. 4 (July 1933), 687-701.

Long, William Joseph, *American Literature*. New York: Ginn and Co., 1923.

Lovejoy, Arthur O., *The Revolt Against Dualism*. New York: W. W. Norton & Co., Inc., The Open Court Publishing Co., 1930.

Lucas, Henry S., *The Renaissance and the Reformation*. New York: Harper and Brothers, 1935.

Lunn, Arnold, *The Flight from Reason*. New York: The Dial Press, Lincoln MacVeagh, 1931.

Lunn, Arnold and Haldane, J. B. S., *Science and the Supernatural*. New York: Sheed and Ward, 1935.

Lynd, Robert S., *Middletown: A Study in Contemporary American Culture*. New York: Harcourt, Brace, 1929.

Mack, Henry W., "Comparative Content of Educational Philosophy Textbooks," *Education*, XLIX (December 1928), 236-244.

Maclean, John, *History of the College of New Jersey from Its Origin in 1746 to the Commencement of 1854*. Vol. I. Philadelphia: J. S. Lippincott and Co., 1877.

Maher, Michael, *Psychology*. New York: Longmans and Co., 1902.

Mangold, George B., *Social Pathology*. New York: The Macmillan Co., 1932.

Mann, Horace, Extracts from Horace Mann's *Seventh Annual Report to the Board of Education in Massachusetts* in Henry Barnard, *National Education in Europe*. 2nd edition. New York: Charles B. Norton, 1854.

Maritain, Jacques, *The Things That are not Caesar's*. London: Sheed and Ward, 1930.

——, *Freedom in the Modern World*. Translated by Richard O'Sullivan. New York: Charles Scribner's Sons, 1936.

——, *Three Reformers, Luther, Descartes, Rousseau*. New York: Charles Scribner's Sons, 1929.

Maritain, Jacques, Wust, Peter and Dawson, Christopher, *Essays in Order*. New York: The Macmillan Co., 1931.

Martin, Everett Dean, *The Conflict of the Individual and the Mass in the Modern World*. New York: Henry Holt and Co., 1932.

Martin, George H., *The Evolution of the Massachusetts Public School System*. New York: D. Appleton and Co., 1894.

Matthews, Brander, Editor, *et al*, *History of Columbia University, 1754-1904*. Published in commemoration of the one-hundred-fiftieth anniversary of the founding of King's College. New York: The Macmillan Co., 1904.

McCormick, John F., *Scholastic Metaphysics*. Part I. Chicago: Loyola University Press, 1928.

McCormick, Patrick J., *History of Education*. Washington, D. C.: The Catholic Education Press, 1915.

McGuire, John, "Atheism in the Public Schools," *The Fortnightly Review*, XXXIV, No. 14 (July 15, 1927), 287-290.

Mercier, Cardinal and Professors of the Higher Institute of Philosophy, Louvain, *A Manual of Modern Scholastic Philosophy*. Authorized translation and third English edition by T. L. Parker and S. A. Parker, with a Preface by P. Coffey, 3d English edition. 2 vols. London: Kegan Paul, Trench, Trubner and Co., Lt., 1923.

Mercier, L. J. A., *"The Trend to Dualism," The Commonweal*, XXIII, No. 4 (November 22, 1935), 92-95.

——, *Address at the Tenth Convention of the Catholic Alumni Federation in Chicago.* Unpublished address, April 1935.

——, *The American Inheritance.* An address before the Springfield City Club, Springfield, Mass., January 13, 1936. Unpublished.

——, *The Challenge of Humanism.* New York: Oxford University Press, 1933.

Merriam, C. E., *A History of American Political Theories.* New York: The Macmillan Co., 1903.

Messenger, E. C., *Evolution and Theology: The Problem of Man's Origin.* London: Burns, Oates and Washbourne, Ltd., 1931.

Messenger, James E., *Interpretative History of Education.* New York: Thomas Y. Crowell, 1931.

Meyer, Adolph E., *John Dewey and Modern Education and Other Essays.* New York: The Avon Press, 1931.

Merz, John Theodore, *A History of European Thought in the Nineteenth Century.* 4th edition. 3 vols. Edinburgh: William Blackwood and Sons, 1923.

Michel, Virgil, "Some Thoughts on Professor Dewey," *The New Scholasticism,* II, No. 4 (October 1928), 327-341.

"Modern Social and Educational Trends," *Research Bulletin of the National Education Association,* XII, No. 5 (November 1934), 227-232.

Monroe, Paul, Editor, "Harvard University, Cambridge, Massachusetts," *A Cyclopedia of Education.* New York: The Macmillan Co., 1912.

——, *A Text-Book on the History of Education.* New York: The Macmillan Co., 1911.

Monroe, Will S., *History of the Pestalozzian Movement in the United States.* Syracuse, N. Y.: C. W. Bardeen, 1907.

Moore, Ernest C., "John Dewey's Contribution to Educational Theory," in *John Dewey the Man and His Philosophy.* Address Delivered in New York in Celebration of His Seventieth Birthday. Cambridge: Harvard University Press, 1930.

Moore, Thomas Verner, *Dynamic Psychology.* Rev. 2nd edition. Philadelphia: J. B. Lippincott Co., 1926.

Morais, H. M., *Deism in Eighteenth Century America.* New York: Columbia University Press, 1934.

Morley, John, *Rousseau.* 2 vols. London: Macmillan and Co., 1891.

Morison, Samuel Eliot, *Harvard College in the Seventeenth Century.* Cambridge: Harvard University Press, 1936. 2 vols.

Mowat, R. B., *The Age of Reason.* Boston: Houghton Mifflin, 1934.

Mowrer, Ernest R., *Family Disorganization.* Chicago: The University Press, 1927.

Murdock, K. B., *Increase Mather; the Foremost American Puritan.* Cambridge, Mass.: Harvard University Press, 1925.

Newman, John Henry, *Discussions and Arguments.* London: Longmans, 1899.

Nize, William A. and Dargan, E. Preston, *A History of French*

Literature from the Earliest Times to the Present. Revised edition. New York: Henry Holt and Co., 1927.

Nunn, T. P., *Education: Its Data and First Principles.* 10th impression. London: Edward Arnold and Co., 1926.

O'Donnell, Charles L., *The Philosophy of Catholic Education.* Washington, D. C.: National Council of Catholic Men. National Catholic Welfare Conference, 1930.

Ogburn, William F., with the assistance of Charles Tibbitts, "The Family and Its Functions," Chapter XIII of *Recent Social Trends.* Edited by the President's Research Committee. New York: McGraw-Hill, 1933.

O'Hara, James H., *The Limitations of the Educational Theory of John Dewey.* Ph.D. Dissertation. Washington, D. C.: The Catholic University of America, 1929.

Osburn, W. J., *Foreign Criticism of American Education Bulletin,* 1921, No. 8. Department of the Interior, Bureau of Education. Washington, D. C.: Government Printing Office, 1922.

Pace, E. A., "St. Thomas' Theory of Education," *The Catholic University Bulletin,* VIII, No. 3 (July, 1902), 290-303.

Paine, Thomas, *Common Sense: Addressed to the Inhabitants of America.* Philadelphia, printed; London, reprinted, J. Almon, 1776.

Parker, Samuel C., *The History of Modern Elementary Education.* Boston: Ginn and Co., 1912.

Patrick, G. T. W., *Introduction to Philosophy.* New York: Houghton Mifflin Co., 1924.

Payne, William, *Rousseau's Émile or Treatise on Education.* Abridged, translated, and annotated. New York: D. Appleton and Co., 1893.

Paxon, Frederick L., *History of the American Frontier 1763-1893.* Boston: Houghton Mifflin Co., 1924.

Perry, Ralph Barton, *Philosophy of the Recent Past.* New York: Charles Scribner's Sons, 1926.

Peterson, Francis Edwin, *Philosophies of Education Current in the Preparation of Teachers in the United States.* A Study of Four State Teachers Colleges, Twelve Normal Schools, and Nine Liberal Arts Colleges. Teachers College, Columbia University Contributions to Education, No. 528. New York: Bureau of Publications, Teachers College, Columbia University, 1933.

Phillips, R. P., *Modern Thomistic Philosophy.* London: Burns, Oates and Washbourne, Ltd., 1934.

Pius XI, "Christian Education of Youth," *Four Great Encyclicals, Labor, Education, Marriage, The Social Order.* New York: The Paulist Press, n.d.

Potter, Charles Francis, *Humanizing Religion.* New York: Harper, 1933.

Powys, John Cooper, *The Meaning of Culture.* New York: W. W. Norton and Co., Inc., 1929.

President's Research Committee, *Recent Social Trends in the United States.* New York: McGraw-Hill Book Co., Inc., 1933.

Queen, Stuart Alfred, Bodenhafer, Walter Blaine, and Harper, Ernest Bouldin, *Social Organization and Disorganization.* New York: Thomas Y. Crowell Co., 1935.

Quick, Robert Herbert, *Essays on Educational Reformers.* New York: D. Appleton and Co., 1899.

Raby, Joseph Mary, *A Critical Study of the New Education.* Ph.D. Dissertation. Washington, D. C.: The Catholic University of America, 1932.

Randall, John H., Jr., *Our Changing Civilization.* New York: Frederick A. Stokes, 1929.

———, *The Making of the Modern Mind.* Boston: Houghton Mifflin Co., 1926.

Ratner, Joseph, *The Philosophy of John Dewey.* New York: Henry Holt and Co., 1928.

Raup, Bruce R., "What Teacher-Training Faculties Believe," *Educational Administration and Supervision,* XX, No. 5 (May, 1934), 141.

———, Educational Philosophies held by Faculty Members in Schools for the Professional Education of Teachers. *National Survey of the Education of Teachers,* Bulletin 1933, No. 10. Vol. III: *Teacher Education Curricula,* Part VII, 409-507. Washington, D. C.: Office of Education, 1935.

Reisner, Edward H., *The Evolution of the Common School.* New York: The Macmillan Co., 1930.

Report of the Commissioner of Education for the Year 1889-90. Vols. I and II. Washington, D. C.: Government Printing Office, 1893.

"Report of the President of Columbia University for 1934," *Columbia University Bulletin of Information.* New York: Morningside Heights, December 15, 1934.

"Report of Rev. James Fraser on American Schools," *Bernard's American Journal of Education,* 19 (1870), 577-580.

Twenty-Eighth Annual Report of the President and of the Treasurer. New York: The Carnegie Foundation for the Advancement of Teaching, 1933.

Rickaby, Joseph, *Moral Philosophy, Ethics, Deontology and Natural Law.* 4th edition. London: Longmans Green and Co., 1923.

Riley, Woodbridge, *American Philosophy: The Early Schools.* New York: Dodd, Mead and Co., 1907.

———, *American Thought, from Puritanism to Pragmatism and Beyond.* New York: Henry Holt and Co., 1915.

Rogers, Arthur Kenyon, *English and American Philosophy Since 1800, A Critical Survey.* New York: The Macmillan Co., 1923.

Rousseau, Jean Jacques, *A Dissertation on Political Economy, to which is Added a Treatise on the Social Compact or the Principles of Politic Law.* The first American edition, Albany: Barber and Southwick, 1797.

———, *Émile ou De L'Education*. Nouvelle edition. Paris: Garnier Freres, n.d.

———, "Lettre à M. Beaumont; et Lettres Escrites de la Montagne," *Oeuvres Completes de J. J. Rousseau avec Des Eclaircissements et Des Notes Historiques*. Troisieme edition. Tome VII. Paris: Baudouin Freres, Editeurs, 1828.

Rugg, Harold, "The Measure of the New Education," *Teachers College Record*, XXXIV, No. 3 (December, 1932), 204-211.

———, *Culture and Education in America*. New York: Harcourt Brace and Co., 1931.

———, *The Great Technology*. New York: The John Day Co., 1933.

Rugg, H. and Schumaker, A., *The Child-Centered School*. New York: World Book Co., 1928.

Rush, Benjamin, *Essays, Literary, Moral and Philosophical*. Philadelphia: Thomas and Samuel F. Bradford, 1798.

———, *Thoughts upon Female Education, Accommodated to the Present State of Society, Manners, and Government, in the United States of America*. Philadelphia: Prichard and Hall, 1798.

Rusk, Robert R., *The Philosophical Bases of Education*. Boston: Houghton Mifflin Co., 1929.

Russell, James E., "Thorndike and Teachers College," *Teachers College Record*, XXVII, No. 6 (February, 1926), 460-461.

Santayana, George, "Dewey's Naturalistic Metaphysics," *The Journal of Philosophy*, XXII, No. 25 (December 3, 1925), 673-688.

Sayers, Ephraim Vern, *Educational Issues and Unity of Experience*. Teachers College, Columbia University, Contributions to Education, No. 357, Bureau of Publications. New York: Teachers College, Columbia University, 1929.

Schilpp, Paul D., *Higher Education Faces the Future, A Symposium*. New York: Horace Liveright, 1930.

———, *Commemorative Essays, 1859-1929, Evolution—Bergson—Husserl—Dewey*. Stockton, Calif.: Privately published, 1930.

Sedgwick, W. T. and Tyler, H. W., *A Short History of Science*. New York: The Macmillan Co., 1917.

Seibert, Theodor, *Red Russia*. Translated by Eden and Cedar Paul. New York: The Century Co., 1932.

Sellars, Roy Wood, *Evolutionary Naturalism*. Chicago: The Open Court Publishing Co., 1922.

Shafer, Robert, *Christianity and Naturalism*. New Haven: Yale University Press, 1926.

Sheen, Fulton J., *Religion Without God*. New York: Longmans, Green and Co., 1928.

———, *Philosophy of Science*. Milwaukee: The Bruce Publishing Co., 1934.

Simpson, B. R., *et al*, "Annotated Chronological Bibliography of Publications by E. L. Thorndike," *Teachers College Record*, XXVII (February, 1926), 466-515.

Slosson, Edwin E., *The American Spirit in Education*. New Haven: Yale University Press, 1821.

Smith, Samuel H., *Remarks on Education: Illustrating the Close Connection between Virtue and Wisdom to which is Annexed a System of Liberal Education.* Philadelphia: Printed for John Omrod, 1789.

Snedden, David, *What's Wrong with American Education?* Philadelphia: J. B. Lippincott Co., 1927.

Sorley, W. R., *On the Ethics of Naturalism.* Edinburgh: William Blackwood & Sons, 1885.

Spencer, Herbert, *Education: Intellectual, Moral and Physical.* New York: D. Appleton Co., 1890.

Herbert Spencer on the Americans and the Americans on Herbert Spencer, being a full report of his interview, and of the proceedings at the farewell banquet of November 9, 1882. New York: D. Appleton and Co., 1883.

Sullivan, James, *An Impartial Review of the Causes and Principles of the French Revolution.* By an American. Boston: Benjamin Edes, 1798.

Sutherland, Edwin H., *Principles of Criminology.* Chicago: J. B. Lippincott Co., 1934.

Suzzallo, Henry, "The Mind of a Scholar," *Teachers College Record,* XXVII, No. 6 (February, 1926), 580-584.

Taft, Kendal B., McDermott, John Francis and Jensen, Dana O., *Contemporary Opinion.* Boston: Houghton Mifflin Co., 1933.

Taine, H. A., *The Ancient Regime.* New York: Henry Holt and Co., 1896.

Thilly, Frank, "Contemporary American Philosophy," *The Philosophical Review,* XXXV, No. 6 (November, 1926), 522-538.

Thomson, Godfrey H., *A Modern Philosophy of Education.* New York: Longmans Green and Co., 1929.

Thorndike, Edward Lee, "Measurment in Education," *Teachers College Record,* XXII, No. 5 (November, 1921), 371-379.

——, "The Quantitative Study of Education," *The Forum,* XXXVI, No. 3 (January-March, 1905), 443-448.

——, "Animal Intelligence: An Experimental Study of the Associative Processes in Animals," *The Psychological Review,* Monograph Supplements, II, No. 4 (Whole No. 8) (June, 1888), 1-109.

——, "The Mental Life of Monkeys: An Experimental Study," *The Psychological Review,* Monograph Supplement, III, No. 5 (Whole No. 15) (May, 1901), 1-57.

——, "The Evolution of the Human Intellect," *The Popular Science Monthly,* 60 (November, 1901), 58-65.

——, "Eugenics with Special Reference to Intellect and Character," *The Popular Science Monthly,* LXXXIII (August, 1913), 125-138.

——, "Darwin's Contribution to Psychology," *The University of California Chronicle,* XII, No. 1 (January, 1910), 65-80.

——, "The Opportunity of the High Schools," *Bookman,* XXIV (October, 1906), 180-184.

——, "The Nature, Purposes and General Methods of Measurements of Educational Products," *The Seventeenth Yearbook of the National Society for the Study of Education.* 1918. Part II: *The Measurement of Educational Products,* pp. 16-24.

——, *Human Learning.* New York: The Century Co., 1931.

——, *Educational Psychology.* 2 vols. New York: Teachers College, Columbia University, 1913.

——, *Education: A First Book.* New York: The Macmillan Co., 1923 (first printed in 1912).

——, *Animal Intelligence, Experimental Studies.* New York: The Macmillan Co., 1911.

——, *Introduction to the Theory of Mental and Social Measurements.* New York: The Science Press, 1904.

——, *Educational Psychology.* New York: Lemcke and Buechner, 1903.

Thorndike, E. L. and Gates, A. J., *Elementary Principles of Education.* New York: The Macmillan Co., 1929.

Thorndike, E. L. and the Staff of the Division of Psychology of the Institute of Educational Research, Teachers College, Columbia University, *The Psychology of Wants, Interest and Attitudes.* New York: D. Appleton-Century Co., Inc., 1935.

Townsend, Harvey Gates, *Philosophical Ideas in the United States.* New York: American Book Co., 1934.

Townsend, H. G., Editor, *Studies in Philosophical Naturalism.* University of Oregon Publications, Humanities Series, Vol. I, No. 1, Eugene, Oregon: University Press, March, 1931.

Trent, William P., *English Culture in Virginia: A Study of the Gilmer Letters, and an Account of the English Professors Obtained by Jefferson for the University of Virginia.* Baltimore: Johns Hopkins University Press, 1889.

Turner, William, *History of Philosophy.* Boston: Ginn and Co., 1929.

Van Becelaire, L., *La Philosophie en Amerique, Depuis les Origines Jusqu' à Nos Jours* (1607-1900). New York: The Eclectic Publishing Co., 1904.

Vann, Gerald, *On Being Human.* New York: Sheed and Ward, Inc., 1934.

Walsh, T. J., *The Quest of Reality.* St. Louis: B. Herder Book Co., 1933.

Ward, James, *Naturalism and Agnosticism.* 2 vols. New York: The Macmillan Co., 1899.

Ward, Leo, *Values and Reality.* New York: Sheed and Ward, Inc., 1935.

Watson, John B., *Psychology from the Standpoint of a Behaviorist.* Chicago: Lippincott Co., 1929.

——, *Behaviorism.* Rev. edition. New York: W. W. Norton and Co., 1930.

Weber, Alfred, Tr. by Frank Thilly, *History of Philosophy* (rev. edition) with *Philosophy Since 1860,* by Ralph Barton Perry. New York: Charles Scribner's Sons, 1925.

Webster, Noah, *The Revolution in France.* New York: George Bunce and Co., 1794.

——, *Ten Letters to Dr. Priestly in Answer to His Letters to the Inhabitants of Northumberland.* New Haven: Read and Morse, 1800.

Welsh, Mary Gonzaga, *The Social Philosophy of Christian Education.* Ph.D. Dissertation. Washington, D. C.: The Catholic University of America, 1936.

Wickham, Harvey, *The Unrealists.* New York: Lincoln MacVeagh, The Dial Press, 1930.

——, *The Misbehaviorists.* New York: Lincoln MacVeagh, The Dial Press, 1930.

Widgery, Alban G., *Contemporary Thought of Great Britain.* London: William and Norgate, Ltd., 1927.

Willmann, Otto, *The Science of Education in its Sociological and Historical Aspects.* Translated from the fourth German edition by Felix M. Kirsch. 2 vols. Beatty, Pa.: Archabbey Press, 1921-1922.

Windle, Bertram C. A., *The Evolutionary Problem as It is Today.* New York: Joseph F. Wagner, Inc., 1927.

Winship, A. E., *Great American Educators.* New York: Werner School Book Co., 1900.

Woelfel, Norman, *Molders of the American Mind.* New York: Columbia University Press, 1933.

Wolfe, John M., Editor, *Character Education, A Symposium of Papers on Its Culture and Development.* New York: Benziger Bros., 1930.

Woodworth, Robert Sessions, "Contributions to Animal Psychology." *Teachers College Record,* XXVII (February, 1926), 516-520.

——, *Psychology, A Study of the Mental Life.* New York: Henry Holt and Co., 1928.

Wyatt, H. G., *The Psychology of Intelligence and Will.* New York: Harcourt, Brace and Co., 1931.

INDEX

279